# Field Guide to Falling Ill

*Essays by* Jonathan Gleason

*Foreword by* MEGHAN O'ROURKE

The Yale Nonfiction Book Prize

THE YALE REVIEW

# FIELD GUIDE TO FALLING ILL

Yale UNIVERSITY PRESS

New Haven & London

Published in collaboration with *The Yale Review*.

Copyright © 2026 by Jonathan Gleason.
Foreword copyright © 2026 by Meghan O'Rourke.
All rights reserved.
This book may not be reproduced, in whole or in part, including illustrations, in any form (beyond that copying permitted by Sections 107 and 108 of the U.S. Copyright Law and except by reviewers for the public press), without written permission from the publishers.

Yale University Press books may be purchased in quantity for educational, business, or promotional use. For information, please e-mail sales.press@yale.edu (U.S. office) or sales@yaleup.co.uk (U.K. office).

Set in Yale New and Tablet Gothic type by Integrated Publishing Solutions.
Printed in the United States of America.

Library of Congress Control Number: 2025941394
ISBN 978-0-300-28294-8 (hardcover)

*Epigraph:* Mark Doty, excerpt from "Charlie Howard's Descent," in *Fire to Fire* (Copyright © 2008 by Mark Doty; used by permission of HarperCollins Publishers)

A catalogue record for this book is available from the British Library.

Authorized Representative in the EU: Easy Access System Europe, Mustamäe tee 50, 10621 Tallinn, Estonia, gpsr.requests@easproject.com

10 9 8 7 6 5 4 3 2 1

For my family, by blood and otherwise

he is beautiful

and like any good diver
has only an edge of fear
he transforms into grace.

—Mark Doty, "Charlie Howard's Descent"

# Contents

Foreword by Meghan O'Rourke     xi

Inheritance     1
Blood in the Water     20
Field Guide to Falling Ill     40
Circulations     67
A Difficult Man     85
Exit Wounds     114
Bitter Joy     135
Gilead     151
Proxemics     169
No Harm     186

Notes     219
Acknowledgments     229
Index     231

# Foreword

\

A young man in the opening decades of the twenty-first century, in a Western country that prides itself on technological prowess, discovers he is living inside an imperiled body. Specifically, the young man lives in the United States, with its uneasy combination of cutting-edge medical interventions and fragmented, often inequitable healthcare. He is a writer—an essayist drawn not only to description but to reflection, to the doubling back and self-correction that the form demands. He is also, as it happens, a person repeatedly drawn into encounters with illness and biomedicine, whether in his own body or those of others. This duality is the terrain of Jonathan Gleason's *Field Guide to Falling Ill*, a collection of essays that explores what he calls the "scenarios . . . situated halfway between medical emergency and human volatility."

Gleason's work, at its core, is an exploration of those moments when our bodies—home to our intimate, private selves—collide with the impersonal machinery of corporatized biomedicine and the sociocultural narratives that shape it. It is also a meditation on language and the ways experience is mediated (and sometimes misshaped) by the words available to describe it. His essays reflect the sensibility of both the witness and the participant, moving between the fluorescent-lit clinic and the writer's desk, between personal history and cultural critique. What makes this book stand apart in our landscape of illness memoirs and narratives of care is precisely this hybrid stance. Gleason is not content merely to record his experiences; he wants to understand what they mean, how they echo across history, and how our technologies shape our contemporary approach to the body as a kind of machine we peer inside of (while failing to tend to the subjectivity of the person who also lies within). As he incisively puts it in "Gilead," an essay about going on PrEP while dating someone who is HIV-positive, "If they wanted to, clinicians could test to see how strictly I have adhered to the regimen—my body stratified like layers of sedimentary rock."

Illness is often framed as a crisis to endure or overcome on the way back to restoring an "intact" self. But as Gleason's work reminds us, illness is also a way of knowing. His essays speak to the precarious beauty of that knowing, and to the ways it connects us—to history, to culture, to one another. In the title essay, Gleason recounts his work as a medical interpreter, a role that requires him to dissolve his own subjectivity in order to channel the words of others. He is a conduit, translating pain and confusion into the language of medical charts and diagnoses. This work coincides with his own sudden health crisis—his arm turns blue, and doctors find a blood clot, "floating like a leaf in water between [his] lungs and brain"—and his introduction, as a patient with deep vein thrombosis, to the very system in which he works.

That dual perspective—interpreter and patient—gives *Field Guide to Falling Ill* its particular charge. It is a book that understands illness not only as a biological event but as a linguistic and cultural one, requiring translation and negotiation at every turn. Disease itself may be a biological fact, but the way we conceptualize it shifts in every era. The language we use to describe ourselves and our diseases reveals not only the state of our biology, but also the shape of our metaphysics. Gleason is particularly attuned to both. His essays are closely observed and vividly peopled with doctors parsing symptoms into charts, or patients whose stories splinter under the weight of language barriers and the system itself. Yet these essays also trace the history of ideas that shape those humans in the clinic, illuminating the vast abyss between modern medicine's desire to treat "a single, predictable illness" and the "irreducible, unpredictable person" who may have that illness. What holds these essays together is Gleason's relentless curiosity, his willingness to pause over the smallest detail—a turn of phrase, a gesture—and consider what it reveals about the human stakes of medicine. Such work, of course, is the inverse of corporatized care's habit of seeing the body "abstracted and reduced to a single dimension."

One of the most striking pieces in this collection, "Blood in the Water," explores how individual experience and stigmatizing cultural narratives collide in the experience of illness. Gleason addresses Gaëtan Dugas—the Air Canada flight attendant infamously, and falsely, branded "Patient Zero" of the AIDS epidemic in North America, a myth popularized by Randy Shilts's *And the Band Played On*. (This claim was debunked in 2016 when a study found that HIV had been present in the United States at least a decade earlier.) The essay is part historical excavation, part personal reckoning, an interrogation of how illness is often entangled with shame and blame. "Blood in the Water" resists the reduction of history into a single cautionary tale. Instead, it opens a space for complexity—for the possibility that we can hold grief, rage, desire, and forgiveness all at once, in the same fragile body.

Why call it a "field guide" to falling ill? The phrase evokes those tidy pocket-sized manuals that help us identify species in the natural world, naming the birds or plants we encounter. But falling ill resists such easy classification. The landscapes of illness are fluid, contradictory, impossible to fully map. And yet, as Gleason reminds us, we need some kind of guide—not to name each disease with scientific certainty, but to help us navigate the uncertainties of finding ourselves suddenly changed by illness. To be sick is to cross into what Susan Sontag called "the night side of life," to a territory none of us willingly visits. And to *have been* sick is to hope, as Weldon Kees put it in his poem "Small Prayer," "That time may find its sound again, and cleanse / Whatever it is that a wound remembers / After the healing ends."

With precision and grace, Jonathan Gleason's *Field Guide to Falling Ill* evokes what it means to be human in a body that is always, in one way or another, vulnerable. To read it is to feel less alone in the night side of life. As someone who has spent years navigating the disorienting terrain of chronic illness, I recognize in Gleason's work not only the existential terror of unexplained symptoms, but also the longing for language that can articulate the experience of being itself, so as to close the gaps between us and render our human suffering legible.

Meghan O'Rourke
March 5, 2025
New Haven, Connecticut

# Field Guide to Falling Ill

# Inheritance

\

What was wrong with them? That's what we wanted to know. The children in my family—not all of them, but some—were sick, and the sickness was brutal. They were my age or younger, the children of my mother's cousin and her husband. Second cousins, technically. But as a child, they were simply my cousins; their parents were my aunt and uncle. At first, doctors were confused. There were no preexisting conditions, no history of severe neurological disease, no visible explanation as to why their children were getting sick.

My aunt and uncle had four children. Their first-born child, a girl my age, never learned to walk or talk. She died before turning three and exists for me now only on the fringes of memories: stretched out, swollen and motionless, on the faded upholstery of a rocker. At Christmases and family gatherings, my aunt would sit by my cousin's side, feeding her patiently—gravely—with a bottle and a stained washcloth. Dampening her forehead her only recourse to care. Their next children were a pair of healthy twins— blessings in a season of grief. We were close and played in the reeds and cattails of lakeshores during family vacations. Their last child, however, was a son who was born frail and elfish. His skin was like rice paper. He died before his second birthday. My aunt and uncle separated afterward.

---

In the 1880s, children in the neighborhoods of New York were falling ill, too. The sickness always started the same: a healthy birth then gradual weakness in the baby's neck and limbs, a withdrawal into listlessness, withering muscles, lolling heads, an eerie apathy swallowing the milestones of early life. The senses would dull. Visual impairment became blindness, and a strangely acute sense of hearing softened into deafness. I have tried to imagine this: the slow dimming of the world one sense at a time, just as fine motor skills begin to develop, just as language begins to solidify into a tool. Eventually, the children experienced seizures, pneumonia, and finally death.

Dr. Bernard Sachs wanted to know why. The son of two Jewish immigrants who had eloped first to Hungary and later the United States, Sachs was born in Baltimore in 1858. He attended Harvard as an undergraduate and later studied medicine in Alsace, Berlin, and Vienna. He worked as an instructor at New York Polyclinic and in hospitals across the city as a neurologist. In the early 1880s, he opened a private practice at 226 East 60th Street, treating patients with Parkinson's, scleroderma, and muscular dystrophy. In 1926, he published the book *The Normal Child*,[1] a child-rearing manual intended for the public. Unlike the popular recommendations of the day, concerned with Freudian fixations and psychoanalysis, he encouraged parents to trust their instincts when raising children. Sachs belonged to a generation of eastern European Jewish immigrants who defined American life as much as their native-born counterparts, but it was the patient he labeled S. who started him down the path that would solidify his most enduring legacy.

S.'s condition was strange but similar to many of the other children Dr. Sachs had treated. She was born healthy, her body well proportioned, her features "beautifully regular,"[2] as Sachs noted in his case report. But by three months old she had become torpid, inert, unable to lift her head. She did not play. She did not respond to familiar voices. She did not seem to care who or what was around her. For a while, one of her few motions was following a point of light dragged across her field of vision, but eventually she became completely blind. In the back of her eye, around the optic nerve, was a cherry-red spot surrounded by a milk-white halo.

There were misleading clues in S.'s birth and heritage. Medicine is filled with such plausible explanations that lead us astray. We like to believe we know the vastness of the world, that everything can be explained through our current models of understanding. S.'s mother was thrown out of a carriage when she was five months pregnant. At first Sachs took this accident as a possible explanation for S.'s condition, even though there appeared to be no damage to the fetus at the time. He noted, too, that on both sides of the child's family there was a predisposition to mental illness. As Sachs wrote in his clinical report on the child, "in the family of both parents, insanity is not unknown."[3] But neither of these possibilities were sufficient to convince Sachs they were the cause of S.'s illness or her death.

In the conclusion of his original paper Sachs wrote, "we have an agenetic condition, pure and simple, affecting the highest nerve elements." As to the cause of this agenetic condition, he wrote: "I am not willing to speculate."[4] He thought, or perhaps hoped, that the disease had something to do with the physical trauma S. experienced in the womb, a latent effect of the fall her mother had suffered during pregnancy, not at all related to heredity. Four years later, however, Sachs encountered another case in S.'s family, a boy whose condition followed the same progression as his sister's: the weakness and listlessness, followed by blindness and loss of hearing, and finally total muscular degeneration and death. "At this time one tooth was just breaking through,"[5] Sachs wrote of that child.

There were other children, too, nineteen by the time Sachs wrote a subsequent 1896 paper, in which he laid out the cases he and his colleagues had seen, complete with the symptoms, prognoses, and possible etiologies of this novel and mysterious illness. The paper was a bone lace of intricate genealogies and loosely sketched familial relationships, but no discernable pattern immediately emerged. The patients were second cousins and siblings. Their parents were often related, though not always. Patient 2 was "a sister of the first child described," but between them a healthy boy was born with no apparent problems. One of the few named children—Mary L.—was brought to Sachs at two years old with a familiar set of symptoms, and two years later her sister—Hattie L.—became sick with "an almost identical condition." Midway through the case study, Sachs described a woman with ten previous children who brought her thirteen-month-old son to the clinic in 1891. Five of her children had already died, and of those five, "three girls were exactly like the child brought to me, and all died before the age of two years, of general marasmus."[6] All of the children described in Sachs's report died within the first few years of life. Most of them had the characteristic cherry-red spot on their retina and milk-white halo surrounding it, and all of them were Jewish.

Sachs did not keep a journal. I have not been able to find any of his letters, if he sent many at all. What we know of his thinking comes largely from his medical writing and his writing on children's development. "The responsibility of developing useful men and women, of building up a fine citizenship rests upon every member of every community," he wrote in *The Normal Child*. "The responsibility rests most heavily however upon the intelligent seriously minded parent, upon the teacher, the clergyman, the social service worker, upon the professing psychologist, and last though not least upon the physician who is so often the friend and adviser of the family."[7]

I wonder if this understanding of his role drew the parents—almost exclusively Jewish themselves—to Sachs. They were first- and second-generation immigrants from eastern Europe, many of them Russian, some of them excluded, not just by native-born Americans, but by their German counterparts, who considered themselves superior. At a time when the authority of doctors was ascendant, on the eve of a renaissance for hard sciences, Sachs was one of America's leading clinical neurologists. There were reasons, in other words, to trust him, both medically speaking and as an adviser and a friend. But he could not do anything for them. The families of the children he treated had come to him for help, for a cure, for relief. All he could do was describe, helplessly, what he observed.

---

Funerals for children are entirely different affairs from funerals for adults. There are too few pictures to string along twine or tack up to corkboards. There are no happy anecdotes to recount, no comfort in the idea of a "full life." Just a piercing sense of tragedy.

The funerals for my cousins took place in a small church in Urbana, Ohio. I remember the smallness of things most, their simplicity. The red chair, the yellow plastic egg, the squat blue table in the white room where we were sent during the wake. I remember the casket, too, which was small.

Driving home from one of the funerals I asked my mother what was wrong with my cousins, why they had died. I was always demanding in my questioning of the world, and she never understood the science well enough to provide a satisfactory clinical answer. She told me they had a disease, something to do with their brains, and that my aunt kept having children, despite the known risks. "But why?" I asked. I don't remember that moment well enough to know if I meant this scientifically or cosmically, if I wanted to know what the specific mechanisms that led to their disease were, or why tragedies like this happen, or why my aunt insisted on continuing to give birth. Maybe I meant it all wrapped up in the single syllable *why*. What I do remember is a quaking fear. The feeling that the car was suddenly incapable of protecting us from the other drivers on the road or the landscape racing past us. I remember the first cold rush of primary knowledge: people die, sometimes young.

My mother did not have an answer for either question. Instead, she said I wouldn't have to worry about it, because all children who die go to heaven. And when I asked her when I would stop being a child, she became frustrated and snapped: "Fourteen." And I remember, for the longest time, hoping that I would die before fourteen. I wanted to avoid the pain of uncertainty.

———

By the time Sachs wrote his 1896 article, he still did not know precisely what caused the disease he was witnessing; it had become clear the cases were linked, not through known pathogens or trauma, but through heredity. Of the nineteen children represented in Sachs's article, all but five were related to at least one other member of the report. Many of them were direct siblings, too many to be a coincidence.

Sachs ended the paper by amending his previous conclusion about the nature of the illness and by suggesting a name for the disease. He considered naming it after its effects—the failure of the cortex to fully develop—but he worried about foreclosing on future studies into the characteristic brain lesions outside of the cortex. "It will be better, therefore," he concluded, "to find a clinical designation, and I would propose the name *amaurotic family idiocy.*"[8] Sachs could not have known it at the time, but *family*, the most familiar and innocuous word in his proposed designation, would go on to have the greatest impact on how the disease was understood and the community it became associated with.

Perhaps you already know the disease I'm talking about, the name we use today. It's a rare disease and a vicious one. Children—and it is almost always children—with this disease do not have the enzymes to break down certain lipids, which collect in their brains, clotting its neurons, ossifying its fatty tissue, building pressure until function ceases. The first thing Sachs noticed in his autopsy of S. was how tough her cortex had become, how his knife grated as he cut away a specimen from her brain. The disease is a genetic disorder caused by a mutation on the HEXA gene. It's an autosomal recessive disease, meaning you need both genes to fall ill with the condition. Carriers move unknowingly through the world with one functioning HEXA gene and half as many enzymes—enough that lipids never accumulate in the brain. Perhaps you love someone who is a carrier and don't even know it; perhaps you are one yourself. Only when two carriers meet and reproduce, only when one of their children has both genes, do they develop Tay-Sachs, the disease Dr. Sachs discovered, and the one later renamed after him.

I didn't die at fourteen. At seventeen I began taking classes at the university in my hometown. I had exhausted the science and math courses at my tiny high school. I already knew what I wanted to be—a doctor—so why not start early? Why not complete my first year of prerequisites now? By then, my cousins had been dead for ten years. My early memories of illness had transformed into an obsession to understand. Knowledge was a charm against fear. If I knew everything about medicine, I would not suffer the fate of my aunt or her children, walking unknowingly into pain and sickness. Maybe, I thought, I could even save other people from that fate.

I needed one credit in history, required by the state of Ohio, in order to graduate high school. Between classes in chemistry and biology, I enrolled in a Western civilization course, covering everything from ancient Mesopotamia to the Cold War. We met in a large auditorium, in the architecture building on the north side of the Ohio State University campus, all smooth brutalist concrete and echoing hallways. In the second half of the course, for an assignment that involved incorporating secondary sources, I discovered Shelley Z. Reuter.

In 2006, Reuter wrote an article, "The Genuine Jewish Type: Racial Ideology and Anti-Immigrationism in Early Medical Writing about Tay-Sachs Disease," and later a book, *Testing Fate: Tay-Sachs Disease and the Right to Be Responsible*, about the way Tay-Sachs was discovered scientifically, first, then interpreted culturally.[9] Of course I chose to write about Reuter. I still thought the world could be explained in terms of medicine alone.

In her article, Reuter defines Tay-Sachs not simply as a biological fact, but rather as a disease *concept,* something with historical and social implications, an illness that is both a product of social-relations and a producer of those relations.[10] Diseases are never just diseases, they have genealogies. And medicine does not exist outside of society, but rather it constitutes a part of broader culture and politics. Doctors practicing medicine are both influencers of that society and are influenced by it. This was the night side of medicine. Its hidden second face. A part I had never considered and one I came to both fear and marvel at.

"The fact that Sachs would choose to include 'familial' in this disease name is significant," Reuter writes, "because it set the stage for the medicalization of family and kinship."[11] If Tay-Sachs was discovered at a different time and in a different context, it would have become a different disease in the way it was filtered through the social body, labeled, and ultimately treated. But from the 1880s through the 1920s, as a wave of Italian and Jewish immigrants entered New York, tension surrounding this group began to rise. Fear of diseases such as typhus, tuberculosis, and cholera, Reuter notes, posed a threat of foreign infections in America, but Tay-Sachs, with its roots in the still nebulous realm of genetics and inherited disorders, reified fictions about Jewish blood, while also presenting a more metaphorical threat to the purity of an imagined American gene pool and the future of the country.[12] Doctors knew that the disease had something to do with heritage and genes, but not exactly how all the pieces fit together, and so they came to rely on pedigrees and race science to prevent the disease and to theorize its causes. Sachs may not have known it, but using the word *familial* in the name of his newly discovered disease played directly into these fears of corruption, the need to reproduce with only "pure" families for the sake of creating untainted offspring.

As Susan Sontag notes in *Illness as Metaphor,* "Epidemic diseases usually elicit a call to ban foreigners, immigrants. And xenophobic propaganda has always depicted immigrants as bearers of disease."[13] Tay-Sachs may not have been specifically mentioned in immigration legislation, but according to Alan M. Kraut, the *American Book of Instructions for the Medical Inspection of Immigrants* listed "Idiocy" as an "Excludable Medical Condition."[14] Dr. Manly H. Simons, medical director of the U.S. Navy in 1908, went a step further, attributing idiocy, deformity, and perversity to lower-class Jews directly. "As a type," he wrote, "Jews are beginning to show mental and physical degradation as evidenced by the great variability of development, great brilliance, idiocy, moral perversity, epilepsy, physical deformity, anarchistic and lawless tendencies."[15] In 1913, the New York surgeon Dr. Alfred C. Reed wrote that these same immigrants were responsible for the "transmission of hereditary taint or predisposition to actual disease."[16] Several years later, a presenter at a 1921 eugenics conference echoed these fears in more sweeping, euphemistic language: "The arriving immigrant of today is the father of tomorrow's citizen and upon tomorrow's citizen and his descendants depends the future of the country."[17]

Jews, the argument went, had to be kept out of the country because they were more likely to suffer from neuropathic tendencies, to come from bad stock, or to suffer from latent trauma stemming from the poor conditions they had fled in Europe. They were depicted as sickly, weak, unable to deal with urban life, and, somewhat confusingly, as naturally criminal and dangerous.[18] No one ever claimed race science was consistent. Of course, many of these beliefs existed before Tay-Sachs or genetics was discovered. The illness was an easily available excuse to justify a latent hatred—a hatred that recalled old fears about Jews as poisoners of wells and spreaders of plague.

Jewishness quickly became the defining feature of Tay-Sachs disease, and once the illness became a Jewish disease, only Jews could have it. Doctors believed the gentile body was immune to the illness, and cases of Tay-Sachs disease discovered in non-Jews were written off as not "genuine." In cases where a diagnosis was undeniable, doctors would take pains to search the history of these families for some hidden Jewish root.[19] Because many apparently gentile families have Jewish heritage, these connections were often easy to find, and the disease could be comfortably reattributed to Jewish blood. Here was the inescapable tautology of illness: to be sick was to be other, and to be other was to be sick.

Sachs, for his part, did not at first believe the disease could be exclusively Jewish. "I can hardly believe that the disease is purely a racial one, for the changes are such as might readily occur under any conditions of life," he wrote in 1896, "and, moreover, cases have been reported closely allied to this form in other races."[20] Sachs held a deep skepticism for the very field he helped lay the foundations of, or at least a skepticism of the way that field would be interpreted and instrumentalized. He maintained a progressive view of genetics, encouraging parents not to fall victim to the "bogy of heredity,"[21] or the false belief that origins were destiny. He was distrustful of IQ, with its specious logic and murky association with the eugenics movement. "I am not one of those who think the ordinary intelligence tests sufficient nor am I obsessed by the 'IQ' fetish," he wrote in *The Normal Child*.[22]

But a decade later, without finding any confirmable cases in gentile families, he was forced to admit what he had observed: that the disease seemed, for whatever unfathomable reason, unique to a single population. He would eventually write that the illness was exclusively observed among the "Hebrews,"[23] though by that point it hardly mattered: the disease had been coded firmly as Jewish.

"I'm sending you a copy of our family tree," my mother wrote to me one spring. She inherited our family tree from her aunt—a woman who had traced our lineage back two hundred years in a fruitless attempt to be inducted into the Daughters of the American Revolution. She'd started working on the tree after a series of deaths in our family had convinced her of the importance of heritage. Her cousin—the mother of my long dead cousins—was the last person to die before she finished. She collapsed on a hiking trail while out for one of her daily ten-mile runs. The paramedics weren't able to reach her before activity in her brain had stopped. She lay in the hospital for several weeks before her body followed her brain out of this world. Her funeral was attended by her healthy twin daughters. She was buried next to her other children. During the funeral the family speculated about what could have caused a heart attack in someone so young. They talked about her recent troubled love life—a new marriage, another child, another divorce—the family history of heart disease, and her children, the ones she had nursed even as she knew they were dying, what toll that could take on the body even years later.

During the fierce Midwestern winter that followed her cousin's death, while wind whistled through loose panes and snow piled up in dirty, ice-glazed drifts along the main roads, my mother installed herself in front of a computer, purchased a subscription to an online heritage database, and began making calls to relatives, determined to finish the work her aunt had started. The hobby that she diligently practiced leans on an idea far less innocent than it appears. By the 1840s, the first genealogical societies had already begun to appear in America—organizations that allowed members to claim lineage to English lords and exploited the desire for status through faked genealogies. At best these were vanity projects for those who already had status, but at worst they represented a sinister notion that lineage is destiny, and that some people are chosen genetically for wealth and greatness. These ideas persist in our obsession over specious genetic tests that promise to map our ancestry back to particular regions of the world. And it does not require extreme views to indulge in racially inaccurate thoughts about heritage. Simply reading about DNA ancestry tests can increase a person's belief in the inherent differences between races.

I received our family tree several months after my mother's message. It came in the mail as a stack of binder-clipped pages that smelled of fresh paper and ink toner. It traced our history through seven centuries, to villages in the German and Italian countryside, and it included a Virginian from Highland County who had participated in the Revolutionary War, just as my aunt and mother had hoped. But I didn't share her enthusiasm for any single name. What struck me as I pored over the document was the sheer volume of connections.

For its crimes during World War II, Germany bears the greatest blame for the dangers of the eugenics movement, but it was the United States whose immigration quotas—enacted through the Johnson-Reed Act of 1924 and based in part on the fear of communicable and genetic diseases—inspired the growing nativist movements in Europe. And it was the United States that became the first country to undertake a systematic program of compulsory sterilization.

Between 1912 and 1932, three international eugenics congresses took place in London and New York City. The logo of the second international congress was a thick tree with a banner reading "EUGENICS" along its boughs, and the caption "like a tree eugenics draws its materials from many sources and organizes them into a harmonious entity."[24] The language of these congresses was often cluttered with metaphors of cultivation: "Only the healthy seeds must be sown," reads the title of a poster from the Eugenics Society archives, as a fit young man walks over tilled land under a yellow sun, tossing handfuls of seeds over his shoulder. But more often these conferences were venues for preaching sterilization. "Check the seeds of hereditary disease and unfitness by eugenics," the bottom half of the poster commands.[25]

Like most dubious public health measures, the burden of these policies was borne out by the already impoverished, disabled, and disenfranchised. From 1897 until 1981, sterilizations were carried out on the intellectually disabled, the physically deformed, the blind, the deaf, and those suffering from epilepsy. Sterilizations extended to ethnic minorities such as African Americans and Native Americans, as well as anyone subject to a correctional facility. By the early twentieth century, at the peak of the movement, some sixty-two thousand people, most of them women, were sterilized in the name of eugenics. It was not until the 1942 Supreme Court decision *Skinner v. Oklahoma*, which stated that sterilization practices in criminal populations could not exclude white-collar criminals, that the notion of sterilization became complicated in the minds of many Americans. And it would not be until the end of World War II, when the policies of Nazi Germany came to light, that eugenics fell out of favor in the United States. Still, a significant number of sterilizations continued until the 1970s, and, as recently as 2010, women in a California prison were coerced into illegal procedures that produced permanent sterilization.

Today, Tay-Sachs is prevented through genetic screening, but in the early twentieth century there wasn't even a test. The gangliosides (the collection of fat, and protein, and sugar) that accrete in the brains of sick children would not be identified until the 1940s, and an accurate genetic test for the disease would not be developed until the 1970s. Before that, every pregnancy was a blind leap into health or illness. It is from this place of uncertainty and fear that one's children might fall ill—horribly, incurably—that I can most understand the desire for purity. The desire to protect one's family. These threats might make anyone scared enough to want to seal their borders against foreign polluters, close ranks around families they know to be safe, invest themselves in the idea of good stock and tainted blood.

———

I remember the lake house where we vacationed in the summers— the swan-shaped paddle boats on gravel shores, the copper fountains and algae-slick cement. I remember playing in the cattails and lily pads of the pond with my healthy cousins. I remember the whispers that followed my aunt, the quiet disdain mixing with pity. "It should be illegal," a family member once said, looking down at my aunt, kicking around in the surf with her two thriving daughters. I remember hearing this and knowing, even as a child, that they were referring to my aunt, to the children she continued to have despite the risks.

When my aunt became pregnant once with a sick child, it was a terrible accident, a mistake of fate and nature. My family had no reason to suspect Tay-Sachs disease; we are not Jewish—not culturally or religiously—though it is likely true that somewhere in the distant past an ancestor on both sides of my mother's family left a Jewish community, carrying with them a single recessive gene for Tay-Sachs. But by the time my aunt's second, third, and fourth children were born the risks were well known. Her insistence on continuing to have children was an intolerable assertion of agency.

As the ethicist Christine Rosen suggests in her article "Eugenics—Sacred and Profane" we live in an age where the presumption is that only healthy children will be born, and "the more lasting significance of our new genetic powers may not be the freedom to reproduce in new ways, but the obligation to reproduce only in the most advanced, most effective and safest ways possible."[26]

My aunt's refusal of medicine—her refusal to act responsibly—chafes not only against a sense of morality, but also against this sense that only healthy children should be born. And yet I believe it was a decision wholly and necessarily within her right. There are rights we need, that we should never indulge, and actions that can be fully immoral that have no place being made illegal. In *Risk of a Lifetime*, a book about the ethics of bringing new life into the world, the philosopher Rivka Weinberg lands squarely on the conclusion that it is unethical to reproduce if two partners are carriers for Tay-Sachs disease, but she also acknowledges her job is to raise philosophical questions, not make practical prescriptions. This is a quiet acknowledgment, I suspect, of how fraught a task it is to tell people they should or should not reproduce, and how troubled that history is.[27]

I remember another part of my memory from the lake house in Ohio. A transgression. In the cottage next to the lake, I went to use the restroom, peeled my wet swimsuit down, then wandered back into a living room lined with paneled wood and shag carpet. In a crib decorated with IV bags and churning machines lay my cousin. He was a year old, nothing but bone and baby's breath, translucent cheekbones making a sharp line beneath the skin. Alone in that room, I stared down at him, waiting for some sign of life.

I must have stood at the crib long enough for my twin cousins to grow tired of the water and my aunt to slip in from the porch to wash the sand from her feet. When I turned to leave, we came face to face. She stood in the doorway, watching me watch her son. I stammered something like an apology, though I didn't quite understand what I was apologizing for, so we stood for a moment, caught in our small cocoon of silence.

I still have a great reverence for medicine. I still think it's admirable to become a doctor. And some days—when the writing is difficult, when the questions look vast and intractable, when it seems like there are no answers at all—I regret abandoning that path. But I did not want to become Sachs: discovering a disease that would escape my control or be used against my people. I decided I did not want to dedicate my life to discovering or curing disease. I realized that medicine is not—in itself—enough to explain itself. It is a system influenced by culture, subject to politics, bounded by human capacities and limitations. We inherit not only its knowledge and wisdom, but also its failures and abuses. I wanted to understand this night side of medicine. I wanted to know, too, not just why people get sick, but why they suffer.

———

In the strictest sense, there is no such thing as a Jewish disease. There are no diseases that afflict only or completely any religious or racial group. In his book *The Missing Moment: How the Unconscious Shapes Modern Science,* the biologist Robert Pollack notes that "Jews are not in fact a single biological family; there are no DNA sequences common to all Jews and present only in Jews."[28] In general, genetic diversity in humans accounts for less than 1 percent of our genome, and "race," as the anthropologist Alan Goodman writes, "fails to explain the vast majority of human genetic diversity."[29] Individual differences within any given population are greater than any difference between those populations, and there is no meaningful grouping of traits in any of the categories that we have historically described as race. We are simultaneously far less unique than we imagine and vastly different from any other member of the groups we are sorted into.

Still, genetic disorders appear more commonly in certain populations. Thalassemia in Sicilian families. Sickle cell anemia in people from Africa. Cystic fibrosis in northern Europeans. To deny these connections is to deny reality, but to overly rely on them is to fall into the same false belief as Americans in the 1920s: the belief that genealogy maps perfectly onto our genetic makeup, or that we can protect ourselves through some false notion of purity. The problem with genes is that they get lost. They spread widely and unpredictably, circulate through populations undetected, and show up in unexpected places. Despite the promises of biotechnology companies like 23andMe, our genes are not perfect proxies for our family history. As hard as we try to build models predicting where we come from, the results that these companies deliver are only overlapping clouds of probability, best guesses based on outliers in our DNA with multiple possible origins. The gene that causes Tay-Sachs is a "single-gene linked trait." Unlike eye color or skin tone, which are expressed through multiple interacting alleles, a single gene controls the manifestation of Tay-Sachs disease in the body, like a widow's peak or attached earlobes, but with devastating consequences. And as a single gene, Tay-Sachs is only one data point in that vast cloud. In isolation, a single gene variation is fairly useless for trying to determine our heritage.

No one is sure where Tay-Sachs comes from, but several theories exist. Pollack suggests that particularly brutal fifteenth-century raids and pogroms on Jewish villages in the Pale of Settlement in Russia left only a few thousand surviving families who rebuilt a community from a decimated population and a diminished pool of genes.[30] Within a small population, traits are amplified, allowing mutations to emerge and take hold as the population increases the way a scar will lengthen as a child grows.

Pollack's theory has its ugliness. If it is true, then so-called Jewish diseases are evidence, not of genetic incursion or polluting forces, but of an ancestry fraught with violence and massacres. I find something sadly ironic in this possibility. Our prejudices are double bladed across history: the hatred and violence of one era spawn the traits we will use to justify our hatred and violence in another era. But the theory also has its beauty. If our attempts to categorize ourselves by name or trait are doomed from the start, if a rare disease can appear like an act of God—unexplainable, untraceable, in the most unlikely place—then perhaps we can all be read as family to one another.

# Blood in the Water

\

Dear Gaëtan,

Happy birthday. I've been reading your letters and thought I would write one of my own. It's strange to write to you when you might not be able to imagine me. It would be hard, I think, when you could not imagine your own future.

I've known about you for years, but only as "Patient Zero." Now I am trying to think of you not as a metaphor, but as a man. Did you have a cross-section of your body you privately loathed, some stock phrase friends knew you by, a gesture as indicating as a fingerprint?

I'm most interested in your letters to Ray Redford. Those relationships—former lovers turned lifelong friends—seem uniquely common to queer folks. "Thank you for your encouraging letter—it is the best medicine so far," you wrote to him in 1982, near the end of your life. "Ray, today is so cold again than I dear not go outside—to get some paper to write. Sorry about these little cards but you would understand if you be here." The urge to write is strong. You put your mind down on what's available, postcards, napkins. I like your charming misspellings. I hope I'm not making you self-conscious by bringing them up. The way *dare* becomes *dear* as if the cold were dear to you. *Dear* because you have the word hanging in your mind, the address of a letter. *Dear* because it is a letter to someone close to you. And something about the mistake *if you be here* blunts and strengthens the sentence. It startles. It makes the phrase into a command. "Be here!"[1] Be here with me. I know these are just little errors, ripples of your native French, catching light on the surface of language. But I've gone looking for traces of you everywhere. There is so little to find.

Dear Gaëtan,
    I'll admit, I'm writing to you for a reason. It began with a mistake: a man, the promise of beauty. There was a place you could go; everyone knew about it. A university gym. A row of private bathrooms with plenty of space, a shower stall, a sink.
    The atrium of the gym was a wall of angled glass. Outside, the afternoon was bright and clear, students marched to their final classes in down coats, breath huffing away like exhaust. I didn't have a membership, but when I got to the front desk, I said exactly what he'd told me to say. "I've just been out for a run." The girl behind the counter winked at me and pressed a hidden button that let me through the turnstile. *How many times has he done this?* I wondered.
    Downstairs, he was sitting on a bench, leaning forward with his hands on his knees. He was exactly what his picture promised, except, maybe, for the patch of thinning hair, which he kept hidden under a baseball cap. He offered me a handshake—heavy and transactional—then led me down the hall. I heard the tongue of a

lock slide into place behind me and he let a black duffel bag drop and deflate on the tile with a low hiss.

We kissed and stripped each other's clothes off. He was athletic, barely an ounce of fat on his stomach, which was freckled and rolled smoothly over distinct muscles. A single curl of amber hair at his navel. He fit his palms around my waist and pulled me so that we faced each other, our hip bones locked in pressure and pleasure, straining to be closer.

From that chapel of passion, everything echoed. Our voices struggled to contain themselves as we rubbed, and pressed, and satisfied a need for spontaneity in a way only strangers can, stopping once when, under the door frame, feet announced themselves and someone tested the door handle before walking away. As we worked, his bag sat on the floor like a well-trained pet. It was a comforting sight, full, I imagined, with all of the proper precautions we were trained to use in health class.

I didn't understand how things worked then, and so when the time came, when every other pleasure had been thoroughly exhausted, and he stood in front of me, beautiful, shuffling his feet, mumbling over how he'd forgotten to bring condoms, I was surprised.

"I'm clean," he swore—disease as filth: a metaphor I hadn't yet learned to protest. As I stood before him pouting about his mistake, I realized the "forgetting" had been a calculated move, that he was after a pristine form of pleasure. In the end, it didn't matter. Testosterone was already blurring the future. I was desperate not to lose what I had come so far to get. I knew this was my opportunity to leave, but I didn't. He took a bottle out of his bag and nothing else, and we embraced again. I understood that sex felt better like this, unmediated—like breaking a promise, like giving in until you forget your body.

Dear Gaëtan,

I've been reading a book about your life: *Patient Zero and the Making of the AIDS Epidemic*, by Richard A. McKay. As I read, I realized that you didn't live long enough to see what they did to you. AIDS barely had a name at the time you died. Could you see it coming: the need for an answer. To assign blame, to find a villain? All of this would land on you. Did you know the nurses at the hospital in New York called you a "Vector of disease"?[2] You might have known you were the index patient in a CDC study of a growing outbreak of pneumonia and Kaposi's sarcoma—patient O—But you couldn't have known what you would become, "Patient Zero." The incubator, the epicenter, the disseminator. "The Man Who Gave Us AIDS," as the *New York Post* declared.[3]

What is the purpose of Patient Zero—the concept, not the man? It provokes. It angers. It narrows the debate down to a binary of right and wrong, good and evil. It imposes narrative cohesion where there is little or none. It does something else, too, McKay suggests: "The term 'Patient Zero' can be read to indicate a human host that originated a disease in our species, but the term can also be read to mean the complete nullification of a patient's perspective."[4]


Dear Gaëtan,

They always use the same picture of you. You look good in it, so maybe you wouldn't mind. In the photo, you're shirtless, thin, tan. On the beach somewhere? It's hard to tell. The background is blank and white. It doesn't matter. You're the star. You and your mop of parted blond hair, full mustache, slightly parted lips, single dip of wrinkles in your forehead. They used it on the *60 Minutes* episode about you: "He was a French Canadian, Gaëtan Dugas, Patient Zero," Harry Reasoner says as the camera zooms in on your face. "One of the first people with AIDS," and the camera jumps closer. "The first person identified as a major transmitter of the disease."⁵ Another cut, and we see just your eyes. The eyes of a killer.

Or so the journalist Randy Shilts thought. He published a book in 1987, *And the Band Played On*, curated from his years as a reporter in San Francisco. The book is subtitled *Politics, People, and the AIDS Epidemic*. It's pretty good. Politics, people, epidemic: the book delivers on its promise. The narrative line is fractured and propulsive, tracking a scatter plot of people—mostly men, mostly gay—falling in and out of sickness from a mysterious cancer sweeping across the country. We're in San Francisco then New York, Haiti then Denmark. Chapters cut like scenes from a thriller, everything's connected, yet nothing's falling into place, not yet. And there you are, looming at the heart of it all, in the shadowy corners of bathhouses and saunas. Shilts admitted that he became obsessed with you. Maybe he needed someone to be obsessed with, or just someone to blame. He was infected with HIV, too, and dying, though he refused to hear his results until after he'd finished his book. I would like to believe he had the best intentions, that he didn't know what he would turn you into. But his book needed a villain and there you were.⁶

I prefer another picture of you. I found this one in McKay's book: you are twenty, on a couch somewhere in Canada. You look so young, nothing like the picture that will eventually make you infamous. You're relaxed, confident. Your hair has this metallic sheen to it, catching every scrap and passage of light. A soft coating of baby fat has yet to recede and reveal the hard, handsome features of your adult face. You are looking at someone you love. The caption tells me it's Ray Redford, your lover at the time, your lifelong friend. But even before I read the caption, I could tell.

Dear Gaëtan,

 I'm back in Chicago. Last week, I went in for a full STI panel at a clinic downtown. I'm sure you know the kind of place: narrow plastic chairs, drafty exam rooms. In the waiting area, I watched a man pull out a rosary, wrap it twice around his palm, and thumb through the beads. We folded into ourselves like birds huddled around our own nests of shame—or I did at least. *There's nothing to be ashamed of*, I said to myself, but I failed to feel it.

 There is a history to this of course: decades of fear-based campaigns, the failure of a comprehensive governmental response, all the talk of individual responsibility in which the culture soaks, and the general discomfort of discussing sex. I always find it hardest to look a nurse or a doctor in the eye and describe forthrightly the mechanical acts that have led me there. Did you ever feel this? Nothing I've read indicates that you did.

 In the hallway, behind a blue curtain, a nurse pricked my finger for a rapid test, and a pipette drank up the blood. She laid the test strip carefully on a metal tray, covered it, then prepared to draw my blood. She was young and kind, careful of my boundaries, asking if each procedure was all right to perform, apologizing for the icy sting of iodine against my skin. "How does that feel?" she asked, wrapping a rubber tourniquet around my bicep. I was amazed at the ease with which she found a vein buried under the flesh of my elbow. While I leaked out two vials of blood, she explained that the blue cast is only an illusion caused by the skin. Deoxygenated blood is in fact just a darker red.

 The rapid test finished its quiet work. When the nurse uncovered the tray, I felt her energy change. She stiffened and frowned. The test was inconclusive—a rote procedure made complicated. She smiled a thin, uncertain smile. Then, realizing her mistake—

showing worry, uncertainty—she suggested we rerun the test. Another pricked finger, another pipette, another sizzle of blood, paper, and chemicals. The second test returned inconclusive as well. What could this mean? I asked. The nurse explained that this happens sometimes. It could mean there wasn't enough blood for the test to run properly, or it could mean the serums of the test are interacting with antibodies of another infection leading to an uncertain result. "Or . . . " she paused there. It could mean that I am in the early stages of infection.

The other test will be more conclusive, she assured me, but they will have to send my bloodwork away to be examined. This could take a little while, but they will call me with the results.

Dear Gaëtan,

When I was young, I was deathly afraid of flying. I was afraid of a lot of things actually: dogs, swimming pools, diving boards, even those helicopter seed pods that spiral down beautifully in the fall—a neighbor convinced me they were poisonous. I was gullible. I would have believed everything they said about you. But I was never afraid of blood until I was taught to be.

I'm still anxious about flying. I've heard you were excellent at your job, that you learned English just to become a flight attendant. I heard that you would challenge passengers for insulting your hair, your makeup, your swishing walk. It's hard to imagine such a thing in the 1970s. And I can't help but feel like they were punishing you for that, for being brash and gilded, so unapologetic. Maybe that was what people were afraid of, more than any illness, the idea that someone could live so without shame.

Dear Gaëtan,

This morning, I stood in my bathroom above the sink, where I'd just flossed, and examined the porcelain bowl now flecked with red. I've spent the day charting the varied and miniscule ways my body bleeds: paper cuts, picked scabs, potato peelers, sometimes inexplicably—a red spot on my pillow in the morning.

The body bleeds more often than it drowns. I learned this from years managing a pool on a university campus. In the mornings, the facility would fill with older patrons who used the pool for water aerobics classes. They had fragile skin: collapsed membranes, patchy with bruises, prone to bleeding. In the evening, children came to swim for a club team. I spent my time covering sliced skin on the soles of feet, plucking splinters that bled for an hour, and providing tissues to staunch bloody noses. Blood was an almost daily occurrence; it neither disgusted nor interested me.

But illness makes the body real: an active player, suddenly more than a vehicle of the mind. It reminds us we are corporeal, weighted, fleshy, vulnerable. Illness makes us conscious of blood (and saliva and mucus and semen)—its agents of transmission—and the way they move through the world. And blood—bright red in the atmosphere—has a unique power to excite and startle. There is something impactful, dangerous, romantic even about blood.

I remember this one evening at the pool when a girl dove so close to a platform that she removed half the flesh from her shin, revealing a white splinter of bone. As she sat howling on the edge of the pool, bleeding into the water, we scrambled to contain the blood. We donned rubber gloves and long sleeves; we ushered pools of blood-stained water into metal gutters; we filled the stadium ceiling with the heavy sounds of mopping—our eyes stung from the caustic bleach vapors. A coach wrapped her leg in a towel and wheeled her off the pool deck in an office chair. Patrons cleared the water and anxiously bathed themselves in the locker rooms, too polite to ask about what could now be lurking in that water.

From a lifeguarding handbook: *One should always assume blood is infectious.*

I've been thinking about my earliest memory of AIDS, about the ways we learn fear. I've been thinking about pools, although I haven't worked at one in years. My lifeguarding certification lapsed a long time ago. Now, when I think about pools—spangled light, blood curling in a smooth arc of fluid dynamics—I think about Greg Louganis sitting for an interview with Barbara Walters, ostensibly to discuss his autobiography, really to talk about his infamous 1988 dive at the Seoul Olympics, when he dove too close to a spring board, caught the back of his head, and bled into the water.

Like any good diver Louganis had a sense of his body in space. He was worried about hitting his hands, not his head. He knew he was going to be close, he says in the interview. He knew this because: "I could feel it in my own body." The mind is too slow to think through a complicated series of acrobatic twists. In an instant of lift and plunge—barely more than a second in total—it has no time to feel anything but an edge of fear and exhilaration. He describes the moment as becoming "lost" in the dive: a moment when time is both stretched and compressed. He was in the water before he even realized he'd hit his head.

I first saw the interview as a child, but by now I've watched it dozens of times, and it is always my body that feels the moment of impact, the instant Louganis's body met the world. The strike is visceral. His head toggles forward unnaturally. The board barely wobbles, asserting its integrity as he falls into the water. The dive footage is slow-motion B-reel. It runs silently over the audio of the interview, but I can almost hear the moment of collision. I flinch as Louganis says "thud" just as his head connects with the board, language standing in for the sound in my head.[7]

Of all the surprising things about that moment, the silence, the interrupted grace of his descent, the awkward fall into the water—like a bird knocked off course—I am most surprised by his composure. The first time I saw the clip, I expected lifeguards to swarm the water. I thought his coach, much closer to the action, would be the one to pull him out. But he swims calmly out of the pool. In both the interview and the footage from the dive, Louganis reaches up and civilly feels the back of his head. The gesture is like an echo across time, a sympathetic pain with a past self. It is also a futile gesture of containment.

"I just wanted to hold the blood in, or, you know, just not let anyone touch it," he says.

I saw the interview as a rerun, long after Louganis had become famous as one of only two Olympic divers to win gold in the platform and springboard events, and infamous as the HIV-positive diver who had bled into the water and allowed an Olympic doctor to suture his wound without gloves. His dive was my first story of contagion as well as a first lesson in fear. Before I knew what a virus was, before I had ever heard the word AIDS, I knew there was an illness, I knew this diver had it, and I knew he was feared because of it. I didn't know anything about diving, though I wonder, watching the interview now, cut with spectacular swan dives and half-pikes, Louganis's body at the peak of performance and spritzed with logarithmic arcs of crystal water, if these images left an impression, if I remember the interview because I saw something in those images to long for—symmetry and beauty, tanned skin and athletic prowess. He brushes the edge of physical law. He breaks the surface of water at thirty-two miles an hour with nothing but a ripple and a David Hockney hiss of foam. He folds himself in half again and again, midair, until he is barely there. I wonder if even his voice, soft and lilting, what I now recognize as gay, was part of an early semiotics of desire. I wonder too if that longing was immediately contaminated by danger.

Dear Gaëtan,

    I have a serious question for you. It's something I've been putting off. Did you mean to do it—everything they said you did? People, multiple people, say you kept sleeping with men, kept forgoing protection, even when doctors warned that you were probably infecting others. This is the hard part: trying to know your mind in the middle of so much uncertainty. Ray once said, "I'm sure, given the times, that he did help to spread the virus. . . . But [he] was no different than the majority of gay men then. If he had more partners than most, it was only because his personality, looks, and job made that easier for him than for others."[8] What does innocence mean in a sea of inconsistent and contradictory information? When even direct observation fails to offer any clues. There were men who died within months while others survived for years. Men with different conditions: PCP vs. toxoplasmosis vs. Kaposi's sarcoma. Men who recovered miraculously from the edge of death and others who died from the very medication that was meant to treat their illness. For most of your sickness, AIDS didn't even have a name. No one knew where it came from. There were theories about poppers and lubricants, and a theory that the disease was caused by repeated exposures to other sexually transmitted diseases, that the immune system was exhausted, and would, with rest, repair itself and return to normal. Doctors told you it was cancer, and you can't spread cancer. And then, of course, there is the low, ceaseless hum of desire. You never lied to yourself or anyone else about that. They told you to stop sleeping with other men like it was as simple as turning off a tap, like there weren't reasons for a group of people, finally blooming into liberation, to be skeptical of the government asking them to tuck themselves back into the closet.

There's a rumor I've read a few times. It goes like this: before going out to bathhouses for casual sex you would cover the lesions from Kaposi's sarcoma with makeup. Under the low light no one could tell. Perhaps the story is true, but its repetition has less to do with truth than with need. They needed someone to fear. They needed a villain and a scapegoat, so they turned your beauty into treachery, something sinister and deceitful. The honey at the bottom of the wasp trap.

What did you think when stepping into a bathhouse, when taking a man's hand and leading him to a room, a dark corner? Did you regret it later? Did you have private moments of believing that you were a monster, a sociopath? Did you shudder with a guilt that was hard to locate? Did it come from the outside or the inside? How much had these things mixed? Was it easier to just shut your eyes? I wouldn't blame you if you did.

Dear Gaëtan,

It's been three weeks since my test. I've been straining my jaw from clenching. I've scoured the soft tissue of my mouth with a toothbrush and spent hours prodding the lymph nodes of my neck and armpits. I've discovered that you can manifest a whole host of symptoms with your imagination alone: headaches, dry mouth, islands of flaking skin. Still, this is only a fraction of what you must have felt.

Recently, I've stopped leaving the house except for work and school. My anxiety feels more manageable in the four walls of my bedroom. I've been using winter in Chicago as an excuse. There's snow up to my thighs here, the street a perilous rink of thawed and refrozen sleet. Ice crystals are snaking across my apartment windows. Depression has thinned another day down to a sunset's last golden thread of horizon.

I can't help but picture vials of blood spinning in a centrifuge, staining Petri dishes. I am sickened by the thought of the disease swirling through me, spreading, proliferating, adding something to me. This is not the correct way to feel—I know—but I can't help it. Retroviruses like HIV work differently than other viruses: they insert their genetic code directly into your DNA, coopting the body's modes of production and making it difficult to eradicate completely. This is just biology. But at my most sentimental, it feels metaphysical, like a violation bordering on sexual. I am ashamed by this making of metaphors though I find them hard to resist. I want my anxiety to be neutral, objective. I want HIV infections to be just another disease. No one thinks of the flu as moral condemnation, no one seems interested in the history of diabetes, no one contemplates the social positioning of kidney transplant recipients. I want illness unbounded from guilt and history. I want it to communicate nothing more than the objective reality of my body.


Dear Gaëtan,

More and more I think of fear as a weapon: something we use on others, something we are victims of ourselves. I read a story once about an HIV-positive man in Michigan who bit a neighbor during a fight and was charged with biological terrorism. Pat Robertson, former host of *The 700 Club,* once claimed that gay men in San Francisco wore rings designed to cut and infect others with HIV when you shake their hands—fear literally taking the shape of a glittering weapon.[9] Sex workers in Florida can have additional years added to a prison sentence for being HIV-positive.

Those rings never existed, adding years to a prison sentence does nothing but criminalize illness, and HIV cannot be communicated through saliva. But I suspect this Michigan man knew that. I suspect he knew something about fear, and its power, too. When you are a victim of something long enough, you learn to use it to your own ends.

Dear Gaëtan,

Online, I watched a video of you speaking at an AIDS Vancouver public forum in 1983. I've heard it's your only surviving audiovisual footage. It's a short video, spliced between talking head interviews with founding members of AIDS Vancouver. But for a moment on screen, you cohere into a whole: speaking, moving, and gesturing. No longer the slivers of paraphrased quotes and descriptions from Shilts's book, not even the still snapshots that plot your life—baby fat youth, to handsome young man, to grown adult. This moving image is as close as we can come. Finally, I can hear your soft French-Canadian accent. Your hair is dark and cropped short (shaved in preparation for chemotherapy). You are the more serious Gaëtan of Vancouver, stolid and methodical.[10]

I had read, before I watched the video, that your questions were difficult and nagging, that you were a pest and a troublemaker. You wouldn't have known, but Brian Willoughby, one of the founding AIDS Vancouver members, leaned over in the middle of your questions and said to the moderator, "Please, if you don't get him off this microphone, he is going to undo any good we've done in the last hour." But the first thing I hear, before you've even reached the end of your question, is uncertainty. Your syntax is tortured and unsure. You ask questions then emend them, embedding qualifying clauses, working the same phrases over into new rhythms, softening them, strengthening them, trying to get them right. The you of the video wants to know if the hepatitis B vaccine, largely tested on gay men, poses a risk of contagion, if there are tests one can ask a doctor to perform, if one is worried about having AIDS. These are difficult questions—ones for which there were no answers at the time—but they are also fair. I hear, too, how you return, again and again, to fear; it's the one thing you're sure of. "It seems like there is a . . . kind of a fear towards those people here, that, who could have symptoms or did have symptoms, or did have the disease . . . but you should, you know, not necessarily fear those people?"[11]

Dear Gaëtan,

"No one dies of AIDS anymore," a friend pointed out to me years ago. "Men who worried about dying young in the early '90s now check their blood pressure, take statins, and exercise," she said. Their deaths are as banal as the rest of ours. This is not true everywhere or for everyone, but it is more and more true here, in the United States, if you are well-off enough to afford the antiretrovirals that not only keep people alive, but healthy. I realize you wouldn't know this; you might not even be able to imagine it. In a world with antiretrovirals, our fears are subtler, lonelier creatures. We worry now about the side effects of medication, the weight gain or the wasting, the uncomfortable conversations we have with future partners.

I have a confession. I've admitted terrible things, true things. If I had met you, I might have been afraid of you, too. About a year before I went in for my own blood test, I was out to dinner with a group of friends at a restaurant. The place had plastic palm fronds buried in pots in the corners and heavy bronze shades half-closed on the windows, giving the atmosphere a dense noir feel. We were having a serious conversation, most of which I've forgotten, but at some point, a friend asked the group whether we would date someone who was "positive." Despite the medication, despite the low risk, most people doggedly admitted that no, they wouldn't. It's just too much of a risk. I can't remember what I said, probably something equivocal. *I'll have to think about it. I have no way of knowing without being in that situation.* Yes, that sounds like me. But now, faced with the uncertainty of my own status, my cowardice resurfaces with an acid taste. If my test returned positive, how would I be able to ask for something I was so unwilling to give?

You know, I barely told anyone about my inconclusive tests or my fears, I suffered through them alone. I wanted people to continue shaking my hand.


Dear Gaëtan,
 You've been exonerated. At least that's what the headlines say: "HIV's Patient Zero, Exonerated." "Researchers Clear 'Patient Zero' from AIDS Origin Story." "'Patient Zero,' Gaetan Dugas, Exonerated by HIV Research." I received the news the other day. The whole Patient Zero thing was just a misunderstanding, a comedy of errors. It's almost funny, the simplicity of it. Proof of your "innocence" sat in a book on a shelf for years. It was only by coincidence that you were connected to several other early instances of an opportunistic infection. The symbol printed next to your name was the letter O not the number zero, and the O meant *out of state*, not

zero for *origin*. A clerical error, albeit a convenient one for people eager to repeat an old story about victims and villains in the spread of a new disease.

I know you weren't the first. The virus had probably been with us since the beginning of the nineteenth century, one hundred years of silent spread. It had made it to the United States by the 1970s, and maybe even as early as the 1950s, the decade you were born into. But firsts are tantalizing with their clear beginnings and promises of clean resolutions. Origin figures are useful: they can teach us whom to fear, whom to blame, whom to hate. The greater horror is that there was no real beginning, no reason, just a senseless world transacting around us.

I know you weren't the first, and yet it must have felt at times like you were. I am trying to imagine the man who experienced this: the fear of being seriously ill without knowing why or with what. The fear of being first—long before a cure, before treatment, before even a thread of explanation. The fear of no narrative to stitch suffering together, to make sense of it. For the most part, even in our most devastating illness, we have a scaffold. Diagnosis, prognosis, a course of treatment, a survival rate. We take for granted that our illnesses, no matter how severe, will at least be known.

In *Devotions upon Emergent Occasions*, that tract of prose from John Donne about sickness and rebirth, he writes, "as sickness is the greatest misery, so the greatest misery of sickness is solitude." His illness was unknown, too. Probably typhus or relapsing fever, but the illness and its mystery were not his greatest form of suffering. It was the solitude they imposed on him. "Solitude is a torment which is not threatened in hell itself," he wrote.[12]

But of course, you weren't alone. You had a family that supported you. You had lovers. You had Redford—the steady earth to your brash, flighty sky. Of his love for you he paraphrases Joni

Mitchell: "I'm afraid of the devil, and drawn to those ones who ain't."[13] I know even less about him than I do about you, but it is through him that you are preserved and resurrected. Not the idea of you, but many of the genuine scraps of the real you that remain.

Dear Gaëtan,

A friend once wondered why I continue to write about medicine, HIV especially. "Isn't it depressing," she asked, "to write about so much death and illness?" I was surprised by her question, and her assumption that there was something morbid or depressing in the work. In my darkest moments, in the bleakest well of self-pity, I have never found it anything but affirming to know that so many people lived full and miraculous lives even in the face of uncertainty and death.

The call came in the middle of a poetry class. My stomach tightened. It was an unknown number, a Chicago area code. I bowed awkwardly out of the room, hurried down the hall, and pushed into a breezeway. By the time I made it outside, I'd missed the call and was left with only the flashing of a pending voicemail.

I would be lying if I said the results didn't matter, but it is also true that I have felt less alone knowing that you made a life in the middle of illness. I could have lived with the results either way. I hung for a moment between the fear of knowing and the ache of uncertainty, then I gave in and listened. A nurse's voice on the other end patiently informed me that I'd contracted a lesser infection in our hierarchy of fear—something treatable, impermanent, and unthreatening. That was all. Weeks of worry for a twenty-second disclosure. They'd send me a prescription, the nurse said. A short dose of antibiotics. Take it with food.

I didn't return to class. I walked home, elated but strangely empty. I threw myself onto my bed, letting the sun fall across my body. The clinic forwarded my prescription to a pharmacy on campus. The process was so simple I couldn't trust it: a single pill and two smaller pills a day later. A friend and I made a feast out of it. We ordered enormous hamburgers with pickle spears and hot sauce from a greasy hamburger joint. We laughed as I struggled to swallow the pill, finally jamming it into the gray meat of the burger and following it with a gulp of water.

Gradually, though, I realized that fear fades like a wound scarring over—slowly, fails to vanish completely. A week after the results, in the tiny supermarket below the train tracks near my apartment, I was still aware when my shoulder brushed a stranger. In my kitchen, I was flooded with adrenaline when a drop of blood landed on the cutting board after I nicked my thumb slicing vegetables. Everywhere I went, I continued to register, in a way I hadn't before, when someone took my hand.

Dear Gaëtan,

I am trying to forget my body if just for a day. So one night I step into a man's apartment near the lake. He is tall and at ease. I nervously roll a wine glass between my thumb and index finger. We chat for an hour in the living room, under a chandelier he's crafted himself out of old ceramic spoons. Then we take off our shirts. We play safe, as instructed. I watch the veins above my clenched fists, blue only by illusion. I picture the blood rushing through me.

When we're finished, we roll over, languid, the world materializing in many slow, still frames. A massacre of sheets and pillows across the mattress. He runs his hands over my smooth stomach and whispers, "I like touching something innocent." His gift of innocence crashes upon me like a baptism of chlorine. I want to feel pure, to be touched, to lose my body the way blood loses itself in water. It almost works. But then I think about you, and what Ray Redford once said, that you were no "ogre and no saint . . . just a young man exploring the world."

It's still winter in Chicago. Cardinals warm their feet on telephone wires. Spring is coming. The next morning, I leave the man's apartment and see that the snow is just a thin crust on the tree lawns. At the corner, I wait for a bus that will take me home to an apartment that will not feel as cavernous as it did. The windows on the bus ride are wide and fogged, I can see myself standing in the bright interior of the crowd: a woman with emerald nails, a teenager wearing impressive headphones, an old woman clutching her bag of groceries with two hands like a kettle weight. I am transparent and confused by the city scene streaming along outside the bus window. Its streetlamps and headlights making me a blurry outline where my body meets the world.

# Field Guide to Falling Ill

\

At work, I am a neighbor. I serve lunch at a public school. I am a nurse practitioner and a Kum & Go cashier. I am a pharmacy technician and a warehouse manager. I am a phlebotomist, a receptionist. I install drywall. I work at a daycare. I am a woman seeking a day-of pregnancy test; a child afraid of needles, wailing in the waiting room; a man with a swollen abdomen on a twenty-day bender. I am diabetic. I have a heart murmur and high blood pressure. I have a history of blood clots, two broken bones in my hand, one kidney, no gallbladder. I am lacking one rib.

I am an interpreter.

Once a week, I wake up at eight o'clock, shower, and drive to a shift from nine to noon at a clinic fifteen minutes from my apartment in the college town where I live. The clinic is free, meaning services cost nothing, meaning we offer as much medicine as possible at no charge, meaning we only treat patients without health insurance.

The clinic is a simple building, a single loop of gray carpeting, a series of vinyl exam rooms, a glass box behind which receptionists sit, filing cabinets on casters that shift back and forth like heavy, rattling curtains. It's a small, aging place; clean and modest. In a back room, a minifridge hums, cooling a supply of free insulin under blue light. From a Dutch door, a pharmacist doles out medicine as if from a stable. She hits a service bell whenever a prescription is filled. In a break room, there's coffee in a donated machine. Some mornings there are pastries, or a tray of withered vegetables, or crumbling Spanish cookies made with lard.

I work when the place is bright and sunlight streams in through the entrance, humming on the multicolored flyers that spangle the door like stained glass. There is always something to announce: utility relief options, workers' rights meetings, programs for free birthday cakes, specialty clinics that offer cancer screenings, dental care and eye exams, an advertisement for a 5K run to support the clinic, a bus schedule with its endlessly changing times crossed out and rewritten in pen.

For my first shift at the clinic, I shadow a man named Brian.[1] Brian isn't exactly who I expected to find working as an interpreter. He's middle-aged, with a graying beard that reaches down to the top of his laminated name tag. The flat, stretched vowels of his speech betray a Midwestern accent. He always has three things on him: pointed leather boots, a faded pair of camo pants, and a coffee mug with the native birds of Iowa darting across its surface.

I follow Brian as he weighs patients, leads them to numbered examination rooms, and takes their blood pressure. As we work, he reminds me of the words for sprain, medical tape, and pap smear in Spanish, snapping off the end of a cotton swab to punctuate a point. In the waiting room, he jokes with the patients about their work and their lives. They are school custodians, fathers of six, mothers expecting their first or third child, landscapers in towns forty-five minutes away. They wear knock-off Oakley sunglasses, work-battered jeans, and clattering pendant earrings. Many have spent a better part of the morning driving into town. We are the only free clinic for miles. I've heard stories of patients driving two hours from Des Moines or the Quad Cities each month for dental clinics, people coming in from out of state.

Each session begins with a question: "You're here for a high blood pressure checkup?" "You're here for an STI screening?" "You're here because you've been having some ankle swelling?" It is important to ask, not to assume anything.

On a chair next to the patient, Brian forms the third point in a narrow isosceles triangle with the doctor. This is the ideal scenography of interpreting, it's a trinity—patient facing doctor, interpreter next to patient, a little behind them if possible, forgettable, ignorable, an internal monologue made audible. I notice how Brian sits, hunched over his own hands, staring blankly at the floor or the exam table. If he doesn't know a particular term, he sails through it with a brief description, barely pausing. He doesn't take any notes; his memory is superb.

When I met him, he'd been working at the clinic for more than a decade. The interpreting gig had originally been a volunteer position, like mine. But he was good enough, and consistent enough, that they offered him a job. By the time I began working there, he knew most returning patients by name, as well as the names of their children, their jobs, and their medical histories. He knew, most importantly, their personalities: who will be irreverent and easygoing, who will be deadly serious, who will need long, difficult explanations, and who will be too nervous to speak.

———

Call it a coincidence, or a curse, or perhaps just convenient narrative timing, but a week after my first shift, I abruptly become a patient.

For years I'd experienced tightness under my arm, tingling in my fingers, swelling at the fingertips—all easy enough to ignore. But suddenly there is a crisis: back pain, a stifled throbbing down my arm, and an unnerving tumescence under my skin. Across my shoulder, a constant tracery of veins announces itself. When I exercise, the backs of my hands turn an alarming corpse-blue, and, at random moments, swimming points of pain erupt at the ends of my fingers. At an emergency appointment that week I tell a doctor about these symptoms. I feel her energy shift, as she leaves the room to "check on something." When she returns a heaviness comes with her. She takes a deep breath before telling me I might—that I probably—have a blood clot in my arm, maybe several.

My life becomes a series of minor emergencies bracketed by one large crisis. I am sent for an ultrasound that confirms there is, in fact, a blood clot in my left shoulder, floating like a leaf in water between my lungs and brain. I call my supervisor to cancel my university classes. I email the clinic to explain I cannot attend my shifts. I text my partner to ask him to meet me at the clinic, and I call my mother just to hear her voice. The doctor offers to put me on a waiting list for a bed on the cardiac floor, rather than sending me to the ER where they will perform the same tests and leave me in a waiting room for hours. But I will have to leave the clinic while I wait, meaning I must sign a liability waiver—protection for the clinic should something happen after I leave. I sign the form, go home, and wait for several hours in my room, clutching my arm like a volatile stick of nitroglycerine. Finally, hours later, I am called back to the hospital.

The morning after they discover the clot, a handsome and charming surgeon visits me on the cardiac floor. "My man," he calls me, fist-bumping my IV-wrapped hand every time he enters the room. He has heavy eyebrows and a swaggering confidence. I like him, even if I suspect "my man" is how he refers to many of his patients. A shortcut to familiarity, without the risk of forgetting or using the wrong name. The surgeon lays out my condition as a problem of dimensions. Nerves, veins, and arteries travel from the head into the torso through a gap between the collarbone and topmost rib like wires through an electrician's hole. In my anatomy the gap is too small, tightened by the surrounding muscles, compressed by years of freestyle swim strokes, overhead lifting, and, I suspect, the saxophone that hung on my shoulder for years. The solution sounds startlingly medieval, something called a rib "resectioning," which in laymen's terms just means a rib removal.

The surgeon explains how he will cut through into the soft well of flesh between neck and shoulder skin just above my collarbone, slice the stabilizing muscle, and pull back two major nerves. Once he reaches the rib, he will saw away the section of bone that has been causing problems. Simple! As he speaks, he mimes parting a curtain with two hooked fingers. He promises I won't miss the stabilizing muscles when they're gone. He tells me that he has performed this surgery dozens of times, and that the resectioning will solve all of my problems. "I'm 99.9 percent sure," he promises. I shudder at the word "saw," the blunt mechanics of it all, but I am comforted by the possibility of a clean, permanent solution.

He notes the risks: bleeding, clotting, infections, a coagulate unlodging and finding its way into my lungs or brain. These problems are not common, but they are possible. "Mostly," he says, "you will have some pain afterwards, and some numbness in your chest."

———

Months before I started my work at the clinic, before the clot began cutting off circulation in my arm, I'd taken a class on medical interpreting. The class was only six weeks long, a crash course in interpreting's basic theories and common problems. We were given a textbook one chapter at a time, chopped up into PDFs, and dialogues to memorize about hypertension and diabetes.

There were five of us in the course: future nurses, doctors, and physician assistants, a social worker, a public health major, and one student missing a single credit to graduate. Once a week, our professor would play the doctor while we took turns as interpreter and patients.

The scenarios were always problems situated halfway between medical emergency and human volatility: Ms. Godinez has seen too many doctors, and now her diabetes medication is off; Mr. Kovalenko has not been taking his HIV medication regularly, and we have to explain how this can lead to more-aggressive viral strains; Mr. Abed's son has retinoblastoma, and, "no, there's nothing we can do. He will lose his sight. The tumor has already taken over his eye." Sometimes the patients were resistant and withholding; other times they were aggressive and demanding, bartering with the doctor as one barters with God: fruitlessly. But there was always a patient, always a problem, and usually a misunderstanding we had to lead them through, patiently.

In class we practiced matching tone and register. We got angry when the mock patient was angry, exasperated when the nurses were exasperated. We practiced slipping into the casual *tu* form when the doctors digressed, and snapping back to *usted* when they got back to business. We went around the classroom and took turns shouting obscenities in Spanish until we were red-faced with embarrassment. "This will actually happen," our instructor informed us. "Trust me. You want to be ready to say exactly what the patient says. That's the job."

In other class periods we discussed theory. We looked at schemas for the mind in the midst of interpreting and read about famous innovators in the field. Danica Seleskovitch was one of our professor's favorites. He was always repeating her advice to "consider sense over words," meaning there is no one-to-one correlation when interpreting; words do not march like ants, single file, across a gulf of understanding. There is more than one path to the truth. Seleskovitch was a French scholar of translation, but unlike other translators of the 1960s, 1970s, and 1980s, who considered translation an art and interpreting a trade, she gave equal importance to both. Before Seleskovitch theorists had imagined interpreting as a process of transcoding, the mechanical act of moving words and structures from one language to another. The metaphors that ping-ponged around the profession were of a conduit, a bridge, a wire conducting information without interference, or a mathematical function—$f(x)$—moving vocabulary and syntax from one language to another.

Seleskovitch thought that interpreting was more than a simple repositioning of words within a grammatical framework. She believed that an extralinguistic process occurred, which involved context, history, and emotion. She theorized a deverbalized state that language passes through,[2] the same state that allows us to retell stories without recalling them verbatim, or to remember the process of driving a car or baking a cake without having to narrate the instructions from our grandmother. It's a state where we experience pain, joy, irritation, and memory as pure, prelinguistic events, unbound from the heavy concreteness of language.

I'm not sure how I feel about this concept of deverbalization—it suggests something mystical I can't fully trust—but I know that many times, as I interpret for a teenager with a pulled pectoral muscle or a woman with a scarred eardrum, I find myself touching these parts of my body, massaging my chest absentmindedly, pressing a thumb to the downy lobe of my ear.

In the recovery room, I wake up vicious with thirst. The sun has moved and deepened. At any moment, someone is retching, moaning, or yelling for a nurse. A paper cup of ice chips glistens with condensation beside my ear, but I can't reach it. My arms are desperately weak and numb with anesthetic. A pressurized tube slithers down the front of my gown. It takes me half an hour to realize it is not just draped over my shoulder, but inside of me.

The greatest risk is not the surgery itself, but infection. "Your chest cavity is all open space," a kind nurse tells me. His station is right next to my bed; he comes over regularly to hold the straw of my water cup up to my lips. "Your incision is weeping blood and lymphatic fluid into the cavity, which has to be drained out." Before another nurse wheels me back to my recovery room, he hands me a gadget that looks like a plastic sextant and tells me to blow into it in spite of the pain. He measures the strength of my breath and teaches me how to read the meter myself. "The more you breathe, the sooner you'll be able to breathe right again, and the sooner you can leave."

For two nights, I lie in the hospital room relearning how to breathe with the tube down my chest. Every breath causes a pleuritic burn to radiate through my chest as my lungs rub against the corrugated tube. Every six minutes I can press a button, and a new injection of painkillers slinks directly into my veins. The painkillers dampen the burning sensation, but they also make me extremely tired and nauseous. I fall asleep athletically, midsentence, then wake up with bouts of hiccups, the mounting need to vomit, or the ache of a swollen bladder. I drink a bottle of strawberry-flavored Ensure and immediately vomit it back up just as the handsome and charming surgeon enters my room. "Oh boy," he says as I deposit a half liter of Pepto-Bismol–colored fluid into a plastic container meant to collect stool samples. I give him a meek thumbs-up, trying to communicate that, despite how things look, I am, in fact, a very easygoing patient.

At home, I stagger out into the sunlight once a day and manage a short unsteady walk around the neighborhood with my boyfriend until my knees begin to wobble like a calf's and my arm pulses. I'm amazed and distraught that I can only make it a block before I must turn around.

On the windowsill of my bedroom, bouquets from friends and family wilt. Their stems soften. A sweet and wretched scent fills my room. The vase becomes a sea of murk, loose petals, and pollen. For a week, I watch the surgical glue dissolve from around the incision, revealing a curdled stretch of purple, distended skin, glistening with disinfectant ointment, eerily reminiscent of an oyster waiting in a tray of ice. I inject spring-loaded vials of syrupy blood thinners into the pinched fat of my stomach. The needle is hair thin. Its medicine sits just beneath my skin, diffusing into my body throughout the day, its shrill, searing pain a strange comfort.

---

After several weeks of recovery, I return to the clinic. I bring a paper bag filled with unused medication—the individually wrapped syringes of blood thinners, a bottle of Dilaudid. "This is some really expensive stuff," the pharmacist tells me, as she peers into the bag with amazement. "I can definitely take the Lovenox." She holds up one of the individually wrapped syringes and examines its plastic casing like a jeweler. "But these painkillers are already open. We can't prescribe them like that."

That morning, I interpret for an older woman who may or may not have MS, a man who needs a refill for his blood pressure medication, and a woman on the phone who needs to come in to redo a blood test. My last patient is a sullen young woman. At first, she seems unwilling, almost unable, to speak. She is short and tan, with a faded blue handkerchief in her hair and the name tag of some institution clipped to her collared shirt. She holds a bag in front of her chest like a shield. Her anger is palpable—it bleeds into the room. She answers the doctor's questions in combative yeses and nos. "How are you sleeping?" "Bad." "Do you exercise?" "No." "Have you ever been diagnosed with diabetes?" "Maybe." Every word punches or writhes its way out of her mouth. Every thought churns wrathfully behind her eyes. I am beginning to wonder what I am doing here at all when the dam breaks. Suddenly, she is describing her daughter who is having accidents at home and at school. The stress of the teachers calling her. The stress of losing hours driving to the school to pick her daughter up. The stress of lost sleep worrying for her daughter. And she tells us about her father, who died recently of pancreatic cancer after a lengthy and painful stay in a hospital. After the doctors had sent him home multiple times, telling him he was fine, until it was too late.

She's switching gears too fast, and my words are trailing far behind her. The doctor looks at me, in fearful confusion. I put up my hand as we've been taught in class to signal her to stop. "Why is your hand up?" She snaps. Her eyes swim with sadness and frustration, an outpouring of emotion that moves in all directions: annoyance becoming rage, rage becoming sadness, sadness breaking, finally, into sharp derisive laughter with nowhere left to go. She describes how the doctors wrote her father off then misdiagnosed him, and all of it after she'd struggled to convince him to go in the first place. "He hated the hospital," she finishes, breathless.

In the tense, windswept still that follows an argument or a

storm the doctor says: "I'm afraid you have high blood pressure." He's helpless. The problem has slipped the bonds of medicine, strayed into a complicated mélange of social services and psychology. "I'll write you a prescription. I can give you some antidepressants, too," he offers. She nods once, sinks back into her sullen silence.

———

The rib is gone but my veins have not healed. "I'm 99 percent sure" weighs on me like a betrayal. When I exercise the backs of my hands turn the dusky-rose color of spent blood. My forearm still goes rigid with fluid collecting in the layers of subcutaneous flesh. From time to time a horrible throbbing erupts at the end of my fingertips, accompanied by panic and dread. I call the surgeon to report these symptoms. "OK," he says, and reschedules a follow-up appointment. The following week another ultrasound confirms what I am already convinced of: a new clot has formed, or the old clot has failed to dissolve. It's unclear if the rib removal has achieved anything at all.

On an operating table again, my body is mapped. My bruises have just begun to fade to a deadened yellow. The pinhole where the internal radiologist inserted the catheter has finally scarred into a puckered white disk. Now, the wounds are reopened. The radiologist leads me to a familiar room filled with screens and lights on curved and movable arms. Under a tent of surgical tarp, I hear the scrape of a guide wire nosing its way through my veins. From the corner of my eye, I can see the radiologist's lurid, gleaming implements, and their fine, clean blades. To get a sharp image, I have to remain awake and hold my breath at precise moments, just as the X-rays pass through my body. "Deep breath," the radiologist commands. A moment later, I hear the rush and whorl of metallic dyes in my skull, the shutter of the X-ray machine. On a screen overhead, my interior resolves—a tree branch lost in fog. I can see the forking tributaries of my body, the ghostly haze of soft tissue, the sharp bands of rib, humerus, and ball-sockets. The radiologist regards the screen gravely. "See here," he says, pointing to a spot under my arm. "That's where the clot is. And here," he indicates a bulging pool of black ink, vaguely the shape of Lake Michigan, "that's where blood is still backing up."

In the recovery room the surgeon is as charming as ever, but a touch less patient. He's diminished in his day clothes: thin tie, brown slacks, nothing like scrubs and the authority they confer. His frown is like the frown of the doctors I interpret for when they lean through the door frame and ask me to follow them. They are deeply competent people, admitting they need help, struck mute before a problem they cannot solve on their own.

"It's a difficult one," the surgeon says, putting his tongue between his teeth. "Your shoulder was the tightest I'd ever worked on." I'm not sure if I should be proud or alarmed by this. I know he travels around the state performing this specific surgery, and I quietly try to calculate how many shoulders and their interior architecture he's seen. He explains that after my surgery they could not remodel the vein as aggressively as they'd wanted. The area was too sensitive and inflamed by the incision. "But now that the site has had more time to heal," he tells me, "we can go in again, carve away more aggressively. This time with the serrated balloons," he says with the unnerving glee of a general plotting a course of attack. When he asks if I have any questions, my first feeling is frustration. I form an accusation before a question. "You promised!" I want to say. Instead, I ask, "Will it work this time?"

The doctor doesn't know. "It should," is all he offers. He prescribes blood thinners until then, instructs me not to "baby" the area, to exercise and stretch, to keep blood flowing. He tells me to let my roommates know what's happening, too, in case some "catastrophe" occurs. I do not ask what catastrophe means; I already know: a clot breaking free, a spill in my brain from my thinned blood, an accident on my bike that precipitates uncontrollable bleeding. The blood thinners are very strong. I am limited to two drinks a day, at most, but quit drinking entirely. The surgeon advises me to avoid head injuries. "Yeah, I usually try to avoid those," I tell the doctor, deadpan, and to my surprise he laughs.

———

Bills begin to arrive, first gradually, then all at once. Just a few small notices at first: a ten-dollar copay for the initial doctor's appointment, a few hundred dollars for the ultrasound they used to confirm the clot. Then the bill for a hospital bed on the cardiac floor, for the expensive blood thinners that fizzed in the IV line, for the procedure to insert a catheter in my arm as well as the care required to remove it. Finally, the enormous bill arrives for the hours I spent on an operating table and all the mysterious equipment used in that time. They're labeled under the umbrella "surgical supplies and instruments."

I'd been trying to ignore the cruel reality of money until then. Nurses encouraged me to focus on healing instead. My health insurance is excellent. My deductible is low-ish. And while in the hospital, I met with a ceaseless parade of medical students and residents—some of whom waited patiently in the corner taking notes, others who interviewed me on lap-sized steno pads—all of this to further defray the cost of care.

For a while I marveled at how disastrous this event would have been at any other time. The condition was terrifying, yes, but at least it wouldn't bankrupt me, not completely, and only because my veins had clotted, finally and fully, at a time when I had university-subsidized, union-negotiated health insurance. I joked with friends about how lucky I'd been. And it is true, I am lucky, but I could not have imagined that this is how luck would feel, like a safety line splitting down to its nylon core, like a fail-safe parachute deploying in the final moments before collision.

Between the initial stay, the surgery, my follow-up angioplasty, and all the trivial bills in between—aspirin in paper cups, plastic tubs to vomit into post-surgery—the cost totals in the thousands, devastating on a grad school salary with an expiration date. I consider asking for a loan from my boyfriend, starting a GoFundMe page for bills—maybe one jokingly for the rib itself. I browse through the "handbook" I was given when I started my grad program, filled with tips on how to make money when in financial dire straits like selling your plasma for seventy dollars a week. "It's very cold inside, so take a jacket," the handbook warns. Instead, I go online and scan for double billings on my itemized receipt. I dip into a small pool of savings from a year I'd spent teaching abroad and pay off a lump sum. Then, helplessly, I schedule the most aggressive payment plan I can budget for, nearly the same amount as my rent, and try not to notice as the money ticks regularly out of my checking account.

---

For weeks the incision, still fresh and weeping, peeks out from beneath my collar, not yet a scar, no longer a wound open to infection. People on the street take notice. Cashiers do a double take. At the clinic, I note patients' eyes wandering to my clavicle, but only one of them ever mentions it: the woman with the cinched bag. I interpret for her again during a return visit. We are supposed to leave the room with the doctors, to be a verbal shadow trailing behind them like an afterthought, keeping ourselves at a distance from the patients. This impartiality is important, but often uncomfortable or impossible. So when the doctor promises to be right back, when it feels too strange to stand awkwardly in the hallway just outside the door, I stay in the room.

When the doctor is gone, the woman asks me about the scar, muted but still snarling out from under the collar of my shirt. "I had to have a surgery," I say. She nods and smiles, then says, "I saw it when we first met. What a pain to be sick."

---

On my drive to work most days I watch a ripple of heat bloom into hard white clouds over the chimney of a power plant by the river. It's midwinter, months since my first shift, months since the surgery. The river is frozen and dusted with dry snow. My arm still is not healed, but I have fallen into a rhythm: shifts on Tuesday and Thursday mornings, specialty clinics on Monday nights, or when needed.

When I arrive at the clinic one morning, two windows have been hit by bullets overnight: dime-sized holes and a shower of glass. No one was injured. The clinic was empty. The windows are boarded up with plywood by the time I arrive. The little free pantry in the parking lot was also demolished, struck, I imagine, with a baseball bat. It lies on the grass like a toppled birdhouse, its post bare; a crushed can of SpaghettiOs leaks and freezes on the asphalt. "That poor pantry," my supervisor says, shaking her head while I hang up my jacket. I suspect this isn't the first time the clinic has been randomly vandalized. I wonder how much it costs to fix.

That morning I interpret for a man I've seen before. He comes to every three-month checkup and tells the same story about experiencing chest tightness, arm tingling, jaw pain—all the symptoms the pamphlets in the waiting room give for a heart attack. He uses proper medical jargon. This makes the interaction easy to interpret—the language of medical literature is universal, its syntax familiar. I tick off a list of the most common symptoms of cardiac infarctions as the doctor looks bored. We do our best to take the patient's pain seriously, even though he interrupts the doctor to extend the session, even though he answers the most basic questions with non sequiturs, even though there has never been any evidence of a heart attack. He pulls his hand through his hair like it's on fire, describing in precise detail the way the pain works its way up his scalp. But the doctor's heard it all before. She has other patients to see—too many. It is clear something is wrong and that it isn't his heart. But I understand why he keeps insisting.

Once, just after the first catheter was inserted in my arm, I was sent home for a few days to await the rib resectioning. At one in the morning, two nights before the surgery was scheduled, my arm erupted in familiar pain. My fingers felt tight and swollen, then turned bright red and wailed in alarm. My arm ached no matter which way I turned in bed. I was sure the clot was shifting unexpectedly in my body, coming free perilously. I was convinced something catastrophic might happen. I called my mother who told me to call the hospital. The nurse on duty said they wouldn't be able to do much without seeing me. So my partner drove me to the emergency room.

The ER at night was a bleary, anxious place—simultaneously dull and electrified—the forty-eighth hour of an amphetamine binge with no sleep. We checked in at a bulletproof window and waited for hours in a curtained-off space while doctors and nurses rushed around, attending to accident victims and overdoses. Around four in the morning the surgeon's resident told us an ultrasound had found superficial clotting, the same as before, but no major change.

He told me I should go home and wait for my surgery, that nothing was wrong—or, at least, no more wrong than it had been. I was surprised not to feel any relief. Here was a doctor telling me what I wanted to hear: that I would be fine. Instead, I felt angry. I wanted to start talking and keep talking. I wanted to describe in bitter detail the pain I'd felt: how familiar it had been, how uncanny and specific the pressure of fluid damming up in my arm was. I wanted to tell the doctor I knew my body better than he did. I reached for the words, but I knew I would not be able to conjure in him the same certainty I felt.

This is the great sorrow of the world: its loneliness. The clinic doctor cannot tell the man with the false heart attack what the problem is, because she can't see it, and he cannot make her feel what he knows deeper than words: that *something* is wrong. We do what we can to help him. A tech wheels in an EKG, glues the electrodes to his chest, and runs the process anyway. The machine chuffs out a cardiogram on pink paper, its normal peaks and valleys testifying to no problem it can diagnose. We reach for the default recommendation: that he go to the ER immediately if he experiences the symptoms again.

---

Every Wednesday in the months following my surgery, I teach a creative writing class for medical students as part of their humanities curriculum. We watch a video about Jill Bolte Taylor, a neuroanatomist who survived a stroke; then we plot her story onto the hero's journey—departure, descent, and return. We read essays about people undergoing experimental treatments for depression and obsessive-compulsive disorder. We wonder what the correct form is for stories without a neat conclusion, stories about chronic pain and autoimmune disorders, stories that unspool raggedly into the future. These narratives, my students tell me, are much more common in medicine than most people think.

The class is something of a release valve. For an hour and a half each week, we meet and talk about literature, but just as often we talk about the students' lives as developing medical professionals. A young man expresses his disappointment at his neurology rotation: "Medicine is about healing people, but over there we mostly just try to keep people from getting worse." Another student, a sharp and opinionated young woman who is always gusting into class thirty minutes late, tells a story about caring for a pregnant woman during a difficult birth. She brought the woman water and a damp washcloth and adjusted her doses of painkillers. All of this seemed like a necessary mercy, but it also cost her precious time. Later her attending physician reprimanded her. This was a nurse's job. They had a schedule to keep. Not every little pain or discomfort could be managed.

In one of our first classes together we discuss the short story "Taking Care," by Joy Williams. In this story a preacher experiences a crisis of faith triggered by his wife's cancer and his daughter's sudden departure to Mexico, leaving him with his infant granddaughter. The preacher is baffled by medicine and, as my students point out, a victim of its institutional apathy and specialized jargon. He describes the doctors as "severe and wise," answering his questions in ways that make him feel "hopelessly deaf." They speak in words he doesn't understand, of "leukocytosis, myelocytes, and megaloblasts." And they insist, as if it were obvious, that there is no such thing as a disease of the blood.[3]

My students see their future in this story, one they are both clawing toward and terrified of in turns. They are wary of the tendency of more-experienced doctors to treat illness rather than a person, a body rather than a mind—but they do not pretend there is an easy solution. There is a problem of subjectivity in medicine: no two people experience illness in the same way. Humanity muddies the water. The manifestation of a disease, the irregularity of symptoms, the way we each perceive pain differently, and how we uniquely express our suffering all introduce unreliability. Medicine is already inefficient, expensive, and time intensive. The desire to help as many people as possible chafes against the desire to offer personal and tender care to each person. This is the terrible paradox my students find themselves in—caught between breadth and depth of care. Treating a single, predictable illness in an objective field is more practical than trying to treat a unique, irreducible, unpredictable person, which would demand an exhausting tromp through the subjective swamp of their interior world, not to mention time and resources. Better, then, to treat the disease itself, the body abstracted and reduced to a single dimension.

I think of my arm, how the doctors' and nurses' temperaments have gradually frayed as months pass without improvements. It was easy for them to be friendly and listen to my lengthy descriptions and complaints when my symptoms were manageable and straightforward. But the longer my veins remain clotted, the more space it takes up in their minds, and the less space that remains for me.

There are worse illnesses, of course, and there are worse things to experience than medical apathy—no treatment at all being one of them. I can't say what it's like to suffer from a severe, chronic illness, the kind that knocks your life into a new orbit. But I can tell you what it's like to be in the postscript of illness, its undead state, where the crisis has passed but recovery isn't certain. It's a dull, heavy place. Each morning I wake up hoping for some internal signal that my arm is improving, and by evening I fall asleep despondent. The problem is not so much that my arm still hurts, or that it still changes color as my heart rate rises, though all of this remains true. The problem is that it isn't improving, not even slightly. I could wait a lifetime if there were any forward motion. Instead, I give up. I take another pill and try to stop waiting at all.

———

In order not to think about my arm, I take long walks through the city, past construction sites where the furrows of tractor wheels are frozen and ribbed with snow. I spend hours in the gym (*don't baby the arm*), comparing the shades of my hands like paint swatches. I continue to take the Dilaudid. I count the pills out carefully, rationing them over weeks until they're gone. I swallow one, then take a bath and sink into the cottony warmth of intoxication, admitting this is more for my mind than the pain in my body. I sign up for more shifts at the clinic, filling out my monthly availability with every possible slot: specialty clinics for dermatology, ophthalmology, and prenatal care. I take evening shifts from six to nine-thirty, followed by nine A.M. shifts the next day. "Are you sure you want both of these?" my supervisor asks, looking over the schedule. I tell her it's fine, not to worry.

Volunteer work is voracious; it needs and needs. There is always more good to do, more money to be raised, more time one can spend. "Careful," Brian warns me at the end of a long shift, my second in as many nights. "This place will take all of you if you let it."

One morning, I come in to work and find the refrigerator in the pharmacy burnt out. The insulin must be moved, box by painstaking box, into the snack fridge. Little paper cartons of Lispro nestle against cellophane-wrapped pastries and browning bananas. As we work Brian shares with me this grand theory of altruism—a law of equivalent exchange. It goes something like this: Volunteer work is a tradeoff. The better the work is in an absolute sense, the fewer concessions it demands, the less of a splash it makes. You could try to change the whole system, but then you'd have to break some eggs, morally compromise yourself in one way or another, in order to really shake things up. Instead, you can do some uncomplicated good, you can help someone for one day, but you don't get to change anything big and you don't get to change it for long.

I'm not convinced of his theory, but the longer I work at the clinic the more I understand what Brian means. Here, there are no heroic surgeries or coding patients, no lifesaving organ transplants or CPR. Here, there are no emergency transfusions or one-in-a-million diagnoses, just a blood pressure cuff that must be wiped clean after each use, another prescription for statins, a new box of diabetes test strips. We treat cancer patients, but we do not remove tumors. The care they come for here is standard and mundane; they receive their chemotherapy elsewhere. In three months, the same patients will return with the same problems and the same complaints. They will be a little older and a little less healthy. We will treat them anyway, schedule their next appointment, and provide them with free refills, as many as possible, as long as we can.

———

I return to the hospital for the more aggressive remodeling of the vein. And on the operating table, the surgeon enters my arm again—another starved morning, another sleepless night on my back, another thousand dollars. A surgery is nothing but a system of gestures, I think, heavy with sedatives. The body is ritualized, wrapped in a stiff gown, cleaned with sponges on plastic tubes that leave a cruel reek of iodine and look like Elmer's glue sticks.

From behind a curtain, the surgeon calls for blades with names that sound like French cutlery. An apprentice hands him objects from a steel tray. I hear them talking about me as if from a distant shore. "He seems uncomfortable." "He says his arm falls asleep in that position." From the other side of the tarp, I am forgettable, a body suspended in a field of medicine, spliced and striated on a series of specimen slides. It must be helpful for the doctors: not to see the grimacing on my face, just my arm and the cold facts of its problem.

After an hour of prep, the catheter is inserted, and the guide wires are in place. It is hard to find a proxy for the feeling, its strangeness and pure violation. It feels like someone is pushing a straw through the bottom of a paper cup, but the cup is some interior membrane of my body. Once inside, the balloon expands with a terrible pressure. Every few minutes, a nurse delivers a dose of fentanyl, and a warm rush of relief fills my body. She reads the sweat on my forehead, deciphers the small gasps as the blades seek their target. She places, when even the painkillers fail to dissolve the deep discomfort, a hand on the top of my head, motherly and firm. I think, as the nurse takes my hand, of the ossified clot being carved away, of the staggering price and the unmatchable pricelessness of this care.

———

Interpreting lives at the intersection of a paradox: a deep intimacy and a necessary distance. We mirror the emotions of the patients, but we do not engage our own. We speak in the first person, but the experiences are not ours. As we listen to a young man with wet eyes and a glistening bottom lip tell us the story of losing his brother to the same cancer he has just been diagnosed with, we are supposed to nod solemnly, be transparent, show sadness only if the nurse, or the surgeon, or the pharmacist does. When we deliver the news that the pregnancy has self-terminated, it is supposed to be with the same balanced tone as the doctor. I repeat after a patient: "I was just so hopeful this time." Care, in this way, sits shrouded in objectivity and remove. To help patients better engage with the provider, we are not even supposed to make eye contact if we can help it.

This is all by design. Impartiality is one of the central tenets of the job. In the 1960s, most patients came to appointments accompanied by spouses, siblings, neighbors, or children—often they still are. Family members and friends, wanting the best for their friend or loved one, might appear to be rational choices for interpreters. They know both the language and the patient, their idioms and presumably their desires. But family and friends have been known to pressure patients into decisions, to leave out essential information while interpreting, or to add context and bias the doctor does not include—sometimes unintentionally. At exactly this point, empathy breaks down, fails to be useful, and becomes instead a hindrance to care.

Perhaps this is why I am skeptical of the plea for more empathy in medicine. Of course, I want my doctors to be nice to me. I want them to know the impact a botched surgery would have on my life, or the way my death would ripple through the lives of those left behind. But I worry that calls for more empathy play cover for material failures. I worry we have the operation backward, that what limits our humanity in the first place are these material concerns. I have seen doctors browbeat patients into compliance, deluge them with commands—to simply take their pills, increase their dosage—or cloak themselves in a protective shroud of medical jargon. I've been that patient myself. Often, we obey. If not, we are labeled noncompliant, and the doctor is absolved of responsibility. I feel for the patients I work with, but I feel for the doctors, too, who are kind, caring, and wise. They are volunteers, offering hours they don't have. They do not have the time to dispel every half-baked conspiracy theory about vaccines that walks through their door. They cannot sit counting out each patient's pills with them, which, more and more, seems to me like the real work of medicine. I think of the med students I teach, how they want to feel deeply and empathetically, to treat their patients as more than objects in a field of illness, and how they are left without the time or the resources to do so. I think of the man with his faux heart attacks pulling his fingers through his hair. I know that some recourse to help him exists, but that it is out of reach, and no kindness or single act of tenderness can offer him the long-term care he needs. I have seen the work of empathy at its most intimate and most powerful. I have seen its limits, too.

———

A friend once told me the theory that language is nothing but an irritant, an abrasion that scrapes and roughens the surface of pure meaning, gives us something to hold on to. This is the only way we understand each other, through this crude tool, this chipped stone. It is amazing that we can communicate at all. I'm not sure where exactly she heard this theory, but perhaps she was thinking of Barthes, who wrote, "Language is a skin: I rub my language against the other. It is as if I had words instead of fingers, or fingers at the tip of my words."[4]

This is the best metaphor I've found for the work: interpreting as a kind of intimacy, a skin you can brush up against, a surface that protects and obscures but that also reveals. You come into contact not just with the content, but with its form; not just words, but with the patterns and structures that contain them. Their cadence and hesitations. Their idiosyncrasies and mistakes. The particular way someone moves through a thought or untangles a problem.

I remember a young man at the clinic for an STI test, recounting a night he regretted, doubling back to emend his story, to add details. The feeling of his anxiety lifting. Or a woman, eight months pregnant, rummaging around in her own experience for the right word to describe her discomfort. I don't remember the word she chose, but I do remember the feeling of her testing out each option—stinging, cramping, burning, stretching. I remember a man who named his pain "crooked."

I don't want to romanticize the work. Most days are rote repetition, the same list of problems and questions. But moments of flow occur, when I can almost feel the churn of a patient's or doctor's mind, the grain and texture of thought. At times, I could almost guess the next thing a patient will say. In these moments, I am tempted to say I know them. But, of course, I don't, not all of them, only the rough, abraded surface of their language.

---

Late that spring, at a final appointment to check my arm, I see only a nurse and the ultrasound technician. There have been heavy rains followed by a cold snap. On my walk to the appointment all the bushes are dressed in gowns of ice, the decorative grass is stiff and beaded. A new strange symptom has emerged; I tell the nurse about it as we wait for the results. It's like a brush fire crackling along the surface of my chest, or water skittering across a hot plate. "Your nerves are just healing," she tells me. They grow a millimeter at a time, groping blindly in the dark, reaching for something familiar and continuous. "Eventually," she explains, "the connections will repair themselves." Their fiery ends will join. The burning will stop. Or, maybe, it won't.

Sometimes I wonder where Seleskovitch's deverbalized space lives, how deep it goes. I know that interpreting engages the predictable regions of the brain: Wernicke's area (comprehension, context, and structure) and its more famous twin Broca's area (grammar, fluidity, linkage). But in moments of surprise and stress I have felt the process seeping in deeper, a network of contexts and experiences beyond the strict limits of language, a taproot of emotional understanding.

Sometimes I wonder about the patient who held her bag between herself and the world until even that wasn't enough. I am supposed to leave these things behind—shred them with my notes or dissolve them in a haze of impartiality—but of course something remains, floating around that deverbalized space, plummeting back into memory like hail. I interpret for her once more, the woman with the bag and handkerchief, six months after our first meeting. She says she's doing better. Her daughter has stopped having accidents. She seems less angry than before. "It's healing," she says, about my scar. You can still see it under the collar of my shirt if you know where to look. The incision by then has tightened and softened into a soft pink dent of skin, tracing the curve of my neck. When she sees it, she puts a finger on the same spot of her body, feels the unbroken skin there.

I don't know if this bridges any divide or cracks open the sealed vacuums of our skulls. Maybe nothing is transferred, and nothing is gained. Meaning might be too fragile to make the journey without the armament of language, and these feelings of connection may simply be a reminder of what we've felt before—pain, relief, worry, understanding. A whisper of our own experiences in the echo chamber of our minds. Maybe it doesn't matter. Maybe what is more important is to simply show up; to speak the words someone says into the room; to remain dispassionate, until you aren't; to offer your time in the stead of money, as much as you can give, as long as you can give it.

After the second angioplasty, my veins remained clotted. The back of my hand still turns an ominous color under stress, but less often. My arm still throbs when the weather changes, when I exercise too vigorously, or for no reason at all. A final ultrasound revealed that the clot was not gone, but something extraordinary had happened. Auxiliary veins had grown around it, feeding blood back to my core, and this, the surgeon promised me, would be enough.

# Circulations

\

### Right Atrium

I was living in a house in the first suburb north of Chicago, working as a lifeguard at a university pool, waking up in the mornings to the familiar voice of a train conductor announcing arrivals and departures. My job had taught me how to find the brachial artery in the arm of a baby or the carotid artery in the neck of an adult, how to perform CPR and dislodge hard candy from a suffocating child's esophagus. In the pool, we practiced saving a life-sized torso of a sneering rubber man who sank like a rock. We felt for the shallow breath of a drowning victim on our cheeks, a flicker of life under the chin. We learned the difference between fibrillation and tachycardia. I liked knowing these things even though they felt distant and abstract, even though afterward none of it comforted me.

Any beginning is arbitrary, but that's particularly true here. The circulatory system is a closed circuit; with the exception of major injuries, nothing enters or exits. But the right atrium is the quadrant of the heart responsible for taking in blood depleted of oxygen before it is renewed by the lungs. Before the heart was properly understood, alchemists, theologians, ancient and medieval philosophers referred to this in mystical terms: the heart was the locus of passion and breath was the *vital spirit*—a metaphor for rebirth and new beginnings.

I knew the man by sight, but not by name. He was tall and thin and slightly hunched, as if he had spent a lifetime on a racing bike. He came into our pool regularly, usually in the evenings, to swim several laps before retreating into the locker rooms. I never thought about him. For the most part, I only noticed our patrons if there was something strange about them—a woman with an absurdly shallow backstroke, an eighty-year-old man doing cannonballs off the high dive, a postdoc perpetually complaining about the temperature of the pool. He was none of these.

It happened like this: A man scuttled out of the locker rooms and over to my chair. He could barely describe what he'd seen. *There's a man laying down in the showers.* He made it sound almost casual. When a coworker and I found him, he was on the ground, under the steady stream of a showerhead, quivering as if electricity were pulsing through him. There was a moment of stillness as I thought, *I can't do this*, before we dragged him to the center of the room and went to work. I did the *compressions* while my friend gave him *ventilations*. We were a crude simile of a heartbeat, we poured secondhand air down his throat.

At one point, I felt his sternum crack like a dry branch and looked down. His body was marbled, blue and white, a summer sky moving across his skin. It was beautiful and terrible, wafting between life and death. In that tense, windowless room, hours seemed to pass before an ambulance arrived and paramedics took over. I was damp with sweat by the time a police officer yanked me to my feet. We stood back and watched a large paramedic hammer on the man's chest—his whole weight funneled into a fist. A team transferred the man to a gurney and began wheeling him away. In the atrium, people stopped and stared. The man's wife was waiting for her husband, unaware of what was happening. For a moment, she watched with the detached curiosity of a bystander to a tragedy. Then, suddenly, it was her life. She recognized the person on the gurney and shrieked. She threw her body onto the stretcher. She pleaded, "That's my husband!" as the EMTs pulled her off. Then they were gone.

## Right Ventricle

There was a boy on the news that autumn. There was always a boy on the news, but this time the story was different. His name was Anthony Stokes. He was fifteen years old and Black and in need of an emergency heart transplant, but the doctors were denying him a spot on the waitlist. He had a condition I'd never heard of, dilated cardiomyopathy, in which the heart's ventricles become swollen and weak. The left ventricle pumps blood into the body while the right ventricle pumps blood through the lungs. If the left ventricle is weakened, blood doesn't circulate properly through the miles of arteries and capillaries coiled around our cells. Stokes's disease had resisted other methods of control. Without the transplant he was given six months to live.[1]

The cruel reality is that our bodies are worth something. An organ's value varies by country. In the United States, it costs a million dollars to medically transplant a heart. It is a small miracle, then, that after death many people give their bodies away for free.

Still, there are not enough hearts to go around. And in the realm of organ donation, in which resources are weighed against all their unknowable futures, patients are necessarily and painfully compared against one another. Age can be a disqualifying factor, as can ill health, incompatible blood types, and even body size. But the peculiar thing about Stokes's case was that it was never clear why he was being denied a heart.

The hospital cited some facts: they brought up his time spent in juvenile detention, his low grades, even his tattoos. They offered these things like evidence in a court of medicine. Together they amounted to a "history of noncompliance," a catch-all term, vague enough to be useful. It meant doctors did not believe Stokes would take his medication regularly or attend his follow-up appointments. It meant they were worried about his future, and that the heart—a million dollars—would go to waste.[2]

"I guess they didn't think Anthony was going to be a productive citizen," said Mark Bell, a friend of the Stokes family, when he heard the decision.[3] It was strange to hear productivity brought up in reference to the death or survival of a fifteen-year-old boy, but my surprise at the ways we kill is fading. Death by injection, death by cop, death by the slow attrition of disease.

In his essay "Black Body" the novelist Teju Cole writes: "The shootings, the fatal choke hold, the stories of who was not given lifesaving medication . . . the black body comes prejudged, and as a result it is placed in needless jeopardy. To be black is to bear the brunt of selective enforcement of the law."[4] The hospital's decision, while shrouded in medical language, was nothing more than a passive and private killing.

## Pulmonary Artery

My family has this genetic curse. My grandfather had his first heart attack in his early forties, my mother her first heart attack at fifty-two. Several of my great uncles died of heart disease at an early age, and few if any members of my family have been completely spared. Your forties is young to have a heart attack, even for a life-long smoker. Fifty-two is very young for a woman who has never smoked. There is a reason most doctors will ask, "Is there a history of heart disease in your family?" It's because of families like mine.

The early spring sun was just melting the last of the ice off the lawns of the Chicago suburb where I lived, when my father called me to tell me that my mother was in the hospital preparing for quadruple bypass surgery. She had spent the past several days struggling to breathe and could no longer make it up a flight of stairs without getting winded. The night before, she'd asked to go to the hospital for a stress test and was immediately admitted for heart surgery.

While my mother lay in the operating room, I took a bus six hours through the cornfields of Indiana and Ohio where signs loomed up in scattered patches along the freeway between turbines and windbreaks. A complete list of the Ten Commandments spanning two successive signs appeared, then another warning: *Hell is real*. The signs were stark against the landscape: black backgrounds with bold white lettering, outlined in red.

When I arrived, it was the early afternoon, and I was practically alone on the bright sidewalk. From the bus stop, I walked directly to a hospital in the center of town, but by the time I found my mother's room, everything was long over, and she was resting under the canopy of an enormous piece of machinery. She looked like a child, swaddled in the palm of a robotic hand. I don't remember a lot of what we said to each other that afternoon, but as I left she apologized, the same apology her father had given her years before: "I'm sorry for scaring you all."

In the hallway, a doctor explained to me that the specific occlusion in my mother's heart is colloquially referred to as *a widow maker,* because of how quickly it can kill, and also, I suspect, because heart disease is seen as a masculine illness. The name reminded me of the forked branches hanging precariously in dead trees across the Midwest. How one autumn a branch from a tree dying a slow death in our front yard fell and shattered inches in front of my sister's toes, a reminder of the violence and randomness of life.

## Pulmonary Vein

In his treatise *On the Usefulness of the Parts of the Body,* Galen called the body a perfect work of God and the heart the organ most closely related to the soul.[5] The intricate musculature, he believed, might be able to store the memories and emotions of the human spirit. He didn't know it yet, but he was theorizing the mind, albeit in the wrong organ. Of course, the heart is not a mind. It's a clenching fist—one of the more mechanical pieces of our physiology. But it is the center of so much magical thinking around our bodies and our souls.

Studies of the heart were stymied by religious dogma in the Middle Ages. In the thirteenth century, Pope Boniface VIII condemned dissections and medical experimentation on corpses, and, eventually, "all practices including cutting up of corpses, blood effusion or dissections were forbidden and condemned by clerical rules until 1480."[6] The rediscovery of the heart was an important turning point in the humanistic trend. Rather than the mysteries of humors and spirit, physicians, scientists, and artists began to focus on humanity and the human body as the source of divinity in the universe.

It's easy to believe we've eliminated that kind of magical thinking in medicine, but a 2008 study titled "In Their Own Words: The Reasons Why People Will (Not) Sign an Organ Donor Card" reveals how superstition and anxiety have persisted around the violability of our bodies, especially our organs, and most especially our hearts. The study worked like this: Participants divided into groups of two called dyads were given a stack of cards on various topics surrounding organ donation. They were put in front of a two-way mirror and asked to discuss the various topics frankly. They were each given forty dollars.[7]

Previous studies had revealed that "two reasons for an unwillingness to donate organs dominate: the fear that doctors will declare death prematurely to procure one's organs, and the belief that organ donation is against one's religion."[8] But, as "In Their Own Words" demonstrated, the reasons people chose to donate or not were complex, varied, and often unarticulated in the minds of potential donors. Major reasons included a belief in a black market for channeling donated organs, general distrust of medical institutions, the fear that one's family members would react badly to one becoming an organ donor, and something the study leaders labeled "visceral/noncognitive" reasons—the feeling that organ donation was "gross" or superstitions about how it violated the body.

Of course, valid reasons to mistrust the medical industry exist, and often mistrust is most concentrated in populations with a history of real grievances, but these are exactly the populations that would be best served by having a greater supply of donated organs.

## Coronary Vessels

This is where we run into trouble. The coronary vessels do not fit smoothly into the flow of blood through the heart. These vessels are outside of the system. They supply oxygen rich blood to the heart itself. Here blood doubles back on its source, supplying the energy that keeps the whole process moving.

I remember a story from my childhood, about Dr. Charles Richard Drew. Drew was an American doctor who participated in the saving of thousands of Allied forces during World War II by engineering a more efficient manner of storing blood for transfusions. Drew was an advocate for desegregation, particularly in the realm of blood transfusion, arguing that there was no scientific basis for keeping white and Black blood in separate banks. And he was—I sensed from the tone my teachers used to talk about him—a symbol for all of the ways white Americans had abused Black Americans.

The most famous story about Dr. Drew took place in the spring of 1950. On his way to a medical convention in Tuskegee, Alabama—exhausted from a night of surgery—he lost control of his car, which somersaulted three times into a field on the side of a highway in North Carolina. As the story goes, Drew and the other doctors in his car were rushed to the nearest hospital—an all-white hospital—where they were denied treatment because of the color of their skin. Although his passengers survived, Drew bled to death in need of the very transfusion he helped to revolutionize.[9]

## Left Atrium

The spring of my mother's heart attack, I sat in a long white conference room at Evanston City Hall. I had been invited, along with my friend and coworker, to receive an award for helping save the man at our pool the previous spring. He had survived his heart attack after an emergency quadruple bypass surgery. The ceremony was meant to celebrate specific acts of bravery within the fire department, but in the audience were a handful of confused-looking civilians including a couple who had fished a lost child out of Lake Michigan and a man who had helped stop a robbery in progress. As people stood up to accept their awards, it was a lesson in a different kind of promise: that we can be saved only by one another.

Stokes went on to survive as well. But it was only after the Southern Christian Leadership Conference became involved on his behalf, and only after a video of his mother, crying and promising that he would take his medication, ran on national news that Stokes was placed on the transplant list. Miraculously—given what I now know about organ transplants—he went on to receive a heart. But following the hospital's decision, doctors were accused of caving to media pressure, news outlets of sentimentality, and the Stokes family of invoking the "race card" in order to receive preferential treatment.

These accusations struck me as a clear reversal of reality, even before I read a study published in the journal *Transplantation,* which concluded that Black Americans are four times as likely to develop kidney failure, but less likely to receive a kidney transplant.[10] Or statistics from the CDC noting that Black men are the group most susceptible to heart disease, but one of the least likely to receive a heart transplant, transplants that take, on average, an additional year on the waiting list.[11] These disparities are driven by the common causes, the higher rates of poverty and lower access to medical care, but they are also complicated by the lower willingness of Black patients to donate their organs after death, a hesitance born, at least in part, from centuries of medical negligence and abuse.

"I feel bad for anyone who might have died waiting on the list because he was pushed to the front," one anonymous internet commenter posted about Stokes's transplant. But the concept of a transplant list that appears commonly on TV medical dramas, with its clearly defined order, turns out to be misleading if not entirely false. While age and urgency are factors in matching a patient with a donor, the transplant "list" is based on a complicated algorithm that considers blood type, body size, and proximity to the donor—organs do not travel particularly well. The list is not so much a list as it is a constantly reordering sea of information, based upon the availability of organs and parameters set by the body of the potential recipient. The idea that someone can jump the line or steal anyone else's spot is a shaky misinterpretation of reality. This idea was summarized in a phrase that popped up, unattributed, across several transplantation organizations: "There is no ranking or patient order, until there is a donor."

## Left Ventricle

Heart disease runs in my family, but so does hypochondria. My father explains it like this: "There's always something wrong with your mother, but then this happens and so you have no choice but to believe her." I find this to be dismissive, and also accurate. My mother overreacts. When I was only a few months old, she locked us both in the bathroom because my grandfather had a cold and decided to come over unannounced. I picture her sitting behind the sliding glass wall of the shower, cradling an infant me, ignoring the pounding on the door. Many of my memories of her involve a disinfectant wipe or a soapy rag. She is often complaining about some nebulous ailment—though that doesn't mean she isn't in pain. She worries about infections, cancers, the metals in our water, and chemicals in sunscreen—though somewhat frustratingly not the damage of the sun itself. During the winters, while I was away at a university on the banks of Lake Michigan, she would often call me and warn me about going near the lake. "It's going to be minus-twenty." "There's a riptide this afternoon." "Wind gusts of forty miles per hour." I would respond to these warnings with annoyance, "Yeah, Mom. Why would I go near the lake? It's winter."

In the nineteenth century, *hypochondria* referred generally to a "depression or melancholy without real cause,"[12] a definition based on the belief that humors, their harmony or discord, controlled health and emotions. But even as these theories faded or were disproven, the word's meaning remained, in popular usage, a groundless, morbid fear for one's health.

The standard dosage in medicine, a friend reminds me, isn't really standard. It's a gendered measurement, calibrated to the body of the average man. Women often underreport or have trouble identifying heart attacks because established symptoms (shooting pains down the left arm, elephant on your chest) are derived from the experiences of men.

Of course, these standards are not just gendered. "Do Black people feel pain?" asks the essayist Tyrese L. Coleman, rhetorically, in her essay "Speculum." She notes that Black patients are far less likely to receive pain medication than their white counterparts, and that doctors are more likely to rate patients' pain as lower if patients are Black. A study by the University of Virginia found that 85 percent of participants with a medical background thought Black people had—literally—thicker skin than whites. And "a considerable number," Coleman notes, "did not understand actual biological fact about the differences between races—for example, that Black Americans are more susceptible to heart disease."[13]

We want to take care of ourselves, naturally and inevitably, first and foremost even. A driver will protect their side of a vehicle over the passenger's, making the passenger's the most dangerous seat in the car. It's an instinct. But hypochondria is this impulse pathologized, so swollen and urgent it swallows everything around it. The danger of hypochondria is that it will convince us that our pain and our anxieties are the most pressing, the most painful, the most deserving of relief in the universe.

For several months after my mother's surgery, I walked through the street noting every pang in my chest and every pulse shooting down my arm. At night, I could feel the even throb of my heartbeat, and it kept me awake with its quiet reminder of mortality. From my house near campus, I watched documentary after documentary about plant-based diets and miracle cures for heart disease. I experimented with veganism. I started absentmindedly finding and counting my own pulse, then I went looking for it in others. "What are you doing?" my boyfriend at the time asked as I felt along his wrist for a groove between the joint and corded tendons where I knew I could find evidence of a beating heart. "Just feeling." At night, unable to sleep, I would listen to his heartbeat: the quick thrum of REM, the lazy whirr of a deep paralytic sleep cycle.

Throughout the spring, I booked several appointments with the university health center, convinced that there was something wrong with me. I was getting dizzy when standing up. I was tired often. I had shortness of breath, I thought. Basically, I was alive and experiencing the daily discomforts of living. But fear makes us gluttons for pain: prick me, extract me, torture my body into health. If it hurts, it's working: this is the principle upon which heroic medicine rests. Doctors in the nineteenth century understood this. They would bleed their patients into pale corpses, suggest purging and sweating as a form of cure. Like religious penance, the agony promised salvation.

Every time I went to the clinic, I saw a different doctor. My follow-up appointments went unattended. A stack of unfilled prescription notes littered my nightstand. I was covering my trail. Deep down, I knew I was being ridiculous. I suspected nothing was actually wrong, and yet I couldn't stop worrying. Eventually, a doctor asked if there had been any recent deaths in the family. I told her about my mother's heart attack, and she asked if I wanted to have my cholesterol checked. I wanted her to check everything. I wanted her to make an impossible promise, that nothing like this would ever happen to me. The cholesterol test was a concession.

A week later, I was disappointed to hear the results had come back normal.

## Aorta

The aorta is the largest artery in the body. It carries oxygenated blood away from the heart in increasingly smaller branching pathways that end in capillaries. A biology professor once told our class that the aorta is as wide as a human thumb. I pictured fitting my thumb into one. "If it ruptures," he warned us, "you would be dead before you hit the ground."

Stokes's death felt like that. I was not expecting it when it came. Two years after receiving his heart transplant—a year after I wrote what I thought would be the end of this essay—Stokes allegedly broke into an eighty-one-year-old woman's house, before fleeing the scene in a stolen car. While evading police he lost control of the car, flew over a highway median, and crashed into a streetlamp, injuring a pedestrian. The pedestrian survived, but Stokes died in the hospital a few hours later.[14]

Online there was a chorus of opinions. Some people were outraged, others were saddened, but everyone seemed to agree that the doctors had made a mistake in giving Stokes a heart, that it had ultimately been a waste. But, as violent and shocking as Stokes's case was, it was similar to the cases of white boys I had known in high school. Boys who were convicted of robbing carryouts at gunpoint. Who entered houses under false pretenses. Who stole hundreds or thousands of dollars in valuables to fuel drug habits. Men who were given probation, let off with reduced sentences, and who were referred to—in at least one post under an online police blotter—as "good boys." Men who likely would have been allowed to stay on a transplant list.

In "In Their Own Words," deservingness was another factor fueling participants' eventual decision to donate or not donate. Those who said they would not donate feared their organs might be used to save people who had "brought their illness on themselves" or that they might go to a "bad person."[15] Prisoners, according to some study participants, should be excluded from receiving transplanted organs, as should smokers and alcoholics—even though smoking and alcohol use are already factors when determining an organ recipient. Participants, the study noted with surprise, even had a crystalized image of what a deserving patient looked like: the parents of young children and people born with their illnesses. "The public," as one exchange made clear, "seems to want to impose criteria that only upstanding citizens receive scarce resources like organ transplants."[16]

Throughout the article there are quoted snatches from the

dyads' dialogues. Verbatim snippets of real conversations, filled with banter, pauses, and verbal tics. Participants discuss their fears that doctors will want to "grab" their organs, that excised pieces of their body will go to a "loser," "SOB," or someone who beats their kids. They joke about coming back from the dead to haunt the undeserving recipient of their heart. They sentimentalize about the twelve-year-old girls and the fathers of three to whom they would prefer to see their organs distributed. Their discussions illustrate not only the general findings of the authors—the common fears and hesitations potential donors feel—but also the great uncertainty of people asked to consider their deaths and the use of their organs.

From Dyad 13:

> Person 2: What if it didn't go to as good a cause as you think it would?
> Person 1: So you'd feel bad about, um, your heart being inside of . . . of a felon of some sort.
> Person 2: Yeah. So, for instance, if you didn't donate your heart, if that person didn't get a heart, then they wouldn't have survived and they wouldn't have . . . I don't know.[17]

I get caught up on that final ellipsis, what it hides or leaves out. It makes the same specious projection made in Stokes's case: that former criminals will be future criminals, that the chance to survive for some is the chance to create more harm, that only the innocent are deserving of care. The ellipsis retreats into silence. It leaves the crime unspecified, open to our imagination, an acknowledgment, I suspect, of an unknowable future and an unwillingness to say precisely what is meant.

Why, I wonder, does the participant falter here? What uncertainty or self-doubt holds them back. They seem unsure of their own reasoning when they say, "... I don't know." I can't know what they wanted to say, but I know that I've reached for that phrase, too, as a way of ending a thought when I know what I'm feeling is real but wrong, when I've been unsure of my own beliefs. I've reached for that toss-away phrase as a way to hold the door open for possibilities, for being better.

## Vena Cava

The vena cava is the largest vein in the body, responsible for returning blood to the heart. The Latin word *cava* means "hollow" because the circulatory system of the body was once thought to be vacant passages, carrying air away from the lungs. But this was a false impression formed because of the way blood congeals and pools in the lowest part of a dead body, leaving the veins empty after death.

The story of Dr. Drew that I was told as a child was not true. He wasn't denied care at the hospital because he was Black; he was denied because of the nature of his injury. His vena cava was damaged, preventing blood from circulating back to his heart. There was nothing the doctors could do for him. "Even the most heroic effort couldn't have saved him," Dr. John Brown, a passenger who survived the accident, later said. "In fact, a transfusion would have killed him sooner.[18]

Of course, many other Black Americans were denied treatment at white hospitals. I suspect that the way his story confirms our prevailing notions of racism is part of the reason the myth of Drew's death spread more rapidly than the truth. But the myth of Dr. Drew, with its distance and easy morals, also promises simplicity, that evil will always appear in its most obvious disguises and conveniently in the past.

I no longer check my pulse with an anxious regularity, though I can still find the spot on my wrist or the throat of a loved one like an instinct. Some days, as I'm running along the paved banks of the river near my home, a sharp pain cuts through me like a thread being pulled through my chest. I imagine I'll die on the spot. Topple over in the rain. But that's not really what it feels like, my mother says. It's just muscles deep in my chest cramping.

If, like my mother and her father, I ever suffer from a heart attack it will be someone else who saves me.

"What are you going to do with them anyway?" a friend says in argument of organ donation. In this I hear an echo of a person from Dyad 14: "Your soul is eternal and, you know, you're in heaven and in heaven, you'll get a new body, and this body isn't important anymore. It rots. So why not?" Jokingly, their partner responds, "People aren't gonna frown upon you when you're in heaven, saying 'Oh, you're the guy without kidneys.'"[19]

He's right that our organs won't do us much good after we're dead, but the act is not as neutral as the speaker implies. The idea of sacrifice is baked into the act of donation, even if, after the fact, it is no real sacrifice at all. Donation is a decision we make when we are still alive, and for that reason it requires something painful and difficult: imagining our death so that someone else might live. Pieces of our body salvaged like heirlooms from a house fire.

Stokes's intentions weren't noble. Very few seventeen-year-olds' are. He never meant to sacrifice himself, even if the outrage surrounding his case felt, at times, like a crucifixion. But sometime after I learned of his death, I returned to an article covering his accident in which someone noted that as the victim of a car crash his heart could be used again.

# A Difficult Man

\

## The Crisis

The early years were chaos. Men ate AL-721 with strawberries at four in the morning, six hours between doses. They fed themselves proteins emulsified in their refrigerators or smuggled in from South America. They meditated, took in only microgreens, disappeared to Canada for a month then returned "enlightened." Men drank their own urine, sometimes with OJ, the same thinned yellow as a mimosa. They took pentamidine or painted their skin nightly with photochemicals until it turned scaly and inflamed. The blisters and searing becoming, somehow, a comfort: proof of treatment, evidence of the virus being scorched from the body. Those who could afford it got on HP23. Those who had special access got on AZT, but they hedged their bets with other treatments. They were skeptical about the effectiveness of new medicines. They had seen other treatments fail. Already friends on AZT were seeing their T cells drop again, after several miraculous months of rebound.[1]

"The 1980s were the darkest, scariest years of the epidemic," the writer and activist Robin Hardy writes, "everything we tried we tried in the dark."[2] The context is essential—the chaos and uncertainty, the apathy from institutions—for understanding why people were so willing to try anything and everything. In the early 1980s, few people were looking for a cure for AIDS. The virus had been identified in 1983, but medical wisdom held that even if a cure existed, it would be too expensive to produce. By that time, the world had eliminated smallpox and discovered antibiotics. Polio had recently been eliminated from the United States. We had landed on the moon. But no one could imagine a retrovirus unwound from its host's DNA.

In this vacuum there were messiahs of new drug treatments, proselytizers and gurus, medicine as a form of faith, with all its vicious contestations. Men became mad scientists. They took aloe extracts, pureed fetal calf, and dapsone—once used to cure leprosy. There were ozone therapy and Reichian orgone boxes with corrugated copper walls, meant to channel cosmic rays through the body. And these therapies, zany as they sound, were the milder variety of treatment. Other options were so extreme they verged on death wishes: men injected themselves with bleach believing it would kill the virus, even if it killed the rest of the body along with it. Gasoline worked, too. In this desperation the essential question of cure is made legible by its extremes: What will kill enough? What will kill most precisely? This was the question asked of AZT, the first drug approved to treat HIV infections.

In 1964, Jerome P. Horwitz, a chemist conducting research with the Michigan Cancer Foundation, first synthesized the chemical that would eventually be renamed AZT. He called his discovery "Compound S," a derivative of herring sperm. Horwitz's job was to test the effectiveness of different chemicals as treatments for cancer, and in that respect his creation was a failure. The chemical was supposed to act as a Trojan horse, interfering with the replication of cancer cells in humans by replacing an essential nucleotide in strands of DNA. But, after failing in animal trials, Compound S was deemed too toxic for humans, and it was shelved, unpatented, for two decades. Horwitz joked at the time that AZT and several similar drugs he had developed were "a very interesting set of compounds that were waiting for the right disease."[3]

This is the first lesson: a drug's usefulness is situational. It rises to meet a need.

Twenty-two years after Horwitz created Compound S, Samuel Broder, a scientist at the National Institutes of Health, was searching for chemicals that might be effective at controlling HIV infections. At the same time, Burroughs Wellcome, a pharmaceutical company known for developing antiviral medicines, had come into possession of Horwitz's compound and discovered that it was effective at controlling viral activity in mice. In the fall of 1984, Broader agreed to accept samples of the compounds from Burroughs Wellcome for testing against live HIV.[4] The trials were a success. Compound S, now called AZT, stopped viral replication in mice, and it was advanced to human trials. "It's a wonderful example of how science works," said Robert Gallo—one of the researchers who discovered HIV—of AZT's rediscovery and the government partnership with Burroughs Wellcome.[5] But not everyone would come to agree.

In an attempt to incentivize the discovery of new drugs, the U.S. federal government allowed companies to apply for full patents on their formulas, meaning the government had no leverage to reduce the cost for the resulting medicine, even though the NIH conducted or supported many of the clinical tests. Horwitz never received much fame or a single cent for his initial discovery of AZT. And the trials for AZT, although initially impressive, were, the longer one looked, deeply troubled by their short time frame, the way the drugs were inconsistently administered, and how comorbidities were treated. The problem was that very few people were looking so closely.

## The Doctor

Dr. Joseph Sonnabend was one of those people. Born in Johannesburg in 1933 to a sociologist father and a physician mother, Sonnabend spent his childhood in Rhodesia, at that time the unrecognized state that would become Zimbabwe, watching his mother take calls in the humid subtropical nights. She was a house doctor, traveling across town to patients in need. It was not a glamorous job, as the real work of caretaking rarely is, but she was deeply dedicated to her profession. From Sonnabend's terse and factual interviews, it is hard to know just how much of his mother's work he saw. He would have been thirteen years old when she died, but her commitment to her patients, the intimacy of her care, the fact that she touched her patients and saw them face to face, seems, in the end, to have made all the difference in who he became.

As an undergraduate student, Sonnabend found something familiar in medicine. He chose to study infectious diseases. But rather than becoming a house doctor like his mother, he wanted to conduct laboratory research, to be accepted into the sacred halls of institutions. He moved to Europe, studied with Nobel laureates and virologists in Geneva, and worked with Alick Isaacs—a codiscoverer of interferon.

For several years Sonnabend moved between London and New York, taking various short-term jobs: a year at the Albert Einstein College of Medicine, three years at Mount Sinai in microbiology. He returned begrudgingly to New York to take a job at the Downstate Medical Center in Brooklyn, where he found "it was not so much an academic department as a business department for private practice plans."⁶ Faculty meetings were concerned with talk about money, donations and grant funding, which department chairs had "pull," and what was fashionable in terms of research. Sonnabend did not get along with the doctors. He brought no money into the department, and when his four-year contract came up, it wasn't renewed.

In New York a restlessness set in that would change his life. "I had a desire to see patients along with research." After fifteen years away from any direct interaction with patients, he wanted "a relationship between theory and practice."⁷ This was no small shift in priorities. Medicine is divided between the world of research and the world of treatment, academics and practice. Sonnabend's desire to move from microbiology research to treating patients as a primary care physician was not a simple change in department, but a categorical move from one world of medicine to another.

He left Downstate angry and entered private practice in Manhattan "out of a sense of total disgust" with the bureaucracy, the money talk, and the changes in how institutions trained new medical professionals.⁸ In 1978 he opened a practice in the West Village, on 12th Street between 5th Avenue and 6th Avenue, treating mostly sexually transmitted infections in gay men. At his practice in the West Village, he noted with suspicion and worry "a variety of unusual things": blood abnormalities and lymphadenopathy, rare cancers and brain infections.⁹ Odd but apparently unrelated data points. The dark gathering of seemingly disparate symptoms. Sonnabend suspected something was wrong, but he couldn't say what. He felt it more than he understood it; a primordial sense detecting a change in the air, a rush of hormones signaling danger. A mounting prodrome. As he wrote in 2009: "Many of us taking care of gay men in the late 1970s became aware that our patients were showing a number of unexplained signs and symptoms. I was one of these physicians. . . . I became aware around 1979 that something very unusual was affecting so many of my patients and realized that there was a developing problem with potentially immense implications."[10]

His patients were some of the earlier AIDS cases in the United States. Of course, AIDS had yet to be named even by its earliest labels: GRID (gay-related immune deficiency), 4H disease (since heroin users were among the patients), CAID (cirrhosis-associated immune dysfunction). These were simply sick people. They had nothing to do with each other. The virus had yet to be detected or even theorized. Few people were aware that a serious problem was emerging.

Sonnabend talked at times of fate laying him at the feet of the coming pandemic. It is hard to read through the facts of his life without a dizzying sense of history, a sense that he was somehow chosen by his temperament and experience to become an essential early figure in the crisis. He entered medicine hoping to be accepted by its exalted institutions, but, in the end, he became like his mother, traveling through the night to see his patients—a house doctor by a different name, taking part in the grueling and often unglamorous work of care.

## The Activist

In those dark years of the epidemic, Sonnabend met a man named Michael Callen. Callen was a self-described "hustler," the lead singer of the band The Flirtations, a member of the People with AIDS Coalition, and a coauthor of the Denver Principles—a manifesto about the rights of people with AIDS to determine their own care. He was also one of Sonnabend's Greenwich Village patients.

We know so much about Sonnabend through Callen, who was

a diligent, if somewhat chaotic, documentarian of his own life. He left his papers and hundreds of recordings to The LGBT Center in Greenwich Village. The tapes include interviews with media outlets, conference recordings, conversations with Sonnabend and other medical professionals, and a miscellany of TV commercials and nightly news sound bites. The quality of the tapes is often bad. Callen's end of the line is much louder than Sonnabend's. At times, his posh, desolate English accent is barely a whisper on the other end. Listening to the recordings, I have to crank up the sound to hear him, causing the background noise to hiss and thrum. I'm startled every time Callen's voice bursts back through my headphones. I drop and shatter a glass when an ear-splitting dial tone interrupts Sonnabend's soft murmurs.

They were an unusual pair, complicated and filled with internal contradictions. Callen was soft yet outgoing in all the ways Sonnabend was both fractious and reserved. But there is both trust and a deep tenderness in their conversations. Their relationship is one of hesitant talent and eager promoter. "You should go, Joe,"[11] is a refrain sprinkled through the interviews as Callen pushes his friend to attend conferences and give interviews. Sonnabend politely demurs, sometimes accepting, sometimes insisting that he has to see patients and therefore can't attend. "You deserve a MacArthur,"[12] Callen says once, without a whiff of irony. He believes in his friend, his greatness, his vision, even when Sonnabend does not believe in himself. Without Callen—his love and support—he may not have made some of the greatest contributions of his life.

"He was my mouthpiece as it were," Sonnabend said in a 1998 *POZ* magazine interview; he had "enormous sexual exuberance," and "embodied a sort of confrontational activism that I understand and respect—not the collaborationist kind." Sonnabend—formal, private, and standoffish—didn't like being in the public eye. Callen, meanwhile, said what needed to be said. He was "a brash person who loved fame and all of that." He had a way of interpreting Sonnabend with a concision that made headlines. When Sonnabend would equivocate, saying things like "AZT is incompatible with life"—abstract, moderated, and polysyllabic—Callen turned his ideas into the punchy parlance of public discourse: "AZT is Drano!"[13]

## The Trials

The first clinical trials for AZT were conducted in July 1985 and halted in September, after "the first clear evidence of effectiveness became apparent."[14] Researchers considered it unethical to delay the release of such a potentially transformative medicine, and by the spring of 1987, the medication had been approved by the FDA. After twenty months of trials, AZT became the most quickly approved medication at that time.

There were 282 people spread across twelve testing centers for the original trial, which were rushed, troubled by a small sample size, and further complicated by the fact that doctors were not given standardized procedures to deal with the pneumonia, diarrhea, and opportunistic infections that accompany AIDS. Some patients received blood transfusions to alleviate their symptoms, while others did not. According to an FDA review, adverse reactions to the drug were sometimes deleted from patients' charts months after being initially recorded. More human problems emerged as well. The trials for AZT were designed to be double-blind experiments. Neither the patients nor the researchers were supposed to know who was receiving a placebo and who was receiving AZT. But due to the extreme side effects of the medication, the difference between patients was obvious. Unconsciously, some researchers may have treated those patients receiving AZT differently than those in the control group.[15] There were also reports that those patients with the real medication were sharing their doses—pooling their pills or giving half to those without—so that everyone could have a chance to live. Although patients were not told whether they were receiving a placebo or the real AZT, the medicine was bitter-tasting, and it came in blue and white capsules that could be split open, meaning patients could easily tell who had been given AZT. The participants did not know if the drugs would work, but they wanted even the slim possibility of success to be shared.

## The Alternatives

While AZT was in the process of being fast-tracked as a singular cure to the AIDS crisis, Sonnabend and Callen were having lengthy conversations in Sonnabend's New York City apartment. They were frustrated that companies like Burroughs Wellcome and their governmental partners were pouring most available time and money into the development of a single, silver-bullet treatment while ignoring perfectly good medications and methods for curing opportunistic infections and controlling the spread of AIDS.

Seized with anger during one such conversation, Sonnabend snatched a piece of paper from his office and in ten minutes dashed off an article for the People with AIDS Coalition newsline about pentamidine—a cheap, available drug that could cure the deadliest opportunistic infection of the AIDS crisis. "Nobody should get pneumocystis pneumonia a second time," the article began, before going on to lay out several possible medicines already available to cure or prevent pneumonia—a list that included dapsone, bactrim, and aerosolized pentamidine. These drugs had been used in child leukemia patients and organ transplant recipients—patients with compromised immune systems similar to AIDS patients—to successfully control *Pneumocystis carinii* pneumonia (PCP). But the National Institute of Allergy and Infectious Diseases (NIAID) refused to recommend them for AIDS patients because specific studies in this population had not been carried out.[16]

Precise and targeted clinical trials are essential to good science, but the total unwillingness to use medications that had proven effective in virtually identical patients suggested a deeper anxiety about another kind of contagion. Child leukemia patients could not be equated with AIDS patients. Immune-suppressing drugs to keep the body from rejecting an organ donation could not be linked even obliquely with AIDS. To Sonnabend and Callen it seemed ridiculous that certain groups received PCP prophylaxis while people with AIDS languished and died, as they waited for a clinical trial tailored to them specifically.

"It is particularly galling to me that 16,929 of the 30,534 unnecessary PCP deaths occurred since May of 1987," wrote Callen after meeting with Dr. Anthony Fauci, then the director of the NIAID, and "the closest person we have to an AIDS czar."[17] Fauci was a mixed figure in the AIDS crisis, an eventual but not an immediate ally to AIDS activists. Callen had gone to him asking that the NIAID issue interim guidelines about the use of prophylactic drugs like pentamidine and bactrim in preventing PCP, but Dr. Fauci turned down the proposal on the grounds that there was no data to support the use of these drugs in people with AIDS.

Dr. Fauci said that there had never been any clinical studies of the effectiveness of pentamidine in AIDS patients, specifically. But physicians like Sonnabend were already prescribing it, off-label, to patients they deemed to be high risks for PCP. No one had undertaken a systematic study of how effective the treatments were, but anecdotal evidence of doctors and patients suggested that the medicine was highly effective. This was one of Sonnabend's great contributions: he paid attention to the actual experiences of average patients and their primary care physicians.

## The Pharmakon

The beauty of old languages is how they pry back the floorboards and reveal the metaphors our language is built on. In ancient Greek, the word *pharmakon* can mean poison or cure. In the original language, it contains both meanings at once; only in translation do we have to choose. Now, we have many words for these concepts, but the distinction between cure and poison is still ambiguous. Most medicines, taken incorrectly or at high enough dosages, can also be a strong poison; and even a poison, deployed correctly, can be curative. "The ambivalent quality of *pharmakon* is more than purely a matter of 'wrong drug, wrong dose, wrong route of administration, wrong patient,'" writes the social anthropologist Asha Persson. "Drugs, as is the case with antiretroviral therapy, have the capacity to be *beneficial and detrimental to the same person at the same time.*"[18]

"AZT Is Not a Poison," reads the title of one 1989 *New York Times* letter to the editor. "We were gratified by your article on our case report of an AIDS patient who developed liver damage on AZT. . . . However, this is an extremely rare side effect of a useful drug. . . . We are concerned that some will seize upon this as a reason to avoid potentially useful therapy."[19] But AZT was a poison, in the way all medicine is also poison. And the fight over AZT was at least in part a fight over conflicting definitions.

Early side effects included nausea, vomiting, headache, dizziness, fatigue, weakness, and muscle pain, but more severe and long-term side effects were common as well. AZT could, ironically, damage the immune system. It could cause intestinal problems, kidney disorders, and anemia so severe that patients required blood transfusions. It could lead to blistering and rashes, irregular heartbeat, extreme tiredness, and yellowing of the skin. Because AZT was first developed as a chemotherapy, meant to scorch the body and the cancer along with it, it destroyed cells indiscriminately and affected nearly every physiological system.

A drug's benefits are relative, depending on what greater suffering it prevents. All of the side effects of AZT combined were still better than dying, or at least less uncertain. The problem was that AZT didn't work, or at least it did not work in the way clinicians had hoped. While it caused patients' T-cell count to rise in the short term, the virus—infinitely protean—adapted, found new pathways around a single obstruction, and rendered the medicine useless. Whether or not the temporary increase in T cells extended life expectancy was, and still is, debated. The side effects were not.

In 1988, a team of researchers studying AZT released their findings in *The Lancet*. They found the drug to be disappointing. The medication damaged blood cells and provided only six months of elevated T-cell count in the body.[20] The original trials, which had lasted only six months and included fewer than three hundred people, missed the drop off in effectiveness that inevitably followed the illusory initial success of AZT. A subsequent trial, known as the Concorde study, ran between 1988 and 1991 in the United Kingdom, Ireland, and France. It found that AZT, despite its initial positive effect on immune cells, did not significantly increase the life expectancy of patients.[21] And so AZT, the drug that the government had endlessly funded and pharmaceutical companies had wrung for all of its value, depended at best on bad science and at worst on a lie.

Why was a drug with such harsh side effects and little evidence of its efficacy approved, while others with few side effects and the ability to extend life were ignored? One answer is money. Pharmaceutical companies and their government partnerships can make or break your career. They decide who gets grant funding and who doesn't. At a time when the entire private-public partnership between pharmaceutical companies and government agencies was focused on developing a single cure for AIDS, AZT and similar drugs received most of the attention and funding. But there were softer interests as well. As Sonnabend said, pharmaceutical companies "promote you and your research. You get a bit of fame and glory. Maybe being on the emotional take is ultimately more insidious than being on the dollar take."[22] He was never "on the take"; his personality—difficult, demanding, principled—seemed to insulate him from these concerns. As a doctor with deep roots in the community and the confidence of AIDS patients, he could have made a fortune testing and promoting drug companies' optimally profitable new products, but he did not.

Pentamidine, on the other hand, was "owned by small corporations that do not have the money to prime the research pump—wine and dine federal officials, fly scientists around the country, provide 30 million capsules of their drug free—all of which Burroughs Wellcome did when AZT testing began. Many physicians critical of the AIDS research effort are beginning to ask questions. They note that many promising drugs are derived from food products and thus not easily patentable, and wonder if any drug company will sponsor research on a substance from which it can derive no profit."[23] In other words, there was little money to be made selling these cheap, unpatented drugs.

The failure of AZT did not in itself have to be a tragedy. Drugs fail all the time. The problem of AZT was how many other potential avenues of treatment were disregarded in the process. As the infectious-disease expert Gordon Dickinson put it: "If you're spending your time working with AZT, you're not working with other drugs that may prove to be of lasting benefit to AIDS patients."[24] Without AZT what other medication might have been developed sooner? How much better might the treatment of opportunistic infections have been? There is no way to know the counterfactual, but it is almost certain that more people would have lived longer.

## The Community

In 1983 Sonnabend, along with friend Mathilda Krim, started the AIDS Medical Foundation, and four years later, in 1987, they founded the Community Research Initiative. Both foundations equipped private-practice doctors with the tools to collect and collate information on the treatments they had been trying. Community research was a radical reimagining of the process of testing and approving medication. It moved the locus of testing outside of governmental and university settings and into the average primary care physician's office. Not everyone was convinced by the idea of community-based research. Some researchers objected that doctors lacked the expertise and training to properly conduct controlled trials. Others, such as Dr. Robert T. Schooley of Massachusetts General Hospital, worried that patients would participate in several community-based drug trials at once, contaminating the purity of the study.[25] This would be a valid concern, a *Los Angeles Times* article notes, if such cross-contamination were not already occurring in academic and clinical research settings.

In 1987, two community-based trials tested the effects and efficacy of pentamidine. As Sonnabend wrote years later for *POZ* magazine: "The Community Consortium in San Francisco provided efficacy data, and the Community Research Initiative (CRI) in New York provided the safety data required by the FDA in the approval process."[26] Sonnabend wrote the protocol and acted as lead investigator for the CRI trials. "I think everything that I've done with respect to AIDS has been predicated on a 'do it yourself' principle," Sonnabend once said. "Since we can't rely on the government, we'll do whatever we need to do ourselves."[27]

The medicines the Community Research Initiative was interested in were not cures, in the sense that they did not stop or prevent AIDS or keep HIV from replicating, but they did keep people healthier for longer. Some patients, perhaps many of them, would have lived long enough to see the virus change—not in its biological nature but in its context—if they'd had earlier access to effective medicines that treated or prevented the most lethal opportunistic infections. More of them might have lived to see the advent of protease inhibitors, the class of drug that changed HIV from a deadly infection to a chronic one.

## The Theory

In May 1983, as HIV was being identified in a lab in France, Richard Berkowitz and Michael Callen published a pamphlet titled *How to Have Sex in a Pandemic: One Approach*, with Sonnabend acting as medical consultant. It's a slim volume, barely forty pages, zine-like, filled with recommendations for safer sex in thick, clumsy Courier font, but it had an enormous impact. Contemporary medical recommendations around safer sex bear a striking similarity to the original recommendations made in Berkowitz and Callen's pamphlet.

In the introduction, the authors lay out the various existent theories of AIDS: the "new agent theory" and the "multifactorial model." The new agent theory held that a novel virus (later confirmed to be HIV), recently introduced through an animal vector, was causing immune damage and eventual death in infected individuals. The multifactorial model, developed by Sonnabend, proposed that patients' immune systems were slowly damaged over time by repeated exposure to various existing viruses, such as Epstein-Barr, cytomegalovirus, and herpes.[28] Of course, these viruses had always existed and always circulated widely, but Sonnabend proposed that the 1970s were a tipping point, a time when these circulating viruses reached a critical mass in the gay population and started causing AIDS regularly enough that doctors and medical institutions began to notice. The exact metaphor Sonnabend used was a pool: if only a few people are jumping in and contaminating the water maybe a few will get sick, but if more people join and the water becomes saturated suddenly many people will begin to fall ill.

In the decades since the AIDS crisis began, the new agent theory has been confirmed again and again, but in the disorienting years of the early epidemic, Sonnabend's multifactorial model was neither unbelievable nor ridiculed. The incubation period of AIDS is long and irregular, making it hard to detect through the background static of disease, especially when only a small number of cases are distributed across a large population. And from the way AIDS emerged, dim and mysterious, as if out of a fog, it made intuitive sense that it was the result of a gradual buildup of damage over time. Susan Sontag, for one, was interested in Sonnabend's model, though she was not entirely convinced. In a 1986 letter she wrote, "Your argument that AIDS is a multi-factorial situation is—to a lay person—persuasive, certainly when I think of how the disease seems to be spreading among gay men. But how would you then account for the fact that some have gotten AIDS from a transfusion of contaminated blood?"[29] Others were more enthusiastic about Sonnabend's proposal. Stuart F. Schlossman, a professor of medicine at Harvard, wrote in 1983: "I had the chance to read your paper entitled 'A Multifactorial Model for the Development of AIDS in Homosexual Men' and found it to be first-rate and of considerable interest."[30]

After the publication of *How to Have Sex in a Pandemic*, Callen began calling himself an "inventor" of safe sex—a questionable but useful hyperbole. He encouraged Sonnabend to do the same. Safe sex may not have been invented as much as prescribed or discovered, but *How to Have Sex* was the first systematic attempt to prevent the spread of AIDS by adjusting sexual practices. For such an early document, I am struck by how effective the recommendations are. Despite its flawed theory, in its broader contours, the recommendations are almost entirely correct. Sonnabend and his coauthors categorized "getting fucked" without the use of a condom as one of the highest-risk sexual activities, while "fisting, though generally a risky activity, to be very low risk in terms of contracting AIDS." Part of the success of Sonnabend's theory is that his multifactorial model theorized a virus as the cause of AIDS, just not the right one. He believed condom use, rather than limiting the number of partners one had, would limit exposure, and therefore prevent AIDS. It was an incorrect theory, but it mapped closely enough to reality as to be useful. Sexually transmitted disease rates plummeted after the publication of *How to Have Sex*. But the important distinction Sonnabend and Callen made—that safe sex did not need to be sex with only one partner, but rather sex with barriers—was not appreciated by every member of the gay community, some of whom were wary of any limitations to their sexual autonomy.

Gay men and queer people, recently liberated in the 1960s and 1970s, were fearful of being banished back to the closet or boxed into monogamy. This wasn't what Sonnabend's pamphlet recommended, but any whiff of sexual moralizing or restraint was too much for some, and certain lines of *How to Have Sex* suggested a less than perfectly progressive assessment of this new liberation: "Sex and 'promiscuity' have become the dogma of gay male liberation," the authors wrote. "Have we modified the belief that we could dance our way to liberation into the belief that we could somehow fuck our way there? If sex is liberating, is more sex necessarily more liberating?" It did not help that in 1982 Callen and Berkowitz had published an article titled "We Know Who We Are: Two Gay Men Declare War on Promiscuity," inadvertently blaming promiscuity for the spread of the mysterious illness that would later be identified as AIDS.[31]

But Callen and Sonnabend refused to amend their stance. And so, their anti-institutional streak—a mix of righteousness and arrogance—led Sonnabend to two of his greatest contributions: community-based research, and his systematizing of safe sex. But it was this same combination of personal qualities that led him ultimately to diminish his own reputation.

## The Cost

In March 1987, Burroughs Wellcome released AZT. Here was the silver bullet. The promise of an AIDS cure. In the wake of this release, it was no longer enough to simply extend lives or cure opportunistic infections. Only a singular, totalizing cure would suffice, and so Samuel Broder of the National Cancer Institute called the use of pentamidine redundant because AZT, the mythic monotherapy, would soon cure not just the incidental infections but the virus itself.[32]

When AZT was first released, it cost ten thousand dollars a year. Burroughs Wellcome justified the price by claiming that the medicine was costly to produce, that cheaper alternatives would eventually cut into their profits, and that they needed to recoup the millions they'd invested in its research and development. But Burroughs Wellcome admitted to making twenty-five million dollars from AZT in its first six months on the market, and cheaper, more effective alternatives took years to materialize. Meanwhile, AZT became one of the highest-revenue-generating drugs of its time.[33] For a short period, federal grants covered some of the expense of AZT, but when those grants ran out patients who were not independently wealthy had to either forgo the medicine or allow the costs to eat their savings down to thirty-one hundred dollars—the level at which they could apply for Medicaid.

Although Burroughs Wellcome provided the raw material for clinical trials, it took on very little risk in the drug's production. "Indeed, one of the obstacles to the development of AZT," wrote Samuel Broder, "was that Burroughs Wellcome did not work with live AIDS virus, nor wish to receive samples from AIDS patients."[34] That Burroughs Wellcome would not even touch the patients they supposedly wanted to help seems, in hindsight, especially cruel.

The government could have challenged Burroughs Wellcome's patents on the drugs, but did not. Drug trials conducted via private and public cooperation could have loosened restrictions on intravenous drug users who wished to enter clinical trials for new AIDS medications, but did not. The government could have increased financial support for those who needed AZT, and they did for a short time, but eventually even those policies lapsed.

Listening to tapes 147 through 149 of Callen's recordings, each labeled simply "Sonnabend," I noticed a conspicuous sense of future pervading the tapes. At the beginning of tape 147, Callen acknowledges that "some poor queen is going to have to transcribe these,"[35] and I paused my transcription with an eerie sense of history speaking to me. In the tapes, Callen and Sonnabend vacilate in the certainty that they will be vindicated by history—that AZT will fail, their safe-sex prescription will work, and their multifactorial model will be validated. By this point Callen is sick. His T cells have dropped. He is already thinking about the utility of his activism and recordings, about death and posterity, about how he will be remembered.

Callen's interviews begin professionally. He acts as interviewer, kind but unwavering, asking Sonnabend to clarify his views on a range of topics: Is HIV the cause of AIDS or pathogenic at all? Should rimming have been reclassified as a high-risk activity? What is the best course of treatment for various patients based on their unique arrangement of opportunistic infections? Their ostensible purpose is to record Sonnabend in his own words on his multifactorial theory of AIDS, but the tapes lapse constantly into the unselfconscious banter of two friends catching up. They bicker:

"What archives? You never told me about those things," says Sonnabend.

"Yes, and you never followed up," counters Callen.

"Well, they're not that interested or they would have called me."

Their conversations become dense with references: friends, patients, former lovers, past slights, names shorn of context, savory but baffling morsels of gossip. "Is he still with that horrible man?"[36] It's clear to both of them who the "horrible man" is. They speak in the language of long friendship. They have no need to explain.

Once, when discussing a friend and patient of Sonnabend's whose T cells have dropped to fifteen per cubic milliliter of blood, the reality of Callen's situation enters the room. "He's worse-off than you," says Sonnabend. "No," corrects Callen, "I'm around seventy-five."[37] The threshold for an AIDS diagnosis is two hundred.

Callen himself lived for nearly ten years with HIV, so long people wondered publicly if he had AIDS at all. At one point he had to reveal his medical records complete with X-rays of his Kaposi's sarcoma–scarred lungs for the public to believe him. Callen was certainly lucky, but it was also Sonnabend's care, his focus on keeping patients healthy for as long as possible rather than striving after a potentially illusive cure, that allowed him to live so long. I wonder if Callen ever questioned his friend's authority, if he ever wondered if he himself should get on AZT. I find no evidence of this in any of his recordings. Publicly he was an unwavering supporter of Sonnabend, even when he was wrong.

## The Lawsuit

It is important to understand how often Sonnabend was right, how frequently he was questioned, how many enemies he created for the right reasons, to understand why he clung for so long to a debunked theory. Looking at the long stretch of his life, I am impressed that he did not descend into complete paranoia. Enemies were at every turn: in the medical establishment, in the government, in his own community, even in the apartment building where he practiced. And while some of these enemies might have been invented, exaggerated, or self-imposed, there were genuine attempts to limit his practice and influence.

In 1983, the 49 West 12th tenant corporation—the co-op from whom Sonnabend rented an apartment where he treated his patients—denied him a new lease. The co-op had ostensible reasons for the denial. The board claimed that Sonnabend was illegally occupying an apartment across the hall. The claim was true to a limited extent. Sonnabend was using an apartment across the hall from his own, but he had permission from the tenant, a neighbor who allowed Sonnabend to temporarily use her space for his overflow of research and clinical equipment. He did not have money to compensate her for the stay, so he thanked her by painting the apartment. The tenant board took issue with the painting. They claimed he had carried out renovations on the apartment, that his patients were loud and disruptive, and that Sonnabend was delinquent on his rent payments. These were transparent covers for a truth no one had to state out loud because the truth was obvious: the board did not want AIDS patients in the building. Which is of course the treachery of obvious truths: they are often the hardest to prove because no one has to articulate them. You can claim you're evicting someone for painting a neighbor's apartment, for speaking too loudly in the lobby, and everyone, sympathetic or not, will know the real reason why you're being evicted, without any way to prove it.

Lambda Legal took on Sonnabend's case pro bono. They called it the first AIDS discrimination case in the country. In court documents and contemporaneous notes from Sonnabend after his meetings with the co-op's lawyer, the already obvious truth was revealed: Tenants—always spoken about in the aggregate or referenced anonymously as having "expressed their concerns to the board"—had claimed to be worried about Sonnabend's practice and the patients he treated. It is difficult to know whether there was any genuine concern about catching AIDS from casual contact with patients passing through the lobby. But in a deposition, Sonnabend laid out another possible reason for his eviction: tenant-shareholders "feared that their property values in the co-op would be adversely affected by the nature of my practice."[38]

Here, the risk of disease is constructed, not in terms of physical but rather financial contagion; and fear of AIDS, not as a fear of sickness and death, but as the ruin of an investment. It seems likely that these New York tenants—anonymous behind the legal mechanism of their co-op board—knew that there was little risk of actually contracting HIV. New York City was the epicenter of the crisis, and it was also a city where the average citizen knew the most about AIDS. As Sonnabend noted in an open letter to the residents of 49

West 12th Street, "AIDS does not spread by casual contact. This is not only my opinion. It is definitively the prevailing medical and scientific opinion, and indeed government representatives have gone to some length to disseminate this view."[39] The residents of 49 West 12th Street likely knew this as well, meaning they did not really care about having the AIDS patients in their building. They may even have been sympathetic to Sonnabend's difficulties and the illness of his patients, but they did not want those same patients damaging the value of their property through association.

Had Sonnabend lost his case, he would have been forced to move his practice to another building if he were able to move it at all. Treatments would have been missed, valuable time lost. Some of his patients, already transient and fickle, would have stopped coming due to a longer commute, the time away, or simply because they'd fallen out of the habit.

He won his case in the end, and his practice continued, but for all the grit and community New York celebrates in the narrative identity of the city, it required a legal order for Sonnabend to be able to continue practicing. In a recorded conversation between Sonnabend, Callen, and Lambda Legal, an unnamed man asks: "Why bother having that extra problem in your life?" The tape lacks perfect context. Maybe this is simply a prudent question for a legal team preparing a plaintiff for his defense. Maybe the man is truly skeptical of Sonnabend's claim on the apartment. Either way, his question ghosts the unspoken sentiment of the co-op board. Why not protect the value of the building you co-own, the imagined purity of the air in your lobby? Why not choose the easiest way to live, the most cautious and least generous? Is there harm if you can't see it? Is there harm if it's sublimated across dozens of patients, their minor inconveniences at accessing care?

Sonnabend responds tersely as ever, evoking the city's narrative of itself: "Because one lives in a city where AIDS is a real problem."[40]

## The Fall

The story of how Sonnabend lost his credibility is both frustratingly simple and narratively familiar, a story lifted right out of Shakespeare's histories or a Greek tragedy: a leader gains power then refuses to listen. A doctor, unbowed by early pressure, forgets his own fallibility. He was a man in love with his worldview, one strengthened by repeated questioning and repeated triumphs. When he died in 2021, obituaries ran in the *New York Times* and the *Washington Post*. The writers politely rushed through the fact that Sonnabend had clung to his multifactorial model of AIDS well into the 1990s, and that he had denied the role of HIV in the AIDS crisis. Colleagues and AIDS activists—those still alive—praised his contributions to both medical science and the queer community, but despite being the coinventor of safe sex, the first plaintiff in an AIDS-based discrimination case, and the founder of several of the leading community research organizations, Sonnabend is not famous. Even as someone with a long-standing interest in the epidemic, I missed Sonnabend's death for several years.

By the 1990s, the era of acceptable HIV skepticism had passed. The viruses had been witnessed firsthand and accepted as the cause of AIDS. Holdouts were labeled quacks, blacklisted, or looked at with pity and skepticism. Rather than accepting that his theory might be flawed or simply wrong, Sonnabend broadened it. When confronted with contradictory evidence, he discounted it or carved out strange and implausible exceptions to maintain the central integrity of his multifactorial model. When asked how this model—which required AIDS patients to accrue a certain amount of immunological damage from repeated exposure—could exist alongside the fact that some people develop AIDS after only a few sexual exposures, or even just one, Sonnabend proposed that some men's semen could generate a particularly high level of damage with few exposures. Callen supported his novel carveouts and even Sonnabend's most outlandish propositions; he even added to them. On the tapes, you can hear the two working through contradictions, tuning his flawed theory against the mounting evidence, always countering and parrying recriminations against them. "Well maybe the person's semen was a bad match with him . . . I'm sure that's possible," Michael argues in a conversation discussing one such man who developed AIDS after very few exposures. What mechanism could account for these bad matches or this exceptional level of damage? And why hadn't Sonnabend theorized any of this until evidence had accumulated, contradicting his theory? All of this goes unaddressed.

Only in snatches does the possibility of error arise. "Are you more or less convinced that the multifactorial model is correct?" asks Callen in a tape recorded in the late 1980s. He adds, after a brief pause, "in its essential outline. I know you've always said that the details are not important."

"No, I can't say I'm convinced," Sonnabend admits at one point, though this is an outlier.

Hints buried in the tape reveal that he recognized his own contrarian tendencies and knew that he was most comfortable in opposition to authority. In the final minutes of tape 149, Callen and Sonnabend discuss an impending interview, an opportunity for Sonnabend to reaffirm his belief in the multifactorial model. He says, "Even if it sort of ostracizes me again, maybe I'm more comfortable in that situation."[41]

## The End

Some people called Sonnabend a saint. Like his mother he was famous for visiting his patients in the middle of the night. He would come to them to deliver the news of their HIV-positive status in person. Others felt that by the end he had ruined his reputation clinging to a long-disproven idea. But more than anything he was forgotten, as complex lives often are when they fail to live up to clean binaries of history.

I'm not interested in sainthood; it's flattening and false, something assigned by later centuries to instrumentalize a life. Sonnabend was a challenging personality: prickly and demanding, both arrogant and empathetic. He loved his work and his patients, who were also his friends and collaborators. He loved them in a way that was blinding and revelatory in turns. It is convenient to ignore half of him in service of the other, but looking at the totality of his life, it's clear neither half could have existed without the other.

In the archives, I return to a copy of *How to Have Sex in a Pandemic: One Approach*. I'm struck on this second reading by the lyricism of the pamphlet and its flights of tenderness. "From the day we are born we are trained as men to compete with other men. The challenge facing gay men in America is to figure out how to love some one [*sic*] you've been trained to 'destroy.'" I was surprised again, and thrilled, to discover the word *destroy,* the danger of it, the somewhat ambiguous scare quotes buzzing gnatlike around its head, the linking of the destruction of the AIDS crisis, a crisis no queer person asked or was responsible for, with the masculine-tinged drive toward violence.[42] I was surprised, too, by the word *love;* nestled between the dry assessments about the relative risks of rimming and the burgeoning trend of jerk-off clubs are poetic runs and philosophical musings. "It came as quite a shock to us to find that we had written almost 40 pages on sex without mentioning the word 'love' once," write the authors in the penultimate section, a section that is itself titled "Love." Accustomed to the sterile sexual health pamphlets in clinics and waiting rooms, I was not surprised at all. In fact, I was surprised to find any deep or risky attempts at a broader ethic at the heart of their work. I expected a papier-mâché of health statistics and committee-written recommendations. I was surprised that someone would claim love had anything to do with health, with disease, with medicine, by this move beyond the strictures of science. As the section continues, they write, "If you love the person you are fucking with—*even for one night*—you will not want to make them sick. Maybe affection is our best protection."[43]

Reading this I cannot help but think of the doctors and review boards who assessed the original trials for AZT. They would likely have labeled the sharing of medication as "noncompliance," a cruel word, apathetic and clinical. It contains the brutality that defined the AIDS epidemic: the neglect and indifference to suffering. But something deeply hopeful shines in the word—a small form of resistance, a private protest. People found ways to make a life even in the face of unimaginable tragedy and near-certain death. They took care of one another even in the face of institutional apathy and governmental neglect.

At a moment near the end of tape 149, Sonnabend becomes his most real: a man plagued by insecurities and quotidian desires— for love, for sex, for understanding. It is one of the most intimate tapes, almost entirely of Sonnabend and Callen talking about their theory, what they will leave to history, but also about each other.

"Maybe it'll get you some dates," Callen says, in reference to a new underground fund named after Sonnabend.

"Well, I think I'm really past that . . . "

"I don't," says Callen, so fast you can tell he knew exactly what Sonnabend was going to say, even before he said it. "I think you would have a whole new era of creativity if you cleaned out your ducts."

"I think you're right."

"I know I'm right."

"But I'm an old man." In fact, he nearly describes himself as a "dirty old man" but backs away from the description mid-word. Unlike Callen—eternally youthful, with a sharp jaw ending in a small chin—Sonnabend was one of those people who became infamous later in life, and so is suspended in perpetual old age. Nearly every photo shows him bearded with deep recessions in his hairline. Even manicured for the cover of *POZ* magazine his eyebrows are staticlike, wild and overlong.

"There's somebody for you. Trust me . . . You're just a difficult person, Joe," says Callen, and a beat later: "You're very moody."

Here, there comes a disturbance in the tape, a fingerprint of static, or maybe Sonnabend just lapses into a self-conscious mumbling. Whatever the case, it's hard to hear his response, but it sounds like he says, "Well, I'm fucked up." To which Callen replies, "Join the team."[44]

This little beat of intimacy appears at the end of one of their final tapes. They've exhausted the PR plans and the arguments and the gossip. All the old injuries have been trotted out and reworked, and now here they are alone with each other.

I have no doubt that Callen and Joe loved one another, though their exact relationship and how it changed across the years has never been completely clear. They seemed in the end to be close platonic friends and accomplices, the kind forged by a common cause and deepened by an unexpected compatibility.

Callen died in 1993, Sonnabend in 2021—outliving his friend by nearly thirty years—but before he did, he wrote an article titled simply "I Miss Michael Callen." Opening the article, I'd hoped to see Sonnabend's interior world articulated, his feelings of love and loss spelled out. But the article is characteristically factual, controversial, and dry. Largely, it's a biography of Callen and his contributions, which bookend Sonnabend's latest contentious opinion: that antiretrovirals are being prescribed too early!

Callen, it seems, was one of the few people who could elicit any kind of sentimentality from Joe. In that way the article is honest. In place of emotions, Sonnabend arrives with an argument, even after his friend's death, ready to fight. And isn't that the thing about loving difficult men? They will be wrong as often as they are right. They will make enemies of old allies, burn bridges out of senseless pride. They will frustrate you endlessly with their inability to play nice, their overly principled stances, even when they're wrong. A part of you will know that they do it selfishly because they have something to prove, because they have learned no other way of living in the world. But in the end, they will also be difficult for you.

When Sonnabend and Callen hang up on this final call, the recording doesn't end. After three minutes of velvety, crackling silence, I can see voices in the waveform approaching. I know to wait, and suddenly another phone call begins. History loops back on itself. There's no real content here, just a promise. Sonnbabend picks up the phone and says, "Can you give me ten minutes? I'll call you in ten minutes."[45] Callen agrees, then the tape ends.

# Exit Wounds

\

I should start with what happened: I'm on a bus, traveling back to Chicago on the first sweltering day of summer. Actually, the bus isn't traveling yet. We haven't left the "station," which is just a sign stuck into a cement plinth that someone rolls away after the bus leaves. Later, someone will worry about security. Someone will say this was bound to happen.

I'm on the second level of the double-decker bus, putting in headphones, wiggling into a position of apathy against the window, when I hear shouting downstairs. The sound doesn't quite peak or harden into language, but it has a rhythm, and the rhythm is urgent, and then it's angry. What animal instinct awakens that knows something is wrong? In front of me is one row of chairs, then the stairwell leading back down to the first floor. The man sitting in front of me is wide-eyed. He can see down to the lower deck. He is watching what's happening there. He leans back and turns his head to look at me, then bandies his hand around in the shape of a gun.

Fear sharpens me into the moment. Anxiety surges through the crowd. I notice everything: a freckled girl sobs on the phone to her mother, a woman in cutoffs rubs her legs anxiously, a young man in sunglasses and a black T-shirt leans his head against the window and sets his jaw; he looks almost bored. I'm moving without thinking. I cross to the other row, which feels safer, brighter. I'm running on superstition and impulse. People are on the phone to several different dispatchers. They speak in the choked timbre of panic.

In my new seat, I handle the red emergency latch on the window, picture it coming free of its frame, sloughed off like shed skin and shattering against the pavement. I am wondering if it is too far to drop, too dramatic for us to all pile out of the window and scatter like insects, when a police cruiser comes fishtailing into the parking lot in a siege of sound and light. For a moment, time means nothing. It dilates to a ripping point. Fear is miraculous like this: a physical medium. Where does it come from? Dropping over us like a curtain. The officer opens his door as a barricade, kneels in its joint, and fires. No warning.

You don't see the bullets, I realize. Of course not! They are just coils of smoke in the air, a burning smell. They live in the future—sounds reaching me after the fact, six percussive beats as fast as the machinery can reload. They come battering around the aluminum tube of the bus. Errant, angry things. One passes through a window—leaves it a pile of green-tinted baked glass on the pavement. Another goes through our cheap seat coverings with a tearing sound, probably. And a third through the fat and flesh of a passenger's waist. It chips his hip bone like a teacup, then lodges itself in soft plastic. The gunman runs and falls. I can't see him, but I can see the heads of other passengers pressed against the window, following him. They stop dead as he collapses against the sidewalk. Whatever separates us from raw emotion—shouting, weeping, beating your fist against the earth—becomes shell-thin. At a high enough pitch, all emotions are the same.

When it's over, the cruiser is still rocking with the momentum of its entrance.

What tense is there for an event that recurs, for one that is complete and also ongoing, the past but also the present, and by extension likely the future? I want a tense for blurred time and blurred subjects, too, that accounts for the failure of memory—its omissions and additions—that does not just speak to uncertainty but encodes it in the very structure. A tense without time. We don't have language for this: the cruiser rocking, the sun beating, the bullets forever in motion even after they have landed. Time honeycombed, collapsing, piling up on itself.

In the strange, still moment after the bullets stop flying, we look around the bus, worried there might be other gunmen. When a young man stands up, no one is at first sure what's happening, only that his left flank is glossy with blood. Not the bright red of exposed blood in the open air, but blood making his T-shirt dark and wet, so much blood it's consuming his side, as it spreads quickly through the fibers. A savage noise crawls up and out of someone's throat. The woman in cutoffs calls for a towel, an extra shirt, to press into the wound. The man is so calm, standing in the aisle like he's searching the crowd for a familiar face. His seatmate leads him down the stairs, shreds of cotton turning to rust under her hand.

I've been pulled back into that moment countless times, and I will likely be pulled back there again.

---

Every weekday, back in Chicago, I would take the train fifty minutes from my apartment in Edgewater to my job west of the Loop, transferring once at Belmont and getting off at Merchandise Mart. On the L, the air was always tight and netted with voices. In the morning people read the paper; on Friday evenings men in suits flipped ties over their shoulders and cracked open beers. These were normal things, benign, and yet I found myself getting off the train with relief. My brain was having trouble distinguishing what was dangerous and what was safe.

On the streets some days, I would hear the blaring of police sirens or hear a man's harsh voice and step backward in time to that moment of panic on the bus. I have read this is common in PTSD patients. It took me years to name the experience. In fact, someone else had to do it for me. I still balk at the terms a little, unwilling to reduce my experience. I want my suffering to be singular. At times it feels precious to me. I want to keep it unnamed, private, pristine.

I rarely remember my dreams, but after the incident I began thrashing my way out of them. I would be in the middle of a nightmare about fear and helplessness—clawing at the ground for purchase, or trying to mop up the blood of a friend who's been shot in a convenience store, shouting, "*There aren't enough paper towels!*" when abruptly everything comes back online like an engine catching. Suddenly I'm up, shouting. My sister once woke me up while we were traveling together. I was tossing and mumbling in bed. I woke up yelling into the darkness of our shared bedroom. The next morning, I was too embarrassed to ask her what I had been saying. Another night, I startled my boyfriend awake in the same way. "What the fuck. What's wrong?" he asked, rolling over to aim his concern at me. I was sweat-drenched and upright, staring into his closet, slowly piecing together where I was. My fear sublimated into an immediate, irrational fury.

"Nothing! People have bad dreams," I said, wrapping the top sheet around me like a toga before getting up and stalking out of the room.

"Hey, I need that," he said as I left to sleep on the couch, the sheet trailing behind me.

A story ran in the *Columbus Dispatch* a few days after I returned to Chicago: "Man Charged in Megabus Hijack Attempt Tells Courtroom He Is Mentally Ill."[1] In the picture at the top of the article, I saw the gunman's face for the first time. He survived. Despite the seven shots (or was it six? memory immediately distorts the world), he was only struck in the hand. His gravest injuries were sustained from a fall as he attempted to flee the scene. An ambulance took him to the hospital, and he was released into police custody later that day.

In the photo accompanying the story, his mouth hangs open in a wild shout. He's pressed against his lawyer, a pale public defender several inches shorter who is making a futile effort to quiet his client. The picture is deeply effective if its intention is to inspire fear. The contrast makes him look imposing, unpredictable, crazy. It's a photo of a man caught in the tautology of mental illness: made to look insane by admitting *I'm sick,* punished by demanding relief.

I learn his name, too: Arsenio Rodriguez, like the Cuban bolero musician. Is this a coincidence or does some long, specific story unspool from it? Is his family Cuban? Did his mother love guaracha? What music filled his childhood home? What records collected dust on the shelves? The article doesn't cover that. There isn't space. Instead, it delineates his criminal record: a stone thrown through an ex-girlfriend's window and a subsequent restraining order; an incident at a Rockville, Maryland, bank, in which he screamed at a teller but was never prosecuted; a second restraining order granted by Prince George's County that December; and pending charges for malicious destruction of property, second-degree assault, disorderly conduct, and trespassing.[2]

Arsenio's rap sheet can be read in two ways. On the one hand, this long string of violence and outbursts could be read—and for the most part it was—as the reason Arsenio should be separated from the community. But on the other hand, could there be a clearer indication that Arsenio was losing his mind, that he needed help and treatment, than a rock thrown through a window, than screaming at a bank teller? In this other reading violence works as a form of language: a call or a plea, desperate and wordless, a last recourse when all other language fails.

---

"We tend to think of mental hospitals as snake pits, hells of chaos and misery, squalor and brutality. Most of them now are shuttered and abandoned and we think with a shiver of terror of those who once found themselves confined in such places," Oliver Sacks writes at the opening of his book *Asylum,* a joint project with the photographer Christopher Payne, about one of America's most expansive state-run institutions.[3] The book is both a linguistic and visual interrogation of the now-vanished world of state psychiatric hospitals. Next to Sacks's prose are sepia-toned photos, postcard lithographs, blueprints, and photos of the palatial institutions that once housed the severely mentally ill. The photographs are grand and elegiac. The vast grounds and ornate ballrooms. The chapel-like lengths of abandoned hallways and impossibly long scrolls of peeling paint. The industrial mixers and ductwork of a facility meant to feed and warm hundreds. The intimacy of used sneakers, hair curlers, a cupboard filled with hanging toothbrushes, labeled by last name. They all speak to the vastness of the project, its ambitions, and its eventual collapse.

Sacks does not indulge in the pulpy fear-mongering that often accompanies depictions of mental hospitals. His first job as a neurologist in the Bronx State hospital was a generally positive experience. He writes that at the best of times mental hospitals could be places where "one's madness could be assured of finding, if not a cure, at least recognition and respect, and a vital sense of companionship and community."[4] But neither does he glamorize life within asylums. By the 1960s, hospitals were underfunded and unsanitary sites of human rights violations. "One must not be too romantic, about madness or the madhouses in which the insane were confined," he cautions.[5] Within Payne and Sacks's book are the surgical arenas, the straitjackets, the corroded enamel tubs, and the morgue cabinets that most of us fearfully associate with asylums. Still, Sacks and the attending photos suggest that some form of care and protection was lost when we rejected this form of treatment. He links the structure of the illness to the architecture that once cloistered, restricted, and certainly protected—though ambivalently—the people who suffered from it: "There is, under the manias and grandiosities and fantasies and hallucinations, an immeasurably deep sadness about mental illness, a sadness that is reflected in the often grandiose but melancholy architecture of the old state hospitals." Neither condemnation nor approval, the book instead is a testament to the enormous task of dealing with mental illness as manifested through architecture—a task, Sacks suggests, that we have transformed into something small and stopgap.

Of course this narrowing of our ambitions did not happen in a single day, and it was born out of generally good intentions. After the discovery of antipsychotic medication in 1950, large federal hospitals were shut down in favor of smaller, short-term state and community clinics. The promise was that these clinics, with the help of tranquilizers, could treat people suffering from mental illness just as well as large asylums, without the price or the questionable ethics of long-term confinement. The problem was that antipsychotics didn't work as well as they were purported to, and, because of their negative side effects, without supervision many patients stopped taking them altogether.

By the 1990s nearly all large mental hospitals were closed, and underfunded clinics were struggling to deal with the influx of patients. "The 'sidewalk psychotics' in every major city were a stark reminder that no city had an adequate network of psychiatric clinics and halfway houses, or the infrastructure to deal with the hundreds of thousands of patients who had been turned away from the remaining state hospitals," Sacks writes.[6] Arsenio was a single member of this larger pattern of men and women left to rely on the intermittent supervision and irregular care of community health centers.

The *Columbus Dispatch* article did not cover these patterns: the cascade from closed asylums and the overreliance on tranquilizers to random acts of violence and eventual imprisonment. It is probably unfair to expect this level of cultural and historical context from a one-page article in a local newspaper, but the way the article framed the violence made it appear absent of history and loosed from a chain of cause and effect. This absence was at times more horrifying than any specific act of violence itself. The article labeled the attack "random," and I would wonder, in the months of anxiety that followed, what *random* meant. That the attack wasn't targeted? That it wasn't planned? That the logic of the attack did not play by the rules of the sane? Or did it mean that the history was too long, too knotted with failures and false promises to be untangled?

It is easy to pin violence to a single moment. This may be one of its greatest appeals, its clarity, its singularity, its temporal limits and sharp, provocative edges. But violence begins early, spreads soundlessly. This is its more complicated truth; it rarely begins and ends in a single moment. It breaches the surface in a single moment, yes, but its roots are as patient and rhizomatic as a fungus.

Here is one branch: more than age, more than race, more than armed or unarmed, the existence of a mental illness is the greatest indicator of whether someone will or will not be shot by police. In 2015, prompted by a lack of national statistics, the *Washington Post* began compiling information on police shootings throughout the country. Every year, there are approximately one thousand such killings, and of those killed one-fourth suffer from some type of mental illness.[7] I find something compulsive in these figures. Despite implicit bias and de-escalation training, the mood of the country notwithstanding, they repeat with unnerving regularity year after year.

The theory is that relatively rare events over huge populations will not fluctuate without massive social change. But I have my own theory: that something sacrificial is buried in these numbers, a blood offering, a willingness to avoid fear at all costs, even if the cost is another person's life. Online, you can see these lives plotted as a line graph expressing fatal shootings on the $y$-axis and time on the $x$-. Each year is the same steady snail's trail of ink inching up and out at a perfect forty-five-degree angle. But the project also includes brief, single-paragraph descriptions of each reported killing and links to longer articles written by local reporters.

The summer after the incident, I spent many nights in a cafe named Kafein—jagged, lightning-bolt-shaped letters spelled out the name against a black awning—obsessed with these numbers, submerged in research, drinking cup after cup of coffee as light slowly drained from the sky. I knew that I wanted to write about what had happened, but I didn't know how. I imagined that with enough dogged tenacity, research could carry me through some imagined finish line. I filled and labeled folders with juicy slivers of information, stories that I found particularly interesting—the man armed with wasp spray, a sixty-six-year-old woman holding first a pair of scissors then a baseball bat—or stories that seemed to fit with particular themes: "Unusual 'Weapons'" read one folder, "People Calling for Help" read another. I had a document labeled "Notes" that was nothing more than three pages of hyperlinks to associated white papers, book PDFs, and local news articles. After a few weeks I had ten different drafts of an essay that had exploded to twenty thousand words. It was the writer's equivalent of pushing my food around the plate: the shape changed, but nothing was added or lost.

On these nights, I would trudge home feeling like I'd just spent hours trying to spear a thread through a needle's impossibly small eye, my head buzzing with caffeine and atomized bits of violence. My work was taking on the quality of those collages strung with red yarn that are used in movies about serial killers or intricate conspiracies. An image that means only one thing: the character is coming unhinged.

Sometimes, unable to sleep, I would go grocery shopping in the middle of the night. I liked the strip of bright windows against the darkness. The freshly restocked produce, the shuttered meat counter, and rows of cold, glowing milk refrigerators—I found it all very comforting. The only people in the store at that hour were other insomniacs—we barely saw each other, shuffling around the store—and undergrads working the night shift at the checkout. Everyone seemed too tired to pose any real threat.

———

No one talks about the waiting. How dull it is to get caught up in tragedy, how hungry you get. Hours pass on the bus, police tape is strung, ambulances come and go. The engine and the air conditioning are off, so the bus gathers heat and stinks like a foot. Sunlight beads on our necks. I surprise myself by getting bored. *I know we were just in a shooting, but can we leave already?* I take calls from friends who have somehow heard about what happened. I hang up on one local news station asking for an interview. When we are finally allowed to get off, we step carefully over the trail of blood, which runs like a ribbon twisting in the wind—widening, narrowing, sun-browned and puckered by specks of dirt. Police instruct us not to disrupt the crime scene. They tell us to leave everything behind. We stumble out covering our eyes with our forearms, blinking in the keen summer light. We enter, unwillingly, into the churn of the criminal justice system. We lose our autonomy. We are led away like toddlers or criminals. The bomb squad pulls our luggage from the undercarriage, and a mechanical arm picks through our wadded underwear. In an alleyway, we press ourselves into a narrow band of shade against an anonymous building. We're given bottles of water and crackers, and after someone asks, we're escorted to a mechanic's shop to use the restroom.

Another bus is summoned. We move from the alley to the air-conditioned interior with delight, but we are still not allowed to leave. We have to be processed first. A detective with a black notepad invites us out one by one to give statements. He's like a caricature of a detective, curt as a French waiter. His face says, "Get on with it," so his mouth doesn't have to. He rattles through questions from his notebook. Mostly I nod or say, "I don't know. I didn't see." Which is true, and, running through his questions, I realize precisely how little I witnessed. I didn't even see the gunman. He was nothing but a voice and a shape indicated by a shower of bullets. Instead, I tell the detective about moving seats, about the girl on the phone with her mother, about the ribbon of blood. I tell him about the police officer skidding into the parking lot and firing. Did he write that down? None of it is useful to the detective. He lets me go back into the air conditioning.

On board another cop is explaining to the crowd that we might be asked to testify. If we're called, he says, with false cheer, it will be all expenses paid, free flight, free room and board. I'm wondering who would want that, when a woman raises her hand like we're in class and asks, "What hotel?"

---

Months after the event and I was still thinking about what happened. My mind had dug a trench in the form of a question: *What would have happened if I hadn't changed seats?* Would I have been the passenger that got hit, the one led off the bus leaving behind a ribbon of blood, or worse, would the bullet have gone right through my stomach? My chest? These events were all long sealed by time. There was no point in continuing to think about them. And yet, I couldn't help myself. Sometimes, I would rub the spot where I had imagined being hit. Sometimes, the fantasy was so strong I would gasp or shudder for no apparent reason.

I saw violence everywhere. Sitting on a train one day, I became fixated on a man who shoved his way on board with a mesh basket stuffed with rumpled clothes and newspapers. He stood in the corner, consumed in his own private thoughts and conversations, shouting from time to time to the rest of the train car. I would not let myself turn to look directly at him, afraid of inviting some kind of confrontation. But from the corner of my eye, I was convinced that he was looking at me, staring even. I was afraid of him, and ashamed of this fear, aware of just how illogical my fear was, but as the sun dropped over the skyline a sense of impending doom surged through me. I heard the bullet first—or was it a brick?—

colliding with the train, blowing through the window behind me. Then I saw the shattering glass, and the bloodied plastic interior of the wagon. Blood from whom? I didn't know. And the train compartment was no longer a train, but the hot, bright bus.

The feeling was so intense, I held my breath waiting for it. I considered changing seats, but instead, when the train stopped, I stood up and walked onto the platform. I told myself that I would get on the next one, but when it arrived, I stood in front of the doors unmoving. Passengers streamed around me. Then the conductor called, the doors rattled shut, and I stood there watching the train curve and vanish down the track. I walked the rest of the way home.

The first time it happened was not the worst or the most spectacular, but it was the most alarming. The volume on the world seemed to get turned down, and I was suddenly convinced that I was going to pass out, or vomit, or drop dead right there on the spot. I was worried about what was happening, and equally worried about making a scene. It was summertime, twilight, and I was eating dinner on a patio with friends. No one noticed that I'd stopped talking; people kept on with their conversations. I could barely understand what they were saying, their words were so muted by my internal panic. That's what it was, I would later identify, a panic attack. It's so obvious when it's over. That first attack hadn't even been that bad, but they got worse.

Another evening, in the throes of a wicked hangover, one that left the world shimmering around its edges like a migraine, it happened again. I was at a Mexican restaurant with friends. I played it cool, tried to breathe, but by the time we were back at their place, playing video games from the homey comfort of their living room, it had become unbearable. I stepped out onto the back deck, taking huge, swallowing gulps of the ice-crusted Midwestern air. I leaned over my knees and panted like a marathon runner. I'd never been so aware of the circumference of my lungs, their cubic volume and tensile strength. I strained my diaphragm for more.

Back inside, I said, "I feel like I'm having a heart attack, but I'm pretty sure I'm just panicking." Strange how both of these things could feel categorically true. Strange how casually the words came out of my mouth. Strange how there was no solution in admitting it. No one was sure what to do, and I stood there feeling ridiculous and alarmed, until someone put me to bed like a child. A friend laid their hand on my back and muttered to me in a soothing voice until the episode had passed.

It was hard to believe that this was panic-induced, even if I had all the typical symptoms. Some days a portion of my face felt as if it were contorting, and to assimilate this feeling I'd become convinced I was having a stroke. I would suddenly feel like my throat was closing, and worry I'd discovered some latent new allergy in the almonds I'd just eaten or the glass cleaner I'd used to wipe down my computer screen. Some days I felt like my body was simply going to stop, shut down like a machine switched off, and I waited in clenched fear of the aneurism or aortal tear that would be the end of me. Of course, any pain in my chest, or back, or arm was a sure sign of a heart attack, and if I scanned deeply enough I could always find and amplify a source of pain. When I was panicked over some imagined mortal illness, the panic was compounded by my fear of completely losing control. And when I wasn't panicked, I worried I was going crazy. It didn't matter that fear of going insane was one of the top symptoms listed in nearly every account I read of panic attacks; my brain could wiggle out of any logic.

*Psychosomatic* is usually just a polite way to call something faked. But when I rush to the hospital after another attack a nurse tells me with sympathy that she's seen patients pass out from panic attacks. The problem might begin in the mind, but that doesn't mean there aren't real effects on the body. *Somatic*—of the body—is at least half the word, an important and coequal player to *psycho*—of the mind. Why do we privilege the body with the real, and burden the mind with the imagined? People have reported losing their sight and their hearing from anxiety alone, even though there was nothing mechanically wrong with their eyes or ears. Perhaps it has to do with demonstrability: you can see the burn, the cut, the cast around a broken bone. What you can't see is the panic, the depression, the numbness. Perhaps in this way passing out, losing your sight, watching your arms go numb and twist into a contorted claw, is the mind's way of proving its pain, demonstrating it in the language of the body.

I'd gone to the hospital one afternoon specifically because my arms went completely numb for no apparent reason. I would have marveled at this if it weren't so terrifying. In the hospital nurses pulled the cellophane backs off suction cups for an EKG and drew my blood. One of them was very young. She was in training; another, older nurse, stood behind her. The younger nurse kept staring at the well of my elbow, its delicate tracing of veins, like she was trying to remember her grocery list. She hesitantly tapped my bicep with two fingers to stimulate blood flow, but had not yet put the rubber tourniquet on. Normally, I wouldn't mind her blundering attempts, but when she looked over her shoulder at the other nurse for encouragement, I spiraled back into panic. "Can you just do it?" I asked the older nurse. Anxiety, it turns out, does not make you patient or particularly kind.

A doctor eventually came in and prescribed me hydroxyzine—an antihistamine—to make me drowsy. I didn't understand what good this was supposed to do, but I tried it anyway. It did make me drowsy, so then I was drowsy and anxious, and still couldn't sleep. I lay in bed for hours watching television and counting the beats of my heart. After a second trip to the hospital, a doctor prescribed me sertraline, a selective serotonin reuptake inhibitor. I started with half a tablet, which I cracked in half by hand. The drug cut my libido and made my eyes bullet-heavy. It didn't seem to help with my anxiety, but it was hard to tell. I didn't go back to the hospital. A friend suggested I keep a notebook of my feelings. "It's hard to evaluate something that's directly affecting your brain," she said kindly. My records were spotty, the results inconclusive.

---

Finally, we are released into a small parking lot. Our parents are waiting for us along with a small cadre of journalists. I'm able to hug my mother who cries into my shoulder, before my father pulls me away for several interviews with local news stations. "I don't want to do this," I say clearly, but it's too late. There's a stampede of reporters, and then I'm stuck. They have film equipment like miniature artillery. A TV personality with big hair and white teeth is already sticking a microphone in my face.

Their questions are practiced and cynical: *What happened? How did you feel? Who called 911? Was a passenger shot? Were you afraid?* I know I am being baited for a sound bite, already slotted into a montage of shattered glass, blood stains, police tape. It's awkward and embarrassing having the floodgates of media unleashed on me all at once, its garish mechanics laid bare. I feel protective of the story. Like somehow it is getting overworked, contaminated. I want to stop touching it, getting my fingerprints all over its pristine surface. I've already repeated the story over the phone to my parents, to the detective, now to the local news. They want to take and shape it for their purpose; they want to shape it into something cheap and familiar. But I'm changing the story too. Already, I realize how each time I recall the memory, I lose a little piece of it. Remembering isn't reinhabiting, it's reconstructing, each memory a memory of what happened compounded with the memory of all the times I've had to reconstruct the original memory.

"Will you be afraid of the people around you from now on?" one especially shameless reporter asks. He hasn't gotten what he wants yet. "There are dangers around every corner," I snap, self-righteously, "we cannot be afraid of the people who surround us." I want to punish him for the question, its inanity and transparent motives. I want him to stop talking; I want to be left alone. I want to shout: "Do you really think I'm that stupid?" But I guess I am. He's getting exactly what he wants: a victim, a story.

For several months, I avoid the clip. I don't want to see myself, how gaunt I looked, how young and vulnerable, with a lock of hair pasted over my forehead with sweat. When I do eventually give in and watch, I keep the sound off. I don't want to hear my voice, which I know will sound high and uncanny, which I will hate in equal parts for its alienness and its familiarity. Sound on or off, it doesn't matter. I know what I'm saying, and I hate, too, that I could not live up to my own words. When a new bus arrived I forfeited my ticket. I had been planning on traveling back to Chicago that night, but when the muffler fell off the back of the bus like some gangrenous limb, something broke. That sharp clang of metal against asphalt rattled around in my head, and I decided instead to spend the night at my parents' house and drive back in the morning.

---

There's a hairline fracture running through the center of this story. The gun wasn't real. It was an airsoft toy spray-painted to look like a hand gun. It shattered when struck by a real bullet, a plastic hail against the pavement. This means that the only real harm was introduced from the outside, that the only real bullets were the bullets of police officers arriving at the scene. It also means that our fear was in the end our greatest danger, and that for a moment two things were true at once—the gun was both a toy and a mortal danger—like Schrödinger's box in which we were the cat. I am tempted to make a symbol out of the gun—for everything that seems threatening but isn't, for all the ways we invite our own destruction—but symbolically is the worst way to interpret the world, and even a fake gun can call up real violence.

"Toy weapon," is a common refrain in the *Washington Post*'s database of police shootings. It is even one of the filtering categories. Nearly 200 of the 5,233 police killings included some mention of toy weapons, and toys are just one of the many items used to justify deadly force. Others include pellet guns, BB guns, screwdrivers, metal pipes, rocks, Tasers, baseball bats, shovels, chairs, chains, wasp spray, pieces of wood, gardening tools, bar stools, flashlights, buckets, walking sticks, wrenches, beer bottles, hose nozzles, broom handles, and batons. Here, the boundary between toy and weapon begins to thin and rupture.

"I'm not terribly afraid of the police being afraid of me," a friend of mine, who suffers from schizoaffective disorder, once wrote. "I'm white, and small. I don't own any weapons and even my worst psychotic episodes have not involved armed threats of violence against officers or anybody else. But I'm afraid that I'll need help and call the police, or that I'll need help and somebody else will call the police and I'll act strangely, or refuse to calm down, or run away, and wind up dead." Schizophrenia presents a peculiar problem, in that a psychotic break almost invariably appears threatening, even when no real danger exists, and one of the most disturbing trends in the stories I collected from the *Post*'s reporting was how often people were calling for help, either for themselves or someone else, before the victim was shot.

In my late-night research, I kept a running list of these cases. There was the thirty-year-old Green Bay man who was shot in his apartment after his mother called the police to request a welfare check on her son. He had called her earlier in the day to apologize to her for being such a disappointment. There was an Arizona man who shouted, "I bet I can outdraw you!" to police after they responded to his 911 call. He was shot six times and later died. There was the forty-one-year-old white man who was shot after his mother called the Ardmore, Maryland, police because her son was suicidal and had ingested rat poison. Also the twenty-five-year-old Black man in Miami Gardens, shot after his mother called 911 because he was standing outside in the cold in nothing but his underwear, holding a broom handle. There was the twenty-four-year-old Bloomington man, and the forty-seven-year-old Denham Springs man, and the thirty-six-year-old Kennewick man: all shot by police after their mothers called 911 concerned that their sons were suicidal. *He said he wanted to die. He said he wanted the police to shoot him.* The pattern—suicide... mother... police... death—was heartbreaking in both its consistency and irony: the mothers who populated these stories were almost always seeking help, and their sons always wound up dead.[8]

I do not pretend that there is an easy solution to the man with a fake but realistic-looking gun taking a bus hostage, or the man shouting "I bet I can outdraw you" to police. But I do know that our first response to fear is often violence, and the reaction to violence is almost always more fear. This is one way of saying that fear nests within other fears, a series of concentric circles. After my experience on the bus, I did not go out and buy a gun, but for a long time afterward my first reaction to any disorder, no matter how innocuous, was a desperate hope someone would put an end to it. I wanted absolute security, and I wanted it at any cost.

———

What did Arsenio fear? I don't know exactly. Even he had trouble articulating this. What did he want? He demanded the keys to the bus, and when the driver told him the bus didn't have keys he demanded the bus driver's wallet, his rings, and the bracelet on his wrist. Arsenio wanted—needed—to get to Indianapolis, no matter how illogical this desire might have been. I did not hear any of this. The driver recounted his experience, as we sat together on our air-conditioned bus in the alleyway. But I can still hear Arsenio's voice screaming at the bottom of the stairwell. It's a noise that sounds first like anger, then like pain, and finally like fear.

I followed his story as well as I could, as it wound its way through the court system. For two years he was housed in a state penitentiary waiting to be sentenced. There, he claimed he was not receiving adequate medication. There, he once threw a cup of urine on a guard—a fact that was brought up in his eventual sentencing. He was finally sent to a state psychiatric clinic with a two-and-a-half-year sentence and five years of probation. A probation period which could easily turn into another eight years of incarceration.

I don't know where he went after his two years. For a while, I could see his record in a database of Ohio inmates, but the trail went dead when he was transferred to a psychiatric hospital. He would be out by now. The day he boarded the bus and demanded the driver hand over the keys, he was trying to get to Indianapolis. Maybe he made it—to Indy or whatever brighter future that city represented for him.

Where does fear end? Not all at once. The popular myth of tragedy is that it's transformative, life-affirming. The arc calls for some resolution: I take a pill that neutralizes my anxiety, I visit a specialist who unlocks a hidden chamber in my brain, I spend my tax return on a one-way flight to Santiago and spend two months drying out in the maids' quarters of someone's house. Or I manage to dig myself out through research and sheer will. Perhaps reading about people brutalized by institutions transforms our fear into empathy—the process as its own product. The most honest answer is also the least satisfying: all of this happens to some extent or another, but none of these are the flipped switch or the tidy conclusion I'm looking for. One day, I get on a bus and am no longer as anxious as I used to be.

The bus route connecting Columbus and Chicago has since been closed for lack of demand. I no longer live there anyway. I still sometimes jump when an air-conditioning unit purrs to life on an empty street, when a steel plate collides with the pavement. I am left red-faced and sweating. Some days I feel nervous boarding a bus, but they are fewer and fewer. Some days, I wake up shouting, from a dream where I've been shot, or a friend has, on a street corner or in a convenience store. It's never on a bus for some reason, and there are never enough paper towels.

# Bitter Joy

\

I spent the last summer I lived in Ohio working for a landscaping company in a town called West Jefferson. The center of operations was only thirty minutes from my parents' house, but might as well have been another country. On one of my first days, I stopped at the side of the road where a disk of fog was turning over a soybean field. I had never seen anything like it. I got out of the car to bend and run my hands through the mist.

It was a shit job, though, brutal and poorly paid. Most days we were dispatched to lay mulch or plant trees at rich country homes with private ponds and huge novelty windmills. The trees were always crying pungent crab apples that I'd find down my shirt or in my underwear later. We worked for twelve dollars an hour or eighteen after overtime kicked in, which most men counted on, meaning we worked from dawn until dusk Monday through Thursday, Friday if we wanted.

No one told me how to dress or what to bring, so I showed up on the first day in tennis shoes, gym shorts, and a T-shirt. By noon, a shovel had bitten through the soft rubber of one shoe sole and cracked it along the bridge, the sun had fried the back of my calves and triceps to a tender pink, and I'd drunk and sweated out more water than twice what my pathetic sixteen-ounce water bottle could hold. I wound up stretched out in the back of a mulch truck humiliated, on the verge of heatstroke.

One of the men I'd been working with—Joel—came over to give me some advice. I was too tired to sit up, so he loomed over me, hands on his hips. He told me to wear jeans tomorrow even if it was hot. He told me to get a handkerchief for the back of my neck and proper boots for stomping on a shovel. He told me to buy gloves unless I wanted to get blisters and let them thicken into calluses. Then he shoved a milk jug, which he'd rinsed and filled with water, into my lap. Its core was still frozen and rattled around like a tiny iceberg in my lap. "Make one of those too," he said. "And for God's sake, give yourself a break."

That was the same summer I became friends with Marc. He was a few years older than me, had just dropped out of college, moved home, and started sleeping with one of my best friends. Sometimes I would imagine them in the back seat of his car. She'd told me that's where they'd done it. She was worried because they hadn't used a condom.

This must have been why he was over at my house one night when my parents were away. She'd invited him. We were all three standing in the kitchen when he took out a foggy sandwich bag full of pills and offered us some.

We couldn't take them whole, though. There was some chemical in them, he said, that would damage our livers. He went to work on them like a chemist, requesting a bread knife, a mug, and a washcloth. He used the flat end of the knife to crush a series of pills, wiped the blade clean with his thumb, and sucked the residue off like a child. I wanted him to offer it to me: the powdered end of his finger. He had that effect on people. He was handsome, but it was more than that. He had a charming, opiated calm, a faint lisp and a nickel-wide gap between his front teeth. He slept with whomever he wanted, or that was the rumor. This fluidity was intimidating; its uncertainty made it legend. When he looked at you, it was like being sized up against the rest of the world.

He warmed a pot of water over a claw of blue flames, dissolved the pills in the water, and then, with the washcloth, he strained out whatever chemicals we didn't want. We passed the mug around, cupping it tenderly, sipping at it like hummingbirds, then went into the garage and sat smoking a small joint in an old Fiat two-seater set on cinder blocks that my grandfather had been repairing before he died. My friend sat in Marc's lap as we waited for something to happen. I didn't mind that they were kissing or that her heels kept digging into my thighs. The truth was revealing itself in turns. I watched as a collection of bottles and paint cans turned into a city. The orange light pouring in through the window turned slick as Crisco over the surfaces it touched. Shadows grew a fleecy skin, so deep I could plunge my fingers into them. It was all so obvious: the future, the past lined up with the soft clink of a cue ball before a shot lands. I could see our fates—the doom and promise of each of them. We would not be lifelong friends, I knew that, and some of us would live very short lives. I thought about mentioning it to them as it occurred to me, but it hadn't seemed worth interrupting them.

When I took the landscaping job, I was only eighteen, twelve years younger than anyone else on the crew, which earned me the name Junior. The company was something of a halfway house for reformed convicts and recovering addicts. The owner was himself a former heroin addict and now lived in a large country house on the connected property. He and his business offered a second chance to people who undoubtedly needed one, but also profited off the cheap labor and limited options of the down-and-out.

I don't think anyone in the firm bothered to learn my real name. I didn't mind, but it seemed to portend all the ways I had been promised a different life. I lived in the suburbs, in a community that had gentrified and shed its reputation as an "unsafe neighborhood" during the first ten years of my life. I could not articulate these feelings then, but I had the distinct sense that I was touring through others' lives, and I experienced this as a moral failing. I noticed how the son of a dentist—"a rich boy"—was despised, and I worried about being despised, too. The men I worked with didn't hate me. Some of them were kind. For the most part they ignored me, but I was mocked for the car I drove (a used Volvo), for the sunscreen I applied (every few hours), and for the food I ate (derisively referred to as "four-dollar bread"). The mocking was never cruel, though; in fact it now seems to me more than fair.

Some of the men had tattoos on their necks and calves that, from sun damage and time, had spread and thinned into the formlessness of bruises. I remember a woman coming out of her house as we worked to complain about them—the tattoos, the men. She told them to roll down their pant legs and put on long-sleeved shirts in the heat. Homeowners and bank managers seemed to be endlessly complaining about our presence, though they were the ones who had called us.

Some of the men took weekly drug tests as a condition of their employment. On the weekends they served mandatory community service and had meetings with parole officers, which they would recount standing in a circle smoking in the gray, emulsive dawn before we shipped out. If my father, who had gotten me the job, knew any of this, he didn't let on. Growing up in the 1960s, in a house with seven children and one income, he had traditional notions about manual labor, hard work, and character building. But, of course, only those of us who don't have to work to survive get to work to build character.

This divide isn't new, and it tracks with uncomfortable predictability the way we have always assigned victimhood or blame to addiction. In nineteenth-century England, opium was the drug of choice for both agricultural laborers in the Fenland and Romantic poets in the Lake District. The poets were interested in the stimulating effect opium had on their imaginations (the sounds, visions, and strange synesthetic blurring opium could provoke). The laborers used it as a medicine to dull the muscular pain resulting from their work. But while both groups' addictions were equally debilitating, only the laborers were depicted as weak-constituted gluttons prone to addiction. The poets, already rich and well-positioned, instead had their vices romanticized in confessional memoirs.

Some weeks we would be sent to Cincinnati, a two-hour drive in boxy mulch trucks, through miles of waist-high corn, their cobs like overstuffed cigars. There was an unspoken intimacy to these trips. I would fall asleep on Joel's shoulder and wake up to him snoring. Or I would sit in the front seat where he would teasingly offer me cigarettes before taking a long popping drag. "Don't get hooked on anything, Junior," he would say, followed by, "these things are full of fiberglass."

Joel was a check fraudster and some kind of rogue genius. He lived with his sister and brother-in-law somewhere in West Jefferson. He showed me how to dig different-sized holes with the greatest economy. He told me to put talcum powder in my socks and gave me a tin of mink oil to massage into the seams of my boots to protect against the rain and mud. He taught me to untangle the roots of boxwoods, which came wrapped around themselves like straitjackets from their black plastic coffins. I had never been so out of depth at anything in my life, nor had I ever felt the sharp, sardonic comradery of a friend quite like Joel. Brash, ostentatiously masculine, unapologetic. I basked in his acceptance—even if he just enjoyed bossing someone around.

Joel said there was plenty he could teach me and was always imparting wisdom about what he called the "bleak underbelly of the world." Once, as we were finishing a job at a bank branch, long after close, we watched two cars pull into the parking lot. A man in a baggy suit and flip-flops got out of the first car and gave something to the person waiting in the second car. "That's a drug deal, Junior," Joel said, clapping me on the shoulder. I was skeptical of this at first, but then again, he would know a lot better than me.

Sports loomed large in Joel's life. They were the source of both his greatest pride and deepest failure. The check fraud was what had finally landed him in prison for sixteen months, but he had priors that I vaguely knew were related to drugs. In college, he had played football on a scholarship at a small Division 3 school. He wasn't a starter, but he was good. After getting injured he had started using steroids to keep up, but the drugs made him reckless. He skipped too many practices and nearly flunked out. After being ejected from the team, he dropped out and started using. He told me this, as I shook a protein shake for him on a ride back to base camp, with the tone of someone wronged, someone for whom life's promises had been proven a lie. "Motherfucker!" he said of his coach, as if an argument were freshening itself with painful clarity in his mind. I could tell he wasn't talking to me anymore.

I knew that Joel had a daughter. In my mind, she was a pale, curly-haired blonde in a summer dress, though I can't remember if he ever showed me a picture. It doesn't seem like something he would do, but then children can change everything about a man. I do know that he would be absent from work some days. "Custody hearing," someone told me once, and I knew he would be back late, in a bad mood, snapping at anyone who dared to come near him. On one particularly bad day, he joined up with us in the early evening, after all the white-collar workers had left for the day. Fifteen minutes into stabbing uselessly at the ground to dig a trench for a row of bushes, he abandoned his work, went over to the mulch truck, and swung his shovel like a baseball bat into its plate-metal side, leaving a wide V-shaped scar and a litter of red paint chips on the blacktop. In the long hollow ringing that followed, everyone looked down at their feet, ashamed.

The species of pain I experienced landscaping was like nothing I'd known before. This was not the round satisfying pain of sore muscles or the sharp dry stab of desperate lungs that I was familiar with from running competitively for years. The pain of landscaping was gnawing and useless—a bitter and fluid ache that lived in my joints and tendons. It was the pain of repetitive labor, the pain of crouching and shoveling and digging, a pain that would wake me up before dawn, my hip flexors cramping like a much older man's.

It is difficult to talk about pain without talking about poppies. Opium, morphine, heroin, codeine, OxyContin—all designed to solve the problem of pain without causing addiction—are derived from poppies, and each drug has its war. Morphine was invented in 1804, but it became the drug of choice sixty years later during the Civil War, when battlefield medics began using it to control both dysentery and pain. Heroin was the drug of punk rock and Vietnam and cities collapsing under their own weight. Now, most poppies are grown in Afghanistan; during infrastructure projects in the 1950s, the water table of the country was destroyed, forcing salt to the surface.[1] The salt rendered land that had been farmed for years untenable, but the bitter soil with its dry, gritty constitution was uniquely suited for poppies. OxyContin became the drug of my youth, as well as the drug of the wars in Afghanistan and Iraq. It was the drug of working-class Appalachia and southern Ohio. It appeared to be new, though the premise it was built on was not new at all. Like its predecessors, OxyContin's active ingredient is an alkaloid of the poppy plant, and like its predecessors this new formulation promised to solve the problem of pain without the unwanted side effects of addiction. But one of the natural laws of opioids seems to be that no matter how their molecules are tweaked, no matter how slowly their active ingredients are meted out, they give rise to both profound relief and profound addiction.

Marc knew about pain, too. He worked loading boxes for a shipping company and on the floor of an American Eagle in one of the three malls that surround Columbus. Sometimes we would talk about what this work was doing to our bodies: him shoving boxes around on conveyor belts all day, me on my knees picking through roots. Back pain was the worst, we both agreed. It had a uniquely sickening quality.

We were friends, but not the kind of friends who called each other or made plans outside of a familiar group. I still have his phone number, but I don't think I ever had an occasion to use it. Most often, I would run into him at house parties. I never knew where he was going to turn up, but I arrived everywhere harboring the secret hope that he would be there.

I saw him once at a party that was coming apart at the seams. People had spilled out onto the front lawn hollering and crushing beer cans against their foreheads, the host was making out with someone on the living room couch, and the rest of us were wandering the hallways. I found him in a bedroom, unhooking a laptop from where it was charging on a desk. He looked over when I came in, but didn't seem surprised to see me at all. It was like he'd been waiting for someone to find him.

"Where'd you get that," I asked, shutting the door against the noise behind me. But he either hadn't heard me or hadn't understood. "Come listen to this," he said instead, lowering himself slowly to the ground with a pained grunt. He arranged the laptop, between one knee and the floor, then he played me a song from YouTube, "Everything in Its Right Place," by Radiohead, as we sat on the floor, the quiet of the room made more palpable by the party still rumbling below us like a great unsteady machine.

On days we were not called out to private properties, I drove a truck with a multi-ton tank of water strapped into the bed—a coveted job. I would travel from property to property, following behind the landscaping crew, watering the bushes and saplings that they'd just put in the ground. It was easy, even if it made me nervous hauling that much weight around. Half the highways that summer were under construction and narrowed with orange cones and cement barriers. I was careful to make sure the tank was always full or else the back wheels would fishtail with the sloshing of water.

I listened to the radio as I drove. That summer The National's "Bloodbuzz Ohio" played every hour on certain radio stations. Songs from Arcade Fire's forthcoming album—*The Suburbs*—were sprinkled over the months. It was two years after the housing market had collapsed and dragged the banks along with it. That summer we signed up for student loans, which would eventually break some of my friends. The residual wisdom, a product of 1980s interest rates, was to take anything they offered. Lyrics about owing money to other money we owed had a twisted koanlike truth to their logic. We had four years and six months to pay back the money. It felt like a lifetime away, even if those principal sums would swell with time.

Other days, we worked hauling dead shrubs from the lawns of banks in the Bottoms—a neighborhood so named because it lies below the waterline of the surrounding rivers and is susceptible to periodic flooding. The homes and businesses are built under the assumption of destruction and subject to predatory loans and high insurance rates. Or they were, until a flood wall was built along the freeway, two breweries moved into the neighborhood, and blocks started to be razed and "renewed." Now it is considered one of Columbus's up and coming neighborhoods, and people who have made their lives there are being shifted out.

Perhaps the work we did was a part of that coming change, but we couldn't see it at the time. All we could see was an old man pushing a shopping cart down the cracked sidewalk, and a woman who pulled into the parking lot across from us one morning and emptied out the contents of her car—fast food containers, stuffed animals, laundry baskets full of clothes, cheap picture frames, a whole life—onto a patch of grass before driving away.

I felt like I was always working. But when I wasn't, we were smoking in garage bedrooms or drinking at a wood-paneled bar called Ledo's. We were reckless, but not in any particularly interesting way. Some days we drove down to the quarter-mile—a stretch of freeway that doubled back on itself in such a tight curve it was impossible for cops to patrol. It circled a man-made lake with a little chain of condos draped over a peninsula at its center. We liked to see what speed we could reach before the freeway ran out. I never drove, but I would sit in the passenger's seat and watch out the window. Wild geese passing over the lake. Steam rising off the asphalt after a summer rain.

"As an object approaches the speed of light, time slows down." Marc was the kind of person who would openly share thoughts like this. Grand thoughts about time, the universe, God. He delivered these ideas with such a lack of pretense that they were never annoying. I had heard this before, of course, without giving it much thought, but racing down that stretch of road felt like a proof of concept. At ninety miles an hour, the city and its reflection turned over the water like a figurine on a mirrored plate.

What can I say about that city? At the time, it was vibrating with a mounting boom. My parents, who bought their house for ninety thousand dollars from a man in prison in the early 1990s, rode this rising tide like a raft of foam. Everywhere developers were paying off bureaucrats and planning ways to displace neighborhoods. The prices of huge tracts of homes were changing seismically under our feet. But at those speeds this felt like an arbitrary blip. We could already see the city raptured and empty . . . the thin wash of tropical sea that had once covered this region . . . the glaciers furrowing the earth, plowing boulders hundreds of miles to rest at the feet of hills . . . the Appalachians peaking like the Rockies, then wearing themselves smooth with time. At those speeds we would never have to see our future.

Pain medication was everywhere overnight—left over from hip surgeries, triple bypasses, and tonsillectomies. I barely registered this. No one was talking about addiction. Drugs were the dime bags of weed people bought on campus, not a bottle you could have filled at the pharmacy with a prescription.

I remember, one night, taking drinks from a large bottle of

codeine in a dining room with some friends. The liquid stained the sides of the bottle a fierce orange. A glass hutch filled with crystal figures gently announced our movements. We measured the liquid out with a hollow plastic spoon, then walked to our high school's track and field to lie out and feel the effects.

A decade later, my friend told me that her father had noticed the missing liquid and accused her mother, an addict, of the theft. "I didn't know that," I said, dumbly, lost for an adequate response. How would I? The youthful trespass of that moment didn't square with what I now knew of the epidemic, and it felt as though I'd just been reminded of some money I once borrowed and forgot to repay—a debt so old and now so large it would be uncomfortable, even impossible, to pay back.

By this time, I was regularly receiving text chains from friends warning of drugs laced with unknown chemicals. "Fentanyl found in a brick of cocaine in Columbus," one friend wrote, accompanied by a link to an article and a screenshot of the most pertinent information. These warnings were always sent as chain messages, a scattershot sent to tens of people at once, an underground alarm system trying to filter its way to the most vulnerable. Newspapers were filled with pictures of men and women overdosing in shopping malls and parking lots and playgrounds. In one particularly famous picture a child sits strapped into his booster seat in the back of a van. He's very young, blond, slightly buck-toothed, and wearing a blue dinosaur T-shirt, which clashes with his adult expression of uncertainty and worry. His grandmother and her boyfriend hang in a hammock of their seat belts in the front seat. One of her bra straps is limp around her shoulder. Their mouths are open in the gape of sleep apnea or death. The officer who pulled the couple over, took the picture after the driver fell unconscious. The photograph, released without their consent, was picked up by *Time* magazine and became one of the defining images of the epidemic.[2]

"Photographs of victims . . . are themselves a species of rhetoric," writes Susan Sontag in *Regarding the Pain of Others*. "They reiterate. They simplify. They agitate. They create the illusion of consensus."[3] Sontag was writing about images of war, but she might just as well have been writing about addiction—a problem that the U.S. government has confronted with the violent single-mindedness of military action. If these photos brought attention to the crisis, it was attention stripped of humanity and glossed over by spectacle. If they have helped achieve small justices against the pharmaceutical companies that pumped cities full of addictive drugs, they have also been distractions from any real justice or recovery. If they worked to elicit empathy, they also inspired blame. *How could they endanger a child like that,* was the tone of the responses I heard regarding the *Time* picture.

Addiction, as always, is poised in the delicate space between unbidden harm and self-destruction, between victimhood and degeneracy. And, of course, one is not assigned a role randomly or evenly. Is addiction an illness though? I have heard persuasive arguments on both sides, and I would not want to steal a narrative that has allowed anyone to live, but the underside of this question has always interested me more: Whom must addiction affect before we classify it as illness? What characteristics do we demand as preconditions of care?

In 1986, when Ronald Reagan described the new epidemic of crack cocaine as an "uncontrolled fire," he did not go on to discuss the victims of addiction, the Black communities ravaged by a drug brought to the country, however indirectly, by its own Central Intelligence Agency. Instead, he discussed how drugs menaced America's children, and how their abuse was not, in fact, a "victimless crime."[4] Drug policies, inherited from the Nixon administration and amplified under Reagan, led to a surge of incarceration for even petty drug crimes. But if the War on Drugs campaign of the 1980s and

1990s was based on punishment and fear, the opioid epidemic has become a campaign of pity and disdain. In 2011, just as the breadth of the opioid supply chain was entering public awareness, executives from AmerisourceBergen—a wholesale pharmaceutical distributor responsible for flooding Appalachia with opioids—were rewriting the lyrics of the *Beverly Hillbillies* theme song to include phrases like "Hillbilly Heroin" and "Pillbillies."[5] Disdain might be preferable to criminalization, but neither approach solves the problem of addiction, and both betray the way addicts have been viewed as either enemies or worthless.

The rumor I heard was that the paramedics found Marc in a closet, though it may have been a bathroom. They either performed CPR, or did not. They may have had Narcan, or they may not have. The rumor, later confirmed, was that he had been nursing a heroin addiction. That was the word people used, "nurse," as if it were something tender and wounded that you had to feed with an eye dropper. A downy altricial lump of skin and feathers. Paramedics rushed him to a hospital, and he survived. That much is certain. He spent several months in rehab and recovered.

We tend to think of pain as the domain of the body rather than the mind, but now I am not so sure how clean these distinctions are. Opioids' ability to dissolve physical pain while weaving intense mental pleasure suggests a kind of mind-body monism. Depressed patients experience higher sensitivity to physical pain than nondepressed patients. They are also prone to back pain, headaches, and unexplained nerve sensitivity. And anyone who has experienced long-term physical pain understands that it can lead to emotional anguish. This understanding isn't new. In fact, it's ancient. We've known it all along. In *The Iliad,* Helen pours the drug nepenthe, an opioid, into the wine of mourners who have come to cry over the lost soldiers of the Trojan War. The drug's name means, literally, "to chase away sorrow." Iced poppy tea is still, in some parts of the world, traditionally served at funerals as a balm not for the body but the soul. Even common over-the-counter drugs meant for bodily pain have been shown to block emotional pain. Our inability to unwind opioids' amazing capacity to provide relief from their similarly impressive capacity to create addiction suggests that these two qualities are somehow interwoven. Perhaps to our minds and our bodies they are the same.

    It was not heroin that killed Marc. Though, in the endless ouroboros of addiction and pain, it must have played a part. He went to rehab, got sober, returned to the world. There was no relapse. He died in his home at twenty-seven, in 2016, the result of a mental illness he struggled with his whole life.

    Of the many surprising features of the brief obituary that ran in the wake of Marc's death—its frankness, its specificity: "He stayed sober for two years, three months and 23 days"—I am most surprised by the way his sobriety was described by his family. They called it something "earned," something that required "hard work" to maintain. "He entered eternity drug free," the obituary read. The language deployed around addiction is uncannily similar to the way we glamorize physical labor. The language of bootstraps, perseverance, and hard work. It glosses over the messy, unsteady truth of addiction and recovery just as it euphemizes the often brutal and exploitative work of physical labor, labor that is both idealized and dismissed in the same thought.

The last day I worked with Joel he didn't say anything about leaving. Maybe he didn't know. He lived that sort of life, bold and impulsive, ready at a moment's notice to ride off into the sunset with all the grand self-importance the image implies. He always seemed happiest at the beginning of things. Even in the mornings, a day of predictable drudgery laid out before us, he was bright and energetic, loading the mulch truck with his enviable athleticism, like anything could happen.

I don't know if he ever worked out an agreement to see his daughter. I don't know where he ended up. I never even knew his last name. The next day he was simply gone. "Took a job in Florida," someone said, noticing my confusion. It sounded more like speculation than a statement. Besides the foremen, everyone was transient. They worked the job until they found a better one or simply a different one. It wasn't worth trying to track with any certainty others' plans. The last thing he would say every day was, "Take care of yourself, Junior." He would call it through his open window as he drove off in a hiss of gravel. That was probably the last thing he said to me.

The last time I saw Marc was in a parking garage of a friend's apartment. It was the summer before his first overdose. He sat in the back seat of my car, framed in the rearview mirror, waiting for someone to get a bottle of whiskey from their freezer. We talked about life, work, school. I was several years into a degree I would eventually finish and spend the next half-decade paying off. He was still loading boxes for a shipping job. His arms were vascular and tight, a lean strength developed from repetitive motions. It looked like something had chewed away all the fat from below his skin. He rubbed his throbbing veins as he spoke. Did his back still ache? I didn't ask. But I, too, would have taken something to cure it.

He told me work was going well, that things were looking up, that if he could just hold on a little longer, soon he'd be going places. He didn't plan to be there forever.

# Gilead

\

Dalton lived in a brick bungalow squatting near the curb on the south side of Columbus. When I arrived, he was already standing on the corner, a dog's leash coiled around his palm.

For our first date, we'd gone to a bar in my part of town. Now, he wanted to show me where he lived. On his street, businesses flew German flags and brick roads bled through asphalt. We spent the day walking through a bookstore that was once a mansion—its sublevels and labyrinthine halls narrowed and insulated by rows of yellowing pages—and letting his Great Dane chase and hump other dogs in a swell of dust from a baseball diamond at a nearby park. While couples held hands and pushed strollers, he put his hand on my lower back and something hot cut through me, down the knuckles of my spine. I wanted him right away. Back at his house, we drank gin from a bottle he kept wrapped in a paper bag in the freezer. Then we watched half an episode of something before giving up the pretense and climbing the stairs to his lofted bedroom.

While he ushered his dog into a kennel, I stood taking inventory of the room—a bookshelf with nutrition manuals, a mattress laid directly on the floor, a collection of pill bottles on a dresser. Outside the window, bare branches were haunted with orange streetlights. When he stood up, a tension flooded the room. We must have both felt it. And I thought for a moment it was just the uncertainty that wells up before two people touch. But we didn't touch. He walked away from me, instead, toward the bookcase in the corner where he stood and said, "There's something I have to tell you," and before I could respond: "I'm undetectable." He pronounced the word like a confession and a reassurance, a well-practiced euphemism.

"I assume that's not a problem?" he asked.

"Of course not," I assured him. But we didn't sleep together that night. "I'd like to get on PrEP first," I explained.

All I knew about PrEP then was that friends had been telling me to get on it for ages; most of them already were. I knew that it protected against HIV infections, and I also knew that for at least a short time debate had raged about its exact potentials and dangers. I can remember, when PrEP was still new, a friend posing for a photo with the iconic blue pill clenched between their teeth, the caption proclaiming the benefits of the medicine and its power to end HIV for good. That same year, a widely panned op-ed in the *New York Times*, controversially, blamed PrEP for "The End of Gay Sex," arguing that it had led to a "a sort of historical amnesia" around condom usage, which had "shaped what it meant to be gay in the 1980s and 1990s."[1] It's not that I didn't care about these debates, only that I didn't have a personal stake in them. I'd been living abroad at the time, with intermittent health insurance, and by the time I came home and signed up for a feeble and overpriced subsidized plan, the dust had settled.

PrEP, it turns out, is not so much any specific medicine as it is an idea, an old tool imagined for a new purpose. Since the 1990s, a combination of antiretrovirals has been used to suppress active HIV infections. Drugs in this class disrupt a virus's ability to replicate itself at different points in its reproduction and through different mechanisms of action. Some medications—*analogs*—mimic the essential building blocks of DNA, standing in for something else, similar but not the same, sand in place of stone, chemically identical but with none of the same physical properties. Analogs trick the reverse transcriptase enzyme that HIV uses to construct its helix of DNA inside of a host cell. The enzyme takes up the analog and adds it to the new strain of genetic material, but the analog is unstable. It brings the whole chain to ruin like a loose thread unwinding a scarf. Other medicines clog the replication process; they jam themselves into the protease enzyme like a wrench in a machine, preventing it from chopping new strands of protein into its infectious chunks. Or they block viral RNA from entering a cell at all, like a stone damming the flow of a river.

A variety of medication is crucial. Adaptability is the first challenge of HIV: a difficult, slippery virus. If a single obstruction blocks the virus's way, it adapts and mutates to slip through cracks in the barrier of our immune system. Its quick, error-prone reproduction means that it has the highest biological mutation rate of any known virus. Mutations lead to variants, and variants sometimes render medication less effective. Thus, the variety of antiretrovirals, the four pills a day, the need for daily PrEP, blood draws, and three-month follow-up appointments.

Durability is the second challenge. After HIV enters the body, it hides out in intestinal and muscular cells. It retreats underground when threatened, only to emerge as soon as treatment stops. And so, antiretrovirals can keep a person healthy, but they cannot eliminate the virus completely from the body. This is what it means to be undetectable—the virus is hidden and inactive. In blood tests, the amount of virus is so low it literally cannot be detected. It is a liminal state of illness. People with an undetectable viral load are not sick, and they are not infectious, but they are HIV-positive.

In 2004, Gilead Sciences began to wonder: if HIV infections could not be eliminated, perhaps they could be prevented. For years pharmaceutical companies and government researchers rejected the idea of taking antiviral medication as a protective measure against HIV, but then the CDC demonstrated that large amounts of subcutaneous tenofovir prevented infections in macaques. Suddenly there was proof of concept. Gilead theorized that a low dose of two antiretrovirals—tenofovir and emtricitabine—could stop an infection in humans, even after exposure. The theory went that if enough free antiretrovirals were circulating in the blood, HIV would not be able to get a foothold in the body. The theory worked better than anyone predicted, and in 2012, the FDA approved Gilead's patent for Truvada, not as a new medication, but as an existing drug with a new indication. It became the first medication available as a preexposure prophylactic or PrEP.[2]

The year I moved back to Columbus, advertisements promoting PrEP were everywhere. Signs were pasted onto billboards and under the plexiglass of bus stops. Commercials featuring dancers in mirror-paneled studios and attractive-looking urbanites drinking on terraces played hourly on certain channels. Like many advertisements for pharmaceuticals, these commercials seemed to be selling the glossy promises of a certain life rather than any particular drug. But they were effective, at least in their constant reminder to *get on PrEP*. I did not have a doctor; for a while I didn't even have health insurance. I knew, or I quickly learned, that out-of-pocket expenses for PrEP could be up to two thousand dollars a month. And I knew that if I wanted to access the medication, if I was ever going to afford it, I would need a doctor, and I would need a prescription.

That winter, I attempted to make an appointment with a clinic specializing in LGBT healthcare near my apartment. I submitted multiple online applications but received no response. I tried their different numbers scattered across the internet, only to have it explained to me, when I finally got someone on the phone, that they were not accepting new clients until April.

I tried the medical center at the university near my apartment, putting the phone on my desk as I scrolled through a list of side effects—headaches, abdominal pain, muscle aches, vivid dreaming, liver and kidney problems. Hold-music played over my speakerphone, until, abruptly, the music cut out, and a harried-sounding administrator asked me why I was calling. After I explained my situation, she told me that the university hospitals required a doctor's referral for "that kind of medication." Why? I didn't think to ask. I explained that I didn't have a primary care provider at the moment, and that, "actually, it would be great if I could find one there." But they were not accepting new patients until May.

"What *is* that?" asked a curt voice over the phone at a third doctor's office I tried: some vague health clinic in the suburbs that happened to be covered by my extremely narrow network. I was wounded by her misunderstanding, having rehearsed the exact phrasing of my request for an embarrassing amount of time.

"It's a medicine," I explained. "It protects against HIV infections."

The receptionist considered this for a moment, then: "Yeah . . . I don't think we have anything like that." Her tone of voice told me the conversation was over. She sounded skeptical that such a thing could even exist.

I called the first clinic back, and accepted an appointment in April.

Dalton and I kept seeing each other in the months leading up to my appointment. We ate tacos in a restaurant as the first flurries of winter came down. We drank more gin in a bar with roll-up garage doors for walls while a bonfire cracked and whipped in the parking lot. We went to parties thrown by his friends and by mine. At one, I caught him doing dishes for the hosts and had to shoo him out of the kitchen.

At some point, we started texting each other every day, a simple "good morning :D" or "good night"—a framework buttressing a relationship that could not quite stand on its own, coaxing it on, willing it into life.

On a map he once showed me the little chunk of green lawn that used to be his yard, and told me about the farm fifteen minutes outside the city where he was raised, a place past the outer belt where strip malls and noise fences fall away, the eight-lane highway retreats back toward the city, and cornfields appear dotted by farmhouses and silos. I noticed all the ways his upbringing percolated into his adult life: how he pronounced *f'ustrated* with no *r* and *vernses* with an *n* wedged between the syllables, the way he charmed everyone with a touch of rural chivalry, how he was always commenting on the psychology of animals. "See how Cole uses his neck like an arm," he observed one night of his dog while it nosed its way between us. "That's the Great Dane in him. Very controlling. Very needy." I learned he preferred the country to the city, hated crowds, and spent a lot of time romanticizing vast, mostly unpopulated stretches of America: Montana, West Virginia, the Ozarks. One evening, after leaving a restaurant, I watched him stand in an overgrown lot, arms outstretched, catching snow in his mouth. He preferred the winter to the summer and was always wearing long-sleeved T-shirts, which made me anxious and motherly. "That really doesn't seem warm enough."

One night, as we were lying in bed, he leaned over me and began working his way up my body, placing a hickey on my thigh, my shoulder blade, the soft downy flesh of my stomach. He smiled sheepishly after each long application of pressure. It was a joke—two adults mimicking the rituals of less experienced lovers. "Nowhere visible," he promised, anticipating my objection, continuing unfazed. *Not visible in public anyway*, I thought, suspicious of his motives, but I let him continue. When he reached my collarbone, he left a fresh red crescent just below my neckline. And I wondered, as he finally drew his lips away from my neck, and wiped the mark he had left with his thumb, if he was trying to mark me, to claim me for himself. Did he imagine another man finding these burst capillaries and knowing, or was this just a game?

As a rule, I didn't ask about illness. I wanted to make it into the nonissue it should have been. But one night he told me the story of how he became positive at seventeen. I was frightened to learn this—that he had been tasked with something so great when he was so young. It made me feel, not anxious and not scared, but rather, small and young, as if the world were once again too enormous and wild for me to manage.

"I can't imagine," I told him, and he agreed with a shrug. "You can't."

The medical term for us is *serodiscordant couple*. I heard the phrase for the first time while sitting on the examination table at my new doctor's office. "Discordant?" I asked. It's a strange word. It sounded harsh and sterilized, like a strong detergent. Accurate, I supposed, but also disturbing in the way it rendered our bodies sacs of negotiating serums and incompatible bodily fluids, in discord, out of tune. "It's just what doctors say," he explained. A wave of his hand.

The doctor was funny and a little self-effacing, with a military cut, silver hair, and keen eyes. He asked me how much I drank, then cracked a joke about a local gay bar known for exceptionally potent cocktails. He had treated a friend of mine too, and said at one point, with the joking severity of an uncle, "Tell him he's overdue for an appointment." I laughed at how deadpan he became while saying it. "So, I understand you're here for PrEP?" he asked, eventually. It was not really a question. A resident had already taken my information and briefed him on why I was there. "Good," he said. "This medicine was made for couples like you." His tone was approving, paternal. He seemed to anticipate my discomfort and banish it. I was relieved and thankful. So often I came to these places to be swabbed and tested for diseases that, despite our best efforts, fail to be rinsed of stigma. And perhaps this was why, as he ran through a checklist of my sexual and medical history, I did not correct his assumption that I had been monogamous for the past four months. I nodded, hummed my assent, and I let him move on to checking my glands, my heartbeat.

By that point, Dalton and I were spending at least one night a week together but were otherwise free to do what we liked, to sleep with whom we liked. The open relationship was his idea. "It's just easier," he had said one night, "being with someone like yourself." *Like yourself* being a euphemism for the same status, the same serum. Someone with whom there is one less barrier to intimacy. I was hurt by this at the time. The feeling dropped suddenly into my stomach with the same sinking sensation as realizing your keys are not in your pocket, but I didn't feel like I had any moral ground to object. It was, after all, my anxiety and circumspection around safe sex that were leaving us both less satisfied, and so I played along. I even enjoyed myself. I slept with a pharmacist who worked at a university a few blocks from my apartment. A news producer who shared my name and always showed up at the same parties I did. A couple whose bug-eyed Chihuahua pressed itself against me like a suckling baby and refused to get off. Most of these men I could not bear to see again. There was nothing between us but an arrangement of bodies, that poor approximation of real intimacy.

I didn't mention any of this to the doctor. I did not want to sacrifice the image of competence and maturity I was presenting. Plus, I was afraid of what other complications I might introduce into the already knotty process of obtaining this medication. Instead, I sat quietly. The doctor ordered blood tests and scheduled a return visit. The resident handed me a plastic cup and showed me to the restroom. The omission filled the room like a pleasant scent.

When we were together, Dalton was a tireless optimist. In the time I knew him, his mother wound up in the hospital multiple times with serious but inexplicable illnesses—swelling fingers, shortness of breath, fat, blistering rashes—and his father started hallucinating, seeing people who had been dead for years running through the meadows of his property. Over dinner one evening, he told me about how a neighbor had recently found his father blinking on the side of the road at three in the morning, as the farmhouse he'd been raised in went up in flames—its orange glow the only light source for miles.

He accepted all of this with preternatural tranquility, saying it was his sister who truly suffered. But when we were apart, he would cancel plans at the last minute, citing bad moods, long days, or, most frustratingly, nothing at all. On those occasions, I could feel some dark energy surging through his interior life, carving out a distance between us.

One night, I showed up at his house and found him limping around the kitchen, preparing food for the week: eggs bubbling on the stove and strips of chicken breast stretched across aluminum foil. As I laid my bag on his kitchen table, he pulled a spaghetti squash warm and steaming from the oven, popped it with a butcher's knife, and emptied its guts into a Tupperware container. He looked like a maniac dressed in sweatpants, a tank top, an ankle brace, and one flip-flop. "What happened to your leg," I asked, nodding at the brace. "It's nothing serious," he insisted. I decided to let it go, but later, when I tried to help a pot of salted water out of his hands, he hip-checked me away, saying, "I've got it!" A serious edge entered his voice, and a curtain of broth slapped the floor. It turned out he'd had surgery earlier that week and hadn't told me. He didn't want to worry me, he said, setting the pot down, and rubbing the spill with a hand towel. He was always hiding injuries, downplaying indignities. He never wanted to show his fault lines, his imperfections. I couldn't really have done anything about his surgery, but I wanted to be part of that pain with him—the triviality of it, its minor details. It was obvious that he did not want to be pitied or cared for—or, I worried, maybe just not in the way I could offer.

Here is a fact and a confession: someone who is undetectable can't pass on the virus. It is much safer to have unprotected sex with someone who is HIV-positive, knows it, and is being treated, than to gamble on unprotected sex with someone whose status you don't know. And so I am at least in part responsible for building this barrier between us. I am told by doctors and by friends that my caution is justified, that I am right to advocate for my own health. They use the logic of airplanes: secure your own oxygen mask before helping your neighbor. They avoid the word *fear,* but that's what it is. Fear of opening yourself up to someone. Fear that medical institutions have, in one of many ways, failed them. Fear of breaking the interdiction most gay men are raised on, one so deep it feels, more than learned, carved into my body. I repeat it in my sleep. I have slurred it through a blackout. While straight friends forgo condoms, get on birth control, anxiously buy day-after pills, we are charged with the moral imperative to "play safe." And some good might come from this. We stay healthier; we protect others. But it is impossible to eradicate all risk, and I am left wondering how much trust we owe those we love.

In the examination room, during what was supposed to be my final trip to the clinic, I took a picture of a laminated flowchart pinned to the wall. I'd lost count, by that point, of how many trips I'd made, but I knew the nurses by sight if not by name and had become familiar with the run of the place—the check-in stations, the visitor's questionnaires, the plastic chemical smell of drying hand sanitizer.

The question at the head of the flowchart read: "Are you insured to cover your costs for PrEP? Yes or No." I considered this for a moment, then chose "yes." Getting and staying on PrEP requires regular three-month checkups to ensure that the medication has not affected your kidneys and that you have not somehow become positive. And so, my expensive, high-deductible plan was part of a careful cost-benefit analysis, balancing my monthly payments against the medication, the follow-up appointments, and the lab work. From there the chart quickly descended into madness. There were options for the insured and the uninsured with branches forking for premiums above three hundred dollars and below that. There were lists of dates and percentages and arbitrary-seeming income amounts. There were options for copay cards, Medicaid, specialized state-funded programs, and another HIV-specific program named after the AIDS activist Ryan White. There were tiny red arrows that seemed to circle themselves endlessly, and one thread that led to a statement reading, simply, "If you encounter barriers to coverage, consult a legal advocate."

There was, it seemed, an unending series of half-measures and intricate online application systems that promised affordable medication, if, through persistence, luck, and the proper connections, you could calibrate their temperaments just right. I assume many of these programs are meant to be stopgaps, providing coverage until something better comes along, and I assume without them there would be nothing at all. But this gamut we're forced to run feels moralistic: the system demanding a sacrifice of time, sweat, and frustration—an offering at the altar of hard work. Staring at the chart I was reminded that nothing is free, and that survival has always been privatized, expensive, and profitable for a select few.

Near the end of January, there was a lunar eclipse that coincided with one of the coldest nights of the year. Dalton picked me up from a bar where I was sharing french fries and cups of coffee with a friend. We went back to my place and sat on the front porch of my apartment, on an iron bench stacked with lawn-chair cushions. The eclipse was expected to last for hours, and we were determined to sit on the porch as long as we could, huddled on the edge of shivering, each of our bodies necessary for the other's warmth. I don't remember the moon vanishing, its body shaved away by the minutes and the earth's shadow. It wasn't that kind of eclipse. What I do remember are the sun's rays leaching and spreading across the surface of the moon, turning it red in some places and a deep navy blue in others. It was a beautiful distraction from the fact that eventually we would have to go inside; and that when we climbed the stairs to my room, we probably would not sleep together; and that if we did, it would involve another exhausting negotiation of condom usage and the rehashing of statistics—a conversation that would drain any spontaneity out of the room and undo all the romance of the eclipse.

We skipped the discussion and fell asleep next to each other, but I sensed a strained distance between us. We barely touched except that I continued to roll into him—a heavy dent in the mattress beside me. "I want you to feel comfortable," he'd said after we'd given up and gone inside. It was the same thing he'd said on countless other nights. A statement that had begun to feel like a series of questions: Why don't you feel comfortable? How can I make you feel comfortable? Is there something wrong with us, with me? If I could go back and tell that version of myself anything now, it would be that you can lose someone, not by hurting them or forcing them away, but simply by holding them at arm's length.

In the morning, he was up at six o'clock as usual. The fitted sheet I'd cinched around my window in lieu of curtains was breathing and luminous. Through my sleep, I watched him rake the floor with his hands, gathering up underwear, socks, a Henley into a tight bundle. He cradled it to the bathroom where I heard him spit and run water through his hair. When the door clattered shut downstairs, I knew he was gone.

Spring arrived in a shower of heat and stormy nights. Hyacinths sat throbbing in their flower beds. All the bushes were newly haloed with fresh buds. An envelope came for me in the mail with a letter from the pharmaceutical company and a copay card stuck to the bottom corner with a dollop of rubbery glue. The card rendered my medication free, which felt at the time like a gift but was actually a trap. I would realize this a year later, standing in a CVS in a new town, trying to fill a prescription, watching the price ring up at full retail, the card used up, the half-full bottle I had left now a precious, waning commodity. In that moment, it would become clear to me why patients will sometimes halve their doses, cutting pills down the middle or into fourths, desperate to extend their protection, to save money. But when I first received the card I was thankful simply to have what so many do not.

I went to the pharmacy and came home carrying a paper prescription bag. On my desk, I poured out a small pile of blue pills. Pills I recognized from commercials and billboards, from posters on bike rental kiosks and doctor's offices. Pills that seemed ubiquitous and easily within reach, but which were, in fact, elusive and unattainable. I realized that I'd never actually held one. They are such simple things, larger than I would have thought, waxy, and cornflower blue. On one side they were stamped with the numbers 701 and on the other with the name "Gilead."

I've wondered often about this name, where it comes from and what it means. Gilead might refer to a physical location or a state of mind. In Hebrew, it translates literally to "heap of stones." In some contexts it means a "hill of testament," in others a rocky region in what is now Jordan—a real place. In legends, a balm grew there that could cure any illness, and in some Christian spirituals it is a veiled reference to Jesus. When the prophet Jeremiah mourned for his people, he did so through the metaphor of illness and health: "Is there no balm in Gilead? Is there no physician there? Why is there no healing for the wounds of my people?"[3]

Gilead regularly makes billions of dollars in sales from Truvada, even though the research that made PrEP possible was funded in part by the public at taxpayers' expense. The CDC was responsible for the trials showing that tenofovir worked as a prophylactic in primates, and the National Institutes of Health supported human trials through grants. PrEP, both in concept and as a tangible class of medication, has the potential to end the AIDS epidemic, raising the question: Why is this medication so difficult to access?

In 2019, the U.S. government sued to end Gilead's patent on Truvada. In a country that often defers to corporate interests, this was an exceedingly rare move aimed at coercing a pharmaceutical company to produce cheaper generic medicines. "The lawsuit bluntly accused Gilead of exaggerating its role in developing pre-exposure prophylaxis, or PrEP, ignoring work by government scientists and 'baselessly denying' the validity of federal patents."[4] For four years it appeared the government might succeed in forcing Gilead to lower the price of Truvada, but in 2023, a federal jury in Delaware concluded that the government had no claim on the patent.[5]

A friend once asked what HIV means to me. I had been writing about illnesses for years, especially HIV, but my work tended to live in the past, in pre-answered questions about a more acute form of suffering and loss, questions that had little to do with my life, even if I lived in their shadow. I cannot, for example, remember a time before antiretrovirals, and I was born into a world where HIV was considered chronic but manageable. I didn't know how to answer her question then, but I now see at least one answer in the name Gilead, which recalls old problems of cure and access. We have all the tools to end this disease, and yet we do not. I have heard the well-worn conspiracy theory that the government or pharmaceutical companies or both have known the cure for AIDS for years. They've burned down swaths of the rainforest and shredded research data to keep the cure a secret because there is more money in selling lifelong treatments than curing a disease once and for all. I don't believe in this theory, but I do sympathize with its underlying logic: that people are left to suffer for the sake of profit. It does not take a conspiracy to understand that PrEP does not reach the people who need it most: sex workers, homeless queer youth, Black gay men in the American South. "It's no longer a death sentence," I have heard and read often in the course of my work. "For some people, maybe," I would like to say. And there are abundant reasons to cure a disease that have nothing to do with death.

My side effects are minimal and common. So common that it is hard to know if they are coming from the new drugs, or if they are the result of stress: some stomach pain, headaches, heightened anxiety, and a few weeks of vivid dreaming. I dream one night that I see Dalton in a cafe. In the dream, we are both years older, and we haven't seen each other in a long time. I consider going in and saying hi, but don't. He is alone, and yet I can tell, with the uncanny logic of dreams, that he is in love with someone else. I wake up heartbroken.

Online I attempt to sort through which side effects are normal and which are aberrant, but instead wind up reading about how residue of Truvada seeps into breast milk and is eliminated in urine. I discover, too, that the medicine will deposit itself in my fingernails and in strands of my hair. If they wanted to, clinicians could test to see how strictly I have adhered to the regimen—my body stratified like layers of sedimentary rock. They would see the gaps in treatment while I travel, the days I miss due to moving or due to changes in healthcare, the days I simply forget. Of course, these tests are only run on the rare occasion that someone becomes positive while taking the drug, which is another reason I've embarked on this research.

At an appointment to check my kidneys and liver, the doctor tells me that it takes five days for the medication to take effect. A technician tells me three weeks. In a pamphlet in the waiting room for a follow-up appointment, I read that the drug lowers the risk for contracting HIV in men-who-have-sex-with-men by 42 percent and, confusingly, in the same article, that the protection when taken regularly is nearly 100 percent. A report from Aidsmap reports that, to date, ten cases of people on PrEP have become HIV-positive.[6] An incredibly small number. A statistical anomaly in the strictest sense. Still, I preoccupy myself with these outliers: proof that even the certain is uncertain, the 0.001 percent. Proof, too, that medicine is only half the problem. Everything I have been taught to fear, and all the ways I've internalized those fears, is the other half. I know that my anxiety is magical and superstitious, but I still worry it like a hangnail. I have trouble believing in things I cannot see—the medicines unspooling in my veins, in his.

I have heard that couples become more like each other the longer they are together. Facial expressions, handwriting, waist sizes. Even the immune system is subject to change.[7] I'm sure biological reasons could explain this—shared bacteria, slowly altered habits—but I prefer to think of it as proof of the metaphysical, a material world manifestation of love, working its way into our very cells. Intimacy, after all, is more than just touching and being touched. It's more than sitting next to someone, fucking someone, or even living with someone. "The things most precious to us often risk—or demand—this kind of contagion," writes the essayist Jordan Kisner. "The 'sacred' places of the body are the ones where membranes are exposed: our mouths, our eyes, our genitals, the places where we connect with others and make ourselves vulnerable to them."[8] I keep coming back to this pairing: the sacred and vulnerable, the idea that intimacy is a kind of wound or aperture, a place where you open to meet another, a space where you are most likely to be changed. Intimacy demands something, a dose of pain, an offering of blood, a willingness to be altered by another. It is the small destruction of two selves for a single whole.

Dalton and I never lived together and probably did not spend enough time together for any of these changes to take effect, but I know the taste of his skin—sweet and bitter like the flesh of a grapefruit—and the stench of his sweat—thin and salted as broth. I know that we changed each other in small and sometimes painful ways. And some days I detect his foreign scents in myself. I take this as evidence of a small intimacy, our limits running together like wet ink.

When we finally did it, there was no special occasion. We walked through the city, same as we did most days—a city once again bursting with heat. He stopped to tie my shoe, his lips tightening with the concentration of a familiar act performed backwards, an act of service. Then we were home, in his apartment, his dog in its kennel, us on top of each other in the bed. I wanted to cry with the simplicity of it.

Of course, things weren't perfect. These drugs were supposed to dissolve any distance between us, but they do not, not completely. Our first time was an anxious and imperfect gesture, but still a start. When we were in it, I couldn't stop noticing: his shoulders globed and blessed with a ladder of scars, the short, heightened grunt of pleasure he lets escape, the humid tangle of his unmade bed sheets in my fist, the cool wood paneling of his bedroom wall my hand presses against for leverage as he rocks above me.

"Are you alright?" he asked. "Am I doing something wrong?"

I wanted to laugh at the questions. I must have looked a million miles away.

"No. You're perfect."

# Proxemics

\

My uncle is an architect. From a prison in rural North Carolina, he sends letters stenciled with Corinthian columns, vaulted arcades, the stately domes of governmental buildings. Before his imprisonment he designed sets for local television productions, senior living centers, and hotels. He lived for a year in Rome to study the masters of the golden proportion. He wrote back with stories about a melting church in Spain, which would take over one hundred years to complete—La Sagrada Familia—and about the builders who spent their days in one of the spires, studying the plans from the original architect, Antoni Gaudí, trying to materialize them in the physical world. Some spaces must be imagined before they can be realized.

When my uncle used to visit our house, neighbors would come up to him in the yard and begin talking as if he were my father. There are almost twelve years between them, but they could be twins. All the men in my family look alike, me included—the strong gravity of genetics. I found my uncle's mugshot on the North Carolina prisoner database one afternoon. The blankness in his expression was the most startling, a sudden pair of glassy eyes, a clenched jaw, an uncanny reflection: the same furrow chiseled into our brows, the same down-turned corners of our eyes, my face, my father's face, but scooped clean of all affect.

If you asked my uncle why he is in prison, he would tell you it's for a crime he didn't commit. It is because his ex-wife is out to get him and his most recent ex-girlfriend, too. He would tell you about glitches in the ankle monitor he wore for a year while on probation, about the judge who, very suddenly, decided she didn't like him. He would tell you about flat tires, and work appointments, and engines shuttering to a halt: all the reasons he had to miss court dates or couldn't be home within the window of a certain hour. He might admit, after a while, to some of the lies he told, but he would say that they were told only out of necessity.

―――

"My client is not in a hurry," Gaudí said of his cathedral. What was a century or two for God? Even before he was struck dead by a tram in the streets of Barcelona, Gaudí knew he would never see his life's work completed, and so he left behind schematics and models to guide the inheritors of his work through the process of creation—a process he found more sacred the longer he lived. Learning to construct the cathedral was like "learning another language," one of those inheritors later said. And it was not just "the vocabulary, but the grammar as well." Gaudí's work "expressed meaning not only through the sculpture and other decorations but through the architecture itself."[1]

Once, on a date, a painter told me about a series he'd done based on the work of Edward T. Hall, the anthropologist, cross-cultural researcher, and accidental architect. In the series, he painted intimate encounters at varying distances, so that each successive panel lost more and more of its resolution. The paintings had the effect of drifting away from someone while standing still, or, if a viewer moved in the opposite direction, of cupping a person's face—skin and pores, stray hairs and musculature—into sharp focus. Hall's early career was spent studying the ways people in different cultures communicate: the body language they used, the distances they maintained while talking. In 1966, he invented the field of proxemics: a branch of knowledge about the amount of space we keep between ourselves and others, and how that distance is encoded in culture and its institutions. "This is a frightening thought, in view of how very little is known about man," Hall wrote. "It means that, in a very deep sense, our cities are creating different types of people in their slums, mental hospitals, prisons, and suburbs."[2] He called his book *The Hidden Dimension*.

---

I'm thinking about penitence and penitentiary—two words knitted together by language and history, though their connection is easy to overlook. Penitence, the state of mind, and penance, the self-punishment that follows, now feel heavy with religious connotations, while penitentiary belongs in the brutal and bureaucratic world of courtrooms, parole boards, and lice powder. But the original Quaker penitentiaries were religious, founded on the belief that criminals could be redeemed through isolation and silence, and the first true penitentiary was called Eastern State. Eastern State was, as the sociologist Norman Johnston writes, "without a doubt the most influential prison that was ever built."[3] Jails had existed for millennia. The idea of locking people up to await torture and execution or until they were able to repay their debts wasn't new. The innovation of Eastern State was conceptual: the confinement itself was the punishment.

During the penitentiary's early years, prisoners were given nothing to read but a Bible. Officers would escort them to their cells in black hoods. And on Sundays ministers would shuffle down the halls under shivering light, socks over their boots to muffle the noise, preaching sermons. Cells contained nothing but a bed, a desk, and a doorway leading to a solitary courtyard. Even the architecture was shaped to reflect the notion of penance. While the exterior of Eastern State was built to intimidate, the long halls of its interior were vaulted like chapels, radial in design, and flooded at certain times of the day with great slabs of light. A skylight was chiseled into the roof of each cell—a narrow shaft of blue-white light meant to represent the eye of God. In the austerity of the prison, it must have glowed like something hot and numinous. Prisoners, though, had another name for it: the Dead Eye.[4]

Not everyone was convinced of Eastern State, its humanity or capacity for redemption. "In its intention, I am well convinced that it is kind, humane, and meant for reformation; but I am persuaded that those who devised this system of Prison Discipline, and those benevolent gentlemen who carry it into execution, do not know what it is that they are doing," wrote Charles Dickens in his 1842 travelog, *American Notes for General Circulation*.[5]

I saw the prison once by accident. My friend was living in the Fairmount neighborhood of Philadelphia. We'd gone for a walk and found ourselves suddenly next to an enormous stone wall, edged with ivy and boxwoods and little cherry trees. The structure even today is impossible to ignore, a gothic fortress right in the middle of Philadelphia, complete with the beveled slivers of archer's windows, fake ramparts, and turrets. But there is something off about its impression now—a hulking skeleton, a taxidermied mammoth. "The exterior of a solitary prison should exhibit as much as possible great strength and convey to the mind a cheerless blank indicative of the misery which awaits the unhappy being who enters," wrote the commissioners of Eastern State penitentiary.[6] By the time I saw the prison, there were foam gargoyles draped with chains flanking its entrance. It was Halloween, and in the half-century since the penitentiary closed, it had become a tourist attraction. For nineteen dollars, you could see the inside, visit Al Capone's cell, and stand under ceilings ribbed with exposed beams. In the cold bright morning, it was hard to imagine the place as exhibiting anything more than residual misery and outdated plumbing.

———

In a red folder on my father's desk, he saves every letter his brother sends. He arranges them by date and staples each envelope to the back of its letter. He drafts each return letter by hand—twice—with marginal notes and improvements, arrows indicating how paragraphs and sentences should be shuffled for maximum effect, before typing them up and photocopying a version for himself. I wonder what he thinks as he writes these letters, if this is a distraction, or if he believes a perfect arrangement of words will "cure" his brother.

Their letters are written in the dialect of my childhood, with its small errors and eccentricities: "The car needs washed." "I would of stayed." "I didn't want the police called." Errors, long ironed out of my speech, come rushing back to me with bitter clarity. My father and uncle wrestle over the label of victim, and who owns it. They talk about acceptance and making good out of a bad situation. They both mention "rock bottom" at some point, as they track the path of a prodigal son: sinner, repenter, returned, redeemed.

My father sends books on self-improvement. He believes that prison, as painful as it may be, is the shock his brother needs. In one letter he writes, "I think you can change if you accept that you have made bad choices . . . Right now you have the opportunity to focus on your physical and mental health without the burdens of work and family. I hope you will use this time to exercise and read as much as possible, and explore how you see the world and how you make decisions."

Once an altar boy, my father is no longer religious, so I am surprised how much his letters echo with the language of his Catholic upbringing, how neatly his thinking tracks the notions of the Quakers building the first penitentiaries. But it is easy to renounce a set of rituals, harder to give up a structure of thinking, especially one you have lived with for sixty years.

If you asked my father why his brother is in prison, he would say it is to learn a lesson. He would tell you that his brother is essentially a good man, a smart man who made bad choices, who became too arrogant and entitled. He would tell you about his brother's upbringing in a household with a single income, no mother, and an infrequently-present father, working long hours at an oil refinery. He would admit that his brother stalked his ex-girlfriend, broke his house arrest, and then made up a story about her brandishing a gun at him—a story later proven false in court. But he would admit it with the sadness and sympathy reserved for family members we unconditionally love. Despite the stalking and house arrest, my uncle's eventual charge was for perjury.

―――――

"Personal Distance: At this distance, one can hold or grasp the other person. Visual distortion of the other's features is no longer apparent. However, there is noticeable feedback from the muscles that control the eyes."[7] If animals have distances for hunting, hiding, and living together, why wouldn't we? Hall's proxemics range from intimate distances to public distances, and he uses somatics—the volume of our voices, the detail with which we perceive each other, the smells we can or cannot detect—to categorize these distances.

Cigarettes, soap bars, envelopes, stamps, SIM cards, cell phones, drugs (recreational), drugs (medicinal), needles, ink, messages, viruses, bodies: some of the items that move in and out of prison walls. All institutions, even those that are meant to be hermetically sealed, are heavily trafficked and subject to the same conditions as the outside world. Even our most strictly controlled institution—the prison system—is porous, subject to leakage and contamination. In the case of disease, a community and its institutions are not separate, but interwoven. A city is only as healthy as its least healthy institution, and an institution is only as healthy as what surrounds it.

In Iowa, my roommate, Jay, works as a correctional officer at the prison in the adjacent town. His facility contains a rotating cast of prisoners. It functions as a type of holding unit, temporarily housing bodies until they can be slotted into the appropriate long-term facilities. The average stay is only ninety days, so prisoners are constantly being shuffled in and out, bringing with them whatever they've contracted on the outside. And because it is one of the few facilities with a hospital on campus, many of the prisoners are also patients, also sick. One night, Jay describes watching a man swallow a pen in the cafeteria. "He just downed it like swallowing a vitamin," he says. Prisoners often swallow things to spend a few days in the hospital, he explains, a risky form of relief. One institution and its monotony swapped for another. Usually everything turns out alright in these instances, but sometimes catastrophic consequences arise: ruptured intestines, blocked colons, prisoners forced to haul around colostomy bags in unsanitary conditions. Another day Jay describes one of his duties: "guarding" prisoners with end-stage kidney disease, liver failure, lung cancer. Prisoners who have been reduced, through confinement and illness, to no more than bodies, bodies kept alive with a dialysis machine and a ventilator. They are still shackled to their hospital beds. They are still guarded for the sake of being guarded. Kept alive for the sake of serving out their sentence. "Prison is not the place where you want to get sick," he finishes.

My father worries about his brother, though he rarely talks about it. On a long drive from Ohio where he lives, to Iowa where I was moving, I asked him about my uncle. He became uncharacteristically silent, clenched the steering wheel, stared at the horizon with its bronze sun. In the past two years, I've seen his red hair lighten to white, and his stamina fall. He is more haggard around the jowls now, and something in his eyes, bloodshot and in a perpetual squint, suggests a weariness sleep will not fix. My uncle was sentenced to twenty-one to thirty-five months beginning in 2019, just before the first wave of the COVID-19 pandemic. And so, both his sentence and my father's worry have been compounded by this fear of sickness.

———

"Social distance: Intimate visual detail in the face is not perceived, and nobody touches or expects to touch another person unless there is some special effort. Voice level is normal for Americans. Conversations can be overheard at a distance of up to twenty feet."[8]

In Eastern State, it was the solitude that prisoners feared most. When Alexis de Tocqueville interviewed the inmates there, they told him about the insects and animals—the crickets and butterflies and birds—that they had befriended, and about the terrible slowness of Sundays, the day when prisoners were not allowed to work.[9] Nearly a century later, solitude kept inmates safe as the flu of 1918 swept through Philadelphia. Pennsylvania, with a population of over a million, was an especially hard-hit state. In the first six months, the disease killed sixteen thousand Philadelphians, but the prison was miraculously spared. While the free were working in crowded, unhygienic conditions on factory assembly lines or in meat-processing facilities, prisoners were not only allowed but forced to keep their distance from others.[10] Now, the original purpose, as ineffective as it was, has been abandoned. Even the pretense of rehabilitation and isolation are gone. Now, it is the overcrowding, the doubled-up cells, and shared air that put this same population most at risk.

Facts and statistics. The average size of an American jail cell: six feet by eight feet. Weekly turnover rate in U.S. jails: 55 percent. Percentage of prisoners awaiting trial: 75 percent. Percentage serving short sentences: 20 percent. Cases of COVID-19 documented in U.S. prisons: 661,000.[11] Copay for a doctor's visit in prison: $4 (roughly equivalent to $580 for a minimum-wage worker on the outside). Hourly pay for the incarcerated: 5¢ an hour.[12]

———

My father comes from a large Irish Catholic family, seven siblings in total, though there are fewer of them now. His brothers and sisters have made the drive down to North Carolina to visit their brother. Afterward, they bicker over gas mileage, takeout bills, and room rentals. My father has never gone. He says he doesn't want to see his brother after years of being lied to. I suspect he also does not want to see his closest sibling and best friend reduced to those conditions.

Instead, my father pays for his brother's phone bill, even though he's not allowed to have a cell phone in prison, even though the two are no longer speaking. Someone (we suspect a girlfriend on the outside) burns through the data and minutes anyway, and my father pays for more. I don't know how much money my father has sent to his brother. In fact, I don't know if he sends him any direct payments at all. What I do know is that he pays for a storage unit in Charlotte so that the few remaining objects tying his brother to a previous life—his mattress, his clothing, his collection of Precision watches—are not pawned or left out to be scavenged on the street. I know that he wants his brother to have some type of life to return to.

There is a saying that floats through my family, a kind of trite motto that I have believed in and rolled my eyes at in turns. "Your siblings are the people you'll be closest to in the world." Your parents will likely die when you're middle-aged; your partner, if you have one, you'll meet later in life; but your siblings are a life sentence. My uncle has two sons a few years apart, and I heard this idea echoed again in his letter. He reminds them that they will be each other's friend and ally across their lives. I can't help but think of him and my father. I have one sibling, a sister three years younger than me. I see her most often in the house where we both grew up, for holidays and weddings, occasions when I fly home to Columbus where she and my parents live. In their house, she is always shaking her head, complaining of all the clutter our parents have acquired over the years: an attic of stained mattresses and cracked box springs and discarded workout equipment, loose drawers of baby clothes, crushed paint tubes, melted crayons, and greening pennies—the detritus of life. It took me a long time to realize why this excess bothers her so much. It's because she imagines a world without them, when there will be only the two of us, and all the stuff of their lives to sort through.

Facts and statistics II. The average amount of money spent on court fees and fines by the families of the incarcerated: $13,000.[13] The cost to send $200-$300 at the Avery/Mitchell correctional institute: $10.65. The cost to send between $0 and $20: $3.45. JPay's annual revenue in 2014: $70.4 million.[14] Things not captured in these statistics: the cost of visitation, the cost of gas, the cost of motels. The cost of missed work and spent vacation days. The cost of lost sleep.

———

"Intimate Distance: At intimate distance, the presence of the other person is unmistakable and may at times be overwhelming because of the greatly stepped-up sensory inputs. Sight (often distorted), olfaction, heat from the other person's body, sound, smell, and feel of the breath all combine to signal unmistakable involvement with another body."[15]

The truth is, at times I find it hard to feel bad for my uncle. In his letters, there's a tone of persecution splashed across every other sentence, a persistent accusation smoldering under the surface of his prose. He spends pages defining his life in contrast to his brother. My father is allowed to visit his children, talk with them, touch them, while he is not. In places, he slips into an oddly formal mode, "appealing" my father's "policy" of isolation, and what it is "costing" them both. At his worst, he couches his harshest accusations in rhetorical questions: What suffering would be enough for you? Maybe you've forgotten how to empathize?

Innocence appeals, with its purity and simplicity, to the dialectics of inside and outside, right and wrong, black and white. It is easy to believe in someone who is innocent, to work for their freedom and better treatment. But my uncle is not an innocent victim of a system; many people are not. He is both the guilty party and a victim at once.

I remember once walking in on my father and my uncle sitting together on the couch after their father's funeral. They didn't see me from where I stood behind them in the doorway. I remember hearing the words "I can't remember her voice anymore," and my uncle crying. I knew that "her" referred to their mother, who had died when my father was twenty and his brother was nine. I'm skeptical of the past as a perfect cipher for making sense of the present. Dead mother to narcissistic personality disorder to disordered relationship with women to prison. What about all the men with dead mothers who turn out just fine? But I do believe in redemption. I believe people can change. I believe in second chances. And I believe we put people, the innocent and the guilty, in the worst situation imaginable and then act surprised when they become exactly what we fear.

---

Prisons are not just tools for punishment or rehabilitation. They are not just architecture and blank time. They are concrete experience, event, and sensation. They are the somatics of Hall's proxemics: razor wire, blacktop, steel, and cinder block. They are the smell of breaded fish frying in a cafeteria, and the particular hardness of concrete, its leaching cold. They are the rattle and boom of cell doors closing in unison and the sudden muffle of sound. They are the unique frustration of waiting an hour for a call only to have the phone break. They are fights over desks and call times. The sickening absence of visitors. The desperate boredom, always the boredom.

My uncle mentions the pandemic in his letters only once, when he talks about the pain of losing visitors, the preciousness of a single fifteen-minute phone call each week. It makes sense why fights are breaking out. And it is all the more heartbreaking that this is what the pandemic means behind bars, not just the possibility of illness or death, but a robbery of one of the single joys many prisoners have left. At one point, my uncle lays out in precise detail the process for sending a letter—you need his prisoner's number, and the facility's specific address. The prison censors certain phrases, and forbids a long list of items. As I read, I begin to notice all the places he's smuggled his prisoner number into the letter—scrawled under his signature, floating above the top margin, hidden in the return address of the envelope the letter came in—quiet requests to write.

———

My friend Colin is a landscape architect. One weekend, in Chicago where I often visit, we sit near the Belmont harbor, and he tells me about the built world and how it influences us. How the spangling of light through planted trees lowers cortisol in the blood. How the "hardscaping" of the harbor where we sit—concrete steps that were once soft grass and huge stone breakers—was meant to prevent coastal erosion, but it also made it easier to banish the gay men who gathered here in the 1990s. Another day, he points to a mangy path that's been stamped into a field. A desire line, he calls it. Architecture reveals our psychology, he explains, how the world we build can chafe against us and our natural impulses.

The work of the artist James Casebere reimagines and rebuilds these spaces. His work consists mostly of intimate photographs of paper models built to resemble public spaces: schools, amphitheaters, and asylums. Arcades of interlaced arches. The branching tunnels of an underground. And of course penitentiaries. Sometimes his work is of the general—hallway, hospital, stacked beds, toilets. Other times it is specific. He has modeled Sing Sing, the tunnels and porticoes of Bologna, and an entire neighborhood of Tripoli.

His photographs are dreamlike, toyish, and eerie in their austerity, too pure in their geometry, too smooth in their surfaces. They are photographs of a model, twice alienated from the real. His work imagines, rather than describes, places of human occupation, but wiped clean of humans. "I was thinking about the circulation of air, water and people, and the way that different plans for prisons developed out of those concerns," said Casebere in an interview with BOMB magazine. "Ventilation and clean air became a concern in the workplace, and in hospitals and other institutions like poorhouses and prisons, partly as a result of the new knowledge that germs are airborne."[16]

Casebere spent time at Eastern State in the 1990s. He understood prisons as essentially a problem of management, and humans, even their emotions, as part of that managerial system. He wanted to make the system visible. His work forces a viewer to confront the spaces we ignore, spaces that form the background static of our lives—those designed for treatment, entertainment, transport, or confinement—and what they imply about the world we've created and perpetuate. In doing so he creates space to imagine a different future. As the novelist Rachel Kushner writes, "Architecture shifts things away from the pieties of the liberal individual who is asked to extend their compassion to some incarcerated person they want to believe is innocent, rather than worthy of something better than prison, regardless of any axis of innocence and guilt. It suggests that maybe we, too, are worthy of something better, as a society. Or we should be."[17]

---

"Public Distance: Several important sensory shifts occur in the transition from the personal and social distances to public distance, which is well outside the circle of involvement."[18] What does it mean to exit someone's "circle of involvement"? For Hall this means no longer smelling someone, no longer registering the contracting of their eye muscles, perhaps no longer even seeing them. The word *involvement*, though, implies something more than these tactile and sensory absences: that a person is so far removed, both physically and conceptually, that we no longer interact with them literally or metaphorically. Perhaps we no longer consider them at all. They disappear behind a wall, into a space we struggle to imagine.

For the most part, prisons don't look like Eastern State anymore. They are now outside of the city, on campuses that look as benign as high schools, hidden in a smoky landscape, mothered by rolling hills with nothing to suggest what they are aside from the high cyclone fences, concertina wire, the men trotting out for their time in the yard.

One night, Jay comes home with a lemon-sized welt throbbing on his bald head. He takes a bag of mixed vegetables out of the freezer and sears it against his temple, then sighs into an armchair. That afternoon, he was tasked with dragging a man out from under his cell bed, where the man was holed up, crouching and kicking at anyone who approached. The simple geometries, the open spaces, the flat surfaces—easy to search, easy to wipe clean—are all part of an architecture meant not only to manage prisoners, but to manage the fear of the people who work there. There should be nowhere to hide, no crevices from which to launch an attack, nothing unexpected that a correctional officer cannot account for. And yet: "It took three of us just to get him out," Jay tells me.

A friend once asked me how I could live with a correctional officer while being antiprison. Didn't those two things negate one another? Didn't I live in a constant state of cognitive dissonance? As if we all don't live with our hypocrisies, our compromises. As if prisons don't hurt more than just the people held there.

———

My uncle's sentence was short, and he was let out early after a parole board deemed him a nonviolent offender—a precious and specious designation. He left behind men much older and much sicker than he, many who were as equally "nonviolent."

My father and uncle are talking again—a fresh and uneasy armistice. They've landed in a strange place. My uncle has spent all his good will. He's overdrawn his credit, and then some. And yet, his brother will never completely abandon him. They're stuck with one another, a painful, filial kind of stuck. Of memories between him and his brother, my uncle says simply "there are so many impactful ones." Of forgiveness—for the brother he still believes abandoned him, for himself—he isn't sure, but he is open to the possibility.

It took 9 years to build Eastern State and 141 years for it to fail. But it took only a few years after the site was abandoned for a forest of mulberry bushes and maple saplings to grow up around the architecture. It took just as long for the roofs and skylights to begin collapsing, for birds to roost in the watchtowers, for trees to begin unmooring the slabs of concrete in the foundation. Eastern State was closed in the 1970s.[19] As it fell into disrepair, prisons were being built en masse across the country. In its strange purgatory between lives, I imagine a quiet place turned even quieter, one of Casebere's models flooded with water and light. A building lost in its own kind of penitence. A reminder that nothing is irrevocable, everything can be redone and remade, and some things can be forgiven.

# No Harm

He worked at night. In the intensive care unit of Mount Carmel West, a hospital on the southwest side of Columbus, Ohio, Dr. William Husel was often one of the only physicians on the floor. He worked treating end-of-life patients, an already difficult and frequently thankless job. To some, Dr. Husel's night work was a sign of altruism, a willingness to take on shifts that others did not want, to treat patients at their lowest point, during the worst time of the day. A time when cortisol levels surge and patients become the most agitated. When families are weary and irritable and ideas about good deaths and lives-well-lived hold the least sway. There is a "60 percent rise in death rate beginning at 2 A.M. and reaching a peak at 8 A.M."[1] In other words, many patients die at night.

To others, the fact that Dr. Husel volunteered for the night shift was a sign he was trying to get away with something. There is less oversight in hospitals at night when fewer doctors and pharmacists are working, and the administrative staff is away. In the hushed corridors and darkened rooms of patients, what might it be possible to do? No murder trial is without its complications, but of the many troubling aspects that plagued the trial of Dr. Husel—the fact that he did not administer any of the painkillers himself, the fact that the majority of his patients were in the process of being removed from life support when they died, or the fact that there is no set federal limit for a legal dose of fentanyl—his guilt or innocence turned on the question of how a jury would read his choice to work at night, how it testified to the impenetrable inner world of the doctor.

Between 2014 and 2018, while Dr. Husel was employed at Mount Carmel, dozens of patients died in his care. On its face, this was not such an alarming fact. Husel was an intensive care doctor, working in a part of Columbus with high rates of poverty, alcohol, and drug addiction. In Franklinton, the neighborhood Mount Carmel West served, the median income is ten thousand dollars and the average life expectancy is sixty years—the lowest in Ohio.[7] So the number of deaths, while high, did not immediately stand out to a staff inured to a particular flavor of suffering and an unusually high rate of patient death. Instead, the first suspicion was a common one: that drugs were being *diverted*—a technical term for the theft of controlled substances in a medical setting. The idea that a staff member might be stealing fentanyl from the hospital for sale or personal use was a simple one. The motives and rationale of addicts were predictable, almost dull, in a state rocked by a stupendous rise in opioid overdoses. But the truth was not so simple. The drugs were all accounted for. They had either been used or properly disposed of, so the doses, while still astonishingly high, were not being stolen. Which left the more unsettling questions of where the drugs were going, what they were being used for, and why.

For months doctors had whispered concerns over the quantity of paralytics and painkillers that Husel prescribed. Nurses wondered privately about the high doses, though nearly all of them administered the medication dutifully. For the most part, friends and family members of patients who had died under Dr. Husel's care went home distraught over the death of their loved ones—a common feeling, sad but final and, ultimately, blameless. But in testimony years later, some family and friends of the deceased would report leaving the hospital feeling unease. They could not put their finger on precisely why, but there was a general sense that the death of their brother, or husband, or friend had not proceeded as it should have.

On October 28, 2018, a pharmacist issued a formal report to his supervisors about Dr. Husel. The pharmacist's concern was triggered by the death of James Timmons, whose palliative extubation (removal of life support) Husel had supervised. Timmons had died ten minutes after receiving a thousand-microgram dose of fentanyl ordered by Dr. Husel. An enormous dose for a man who was already catatonic. After reviewing the report, the pharmacist's supervisors elevated the concerns further, and less than two months later, on December 5, 2018, after an internal review, Husel was fired from Mount Carmel West, and the hospital notified the Ohio State Medical Board of their decision. Six months later, on June 5, 2019, after an external investigation into multiple deaths, Husel turned himself over to police. His arrest marked the culmination of four years of suspicious deaths and rumors. Four years in which as many as thirty-four patients may have had their lives cut short under Dr. Husel's care. He was charged with twenty-five counts of murder.

―――

To understand Mount Carmel West, you must first understand its neighborhood. Part of the horror and intrigue of the Husel case was that, in theory, it could happen anywhere. This is the salacious threat and tantalizing promise of the gritty true crime genre: it could happen to you too. But for the most part it doesn't, and the case of Dr. Husel was always much more likely to occur in a place like Franklinton.

Franklinton is a neighborhood of persistently rotten porches, split cinder block, and trampled zinc fencing. Informally, locals call it "the Bottoms" because the flood line of the surrounding rivers lies above the basements of most houses in the neighborhood. For years, insurance companies refused to secure homes in Franklinton because they were considered too high risk. It is the oldest neighborhood in an already old city. Before Columbus was incorporated, before Ohio was even a state, when the country was just barely a country, Franklinton was already a settlement. The flatness of the Midwest begins here, where the Appalachian foothills ripple out and still, giving way to the flat glacial till that continues mostly unbroken until the Rockies. It is a neighborhood in the near biblical thrall of water and its temperament. Surveyors first settled this low-lying region in 1795, but their encampments were swept away in 1798.[3] Undeterred, they moved uphill and began again. Throughout the nineteenth century, Franklinton experienced routine floods that pushed homes off their foundations and scraped up brick-laid roads like crumpling wallpaper. For decades, the neighborhood was decimated again and again by moderate and periodic flooding. Then, in 1913, a worse flood came. The wooden levees protecting the neighborhood failed. Ninety-four people died.[4] Streets became clogged with loose lumber. Houses tipped once, then twice in the rushing water, until they came to rest oddly on one of the tilted planes of their roofs. Mothers who had carried their children above their heads through the river-drowned city were now grandmothers, themselves carried by those very children to Mount Carmel West. The hospital was the tallest structure in the region, and it rested on slightly elevated land. In more ways than one, Mount Carmel was an institution and a sanctuary.

In 2014, David was a student at Mount Carmel's school of nursing. Later, he worked as a nurse's aide in the emergency room, though never with Dr. Husel. We spoke over the phone in the spring of 2022, just after the trial concluded, about the neighborhood and his experiences living there. While studying and working, David lived in Franklinton, in a home walking distance from the hospital and campus, a house his family purchased in 2004. A generation of siblings have cycled through that house. David's older brother lived there before him, and his younger sister was living there when we spoke. He described the neighborhood first in its broader stereotypes: as a place where no one cares, a place of high crime and little money, where garbage cans are constantly toppled and overflowing, and the front doors are often boarded up and spraypainted. But David knows the place not as an outsider, but as a resident. Really, he tells me, these are just signs of neglect. Trash service is irregular; taxis, police, and even ambulances are hesitant to go there; attempts to develop the neighborhood have, until recently, been failures.

David is a character—brash, talkative, lightly profane—and he has an eccentric's memory for striking details. He talks about random gunshots startling him awake at night, the ache of gunpowder in the air. He describes AC units lifted from windowsills like pies set out to cool in a children's story, and stereo systems pried like gemstones from parked cars. He remembers a pallet of shrubs being snatched from his front yard, and wonders out loud what the thief could have possibly wanted with them. He tells me about the people who would occasionally wander up to his door asking for money, or how a man once knocked on his door to tell a long story about falling asleep on his mattress with a lit cigarette, nearly burning his house down. It took a while for David to realize what the man wanted. When he told the man he didn't have a mattress to spare, the man simply shrugged, unfazed, and moved on to the next door down the block.

That it seemed natural to assume the high doses of fentanyl were being stolen and sold or abused was an old prejudice, a pairing of Franklinton's sizable Appalachian population with opioid addiction and drug dependency, an assumption that the people there are more likely than others to be looking for escape. But David doesn't agree that Franklinton is any worse than other parts of the city. He calls it a down-to-earth neighborhood. A strange place, one that is rough around the edges, but essentially good. He uses the phrase "urban white trash," which is the dominant stereotype of the neighborhood, even though it is one of the few racially diverse neighborhoods in Columbus. When I ask him what his most enduring memory of the neighborhood is, he tells me the story of watching a child running through his alleyway, being chased by a grandmother on an electric wheelchair. Whether she was chasing him as part of a game or to mete out some type of punishment, he isn't sure, but he is sure that Franklinton is not the desperate and dangerous place most people imagined.

---

February 22, 2022, is the kind of cold, overcast day in Columbus where the horizon dissolves directly into the depthless sky and the scattering of buildings that form the city skyline is tossed in a slow roil of fog. Inside, the courtroom has the dull, warm ambiance of a midwinter school day. Proceedings were stalled by the pandemic, and the courtroom, when the trial begins, is clad in plexiglass. Cameramen recording the proceedings must be careful not to catch the reflection of an anonymous juror against the barriers; witnesses have to shout to be heard by the court stenographer.[5]

The first day of the trial is filled with the predictable conventions of an opening argument: a family photo of Husel dressed in white next to his wife and two daughters, an emphasis on his Ohio childhood with a father in mass transit and a stay-at-home mother. There is also the familiar and absolute assertion that, granting some room for error, no criminal acts were committed. But in other ways the case is marked from the beginning as exceptional. Jose Baez, a lawyer who once defended Casey Anthony, Aaron Hernandez, and Harvey Weinstein, acts as lead for the defense. He has the face and confidence of a TV lawyer, which in some ways he is, having transcended his profession with so many high-profile cases. He opens with a stark question: "Have you ever thought of your death?" It is a daring move and an acknowledgment of the defense's steepest challenge: the fact that each patient in question died under Husel's care—there will be no evading this fact—and that the jury will be reminded of these deaths, and perhaps their own, with each new witness. The defense's task, then, is to show that these deaths were inevitable and that they had not been hastened by Dr. Husel. To do this they will have to approach death nakedly.

Baez begins by laying out the complicating features of the case. He highlights the fact that some of these patients, though certainly not all, may have already been habituated to opioids and therefore less responsive to their palliative effects. He notes that many of these patients were sick—some were experiencing multiple organ failures, some were already brain-dead. He tells the jury that no federally set maximum dosage for opioid use exists, only institutional policies and best practices. Finally, he lays out his central, exculpating theory of the case: that the hospital had maintained poor practices for years around drug administration during end-of-life care, and when administrators got scared—when they saw the number of deaths—they went looking for a scapegoat in Husel.

It is a compelling argument, but one troubled by the uniquely large doses Dr. Husel administered.

On day 2 of the trial, the prosecution calls Talon Schroyer, one of the pharmacists who first elevated the concerns about the quantity of fentanyl Dr. Husel administered. Schroyer is a young, wide-eyed, and goateed man. He describes his reaction to the doses as simply "shocked." As he speaks, he widens his eyes as if reliving that shock. He speaks of the "synergistic effect of the medication," or the mutual amplification of effects when vasodilators (used to aid circulation) and opioids (used as painkillers) are combined. If both vasodilators and opioids suppress breathing, when they are used together it is not a matter of simple addition, they multiply each other, become greater than the sum of their parts. Schroyer's testimony begins straightforwardly enough, but it is in this second day of the trial, as his testimony proceeds, that the challenge for the prosecution crystalizes. I had expected, when the case began, to be conflicted, to feel myself torn in two directions, between the desire of this doctor to relieve suffering and the essential preciousness of human life even in its final moments. I had expected to flip sides with each changing of the guard between examination and cross-examination. I had, in short, been prepared for a television trial, one punctuated by bold claims and clear though conflicting narratives.

Instead, what I experience from the moment the prosecution calls their first witness is confusion, interrupted by only brief moments of clarity. The orderly theorizing of opening statements is immediately washed away by the impenetrable bureaucracy and the specialized operations of the hospital system: the nuances of various pain and coma scales (Glasgow versus RASS versus Moscow); the type of vials used to administer fentanyl and their specific forms of delivery (in bolus or infusion); whether a patient had benzodiazepines in their system or not when a particularly high dose of fentanyl was given, and if they did indeed have these benzodiazepines in their system who administered them, and if they were administered how they were approved, and if they were approved, when and where and why. Even simple procedural elements of the case like where the pharmacists sit (in the basement, receiving orders for medication from the hospital above, orders which can be overridden, and then retroactively must be approved by a pharmacist) have to be clarified again and again.

Language is often accused of being inadequate to encompass the size of an issue, but here, in the courtroom, another curious breakdown occurs: the inability of language to order and clarify the technicalities of procedure and the minuteness of detail. Death is profoundly technical. We tend to talk about it as a singular event, a swift moment-by-moment passage from one state to another, but here that passage becomes hazy, and the overlapping complexities of the body enter the legal field uneasily. Patients' hearts stop. Their kidneys fail. Their respiration drops below sustainable levels. Patients are administered CPR under code and intubated. They are delivered pain medication and paralytics whose side effects are weighed against the probability of their suffering. They die and recover, Lazarus-like, and their temporary deaths are recorded precisely in minutes and seconds, though this record is a lie of medical and legal utility. Language has trouble accounting for this overlapping Venn diagram of collapse except in the general, and the general does not count as evidence here.

Here is the essential scenography: Medication in most of the cases was drawn from Pyxis machines (storage cabinets preloaded with drugs that doctors—or more often nurses—can withdraw without having to go to the pharmacy). Normally, these withdrawals must be approved by a pharmacist, but in emergencies medication can be withdrawn without prior approval. This exception is essential, especially in end-of-life care, because a patient's status can change suddenly, and doctors and nurses often do not have the time to seek pharmacy approval for the medications they need. Because Dr. Husel worked at night, with fewer staff members and less oversight, and because he worked with patients in dire circumstances, his use of medication was approved only retroactively. The majority of questionable doses of fentanyl were delivered during palliative extubation, or the removal of life support, specifically the removal of the tube that keeps a patient breathing through a ventilator when they cannot breathe on their own. Dr. Husel himself was not in the room for many of the deaths.

The fact that these patients were sooner or later going to die and the inability to know how long, exactly, they might have lived without the introduction of thousands of micrograms of fentanyl is one of several factors complicating the prosecution's argument. Another is the nurses, who all have a mixed investment in the state's success. It was the nurses, not the doctor, who administered the allegedly lethal doses of painkillers. And it was the nurses who found themselves in a strange liminal space of legal jeopardy: both responsible and not for the drugs, potentially willful actors, potentially obedient followers of orders. Before the trial began, the state had already declined to criminally prosecute anyone other than Husel, but there was still the looming question of the nurses' licensure, disciplinary actions from the state board, and the potential for future civil litigation.

"If a doctor had ordered doses of 1,000 micrograms," an anonymous nurse reported to the *Columbus Dispatch*, "I would think 'Have you lost your mind? Did you mistype a zero?' . . . I wouldn't ever give it, because I know I'd kill them." The largest dose that nurse remembers giving was 200 micrograms, a number she ultimately accepted under particularly unusual circumstances, but one that gave her pause.[6]

Why would these nurses be so willing to deliver a thousand micrograms of fentanyl? Part of the answer might lie in the hierarchy of the hospital. In our interview, David described experiences in which he felt pressure from doctors to do things he wasn't comfortable with. The doctor is the ultimate authority in the room. But another nurse I spoke to wasn't so sure. ICU nurses are tough, swaggering, he said. At least that's the stereotype. They know what they're doing: when to challenge doctors and when the dosing for a certain medication is inappropriate. They're trained to be confrontational for the good of the patient, sometimes even when they're wildly off-base. That's part of the job.

This may be true, but as I watch the trial unfold, what stands out to me is how young the nurses all are. They're freshly graduated, mid- to late twenties, a few years into their work, some of them incredibly inexperienced, all of them at risk of losing a career they've only just begun.

Of all the nurses, Stephanie LeChard, a witness for the prosecution called on day 11 of the trial, is the most striking. She is a young woman with large, cervine brown eyes and visible anxieties. Her testimony is accompanied by constant, stuttering nods, a real-time cardiograph of fear. Her eyes dart often to the judge for reassurance and to someone else, unseen, in the audience—a lawyer, a parent? She rarely looks the state's lawyer directly in the eye. In her testimony, she describes how Husel was patient and methodical, always willing to walk a resident or nurse through both his process and his thinking. Seen one way, his willingness to teach suggests he was a generous mentor willing to take young and inexperienced medical professionals under his wing; but looked at another way, he was a trainer of acolytes, forging a culture of high doses, quick decisions, and extreme interventions in palliative care. At most, LeChard worked six shifts in the ICU prior to caring for Sandra Castle, the patient she has been called to testify about. Sandra was her first palliative care patient. Knowing this, watching her testimony, it seems unfair that she should be here. She's Kafka's own collateral victim—frightened, obedient, disoriented by the jarring turns of fate that have led her here.

Her anxiety, though, inspires more than just sympathy; it is a hindrance to the smooth narrative the prosecution is attempting to lay out. She answers every question with the uncertain lilt of another question. "You rated her arm as flaccid," the prosecution asks. "Is that consistent with being rigid?" "Um . . . no?" she responds, with a long gaping pause between each syllable. She sounds like a child caught off guard by a teacher's question, unsure, unpracticed.

The prosecution's main task is to demonstrate that Husel administered an excess of painkillers in the course of managing his patients' pain. From this perspective, LeChard states things that do not seem especially helpful to their case. "It seemed like the morphine wasn't helping [the patient]," she volunteers at one point under direct examination, a time when she is supposed to be answering familiar and practiced questions from a friendly lawyer. At another point she adds the sentimental detail that there was "a tear running down [the patient's] face."

At several points, the lawyer for the prosecution lapses into frustration. He nearly scolds his own witness. The air crackles with tension, and LeChard looks like she might break down and cry. During one brief pause, as lawyers approach the bench for a sidebar, the judge asks: "Are you okay there?" It's not really a question. Her terror is visible, and the judge doesn't wait for an answer. Instead, he gives her an instruction: "Take a deep breath. Relax."

———

On the bank block of the town where I grew up, I meet with Adam, a nurse practitioner who studied at Mount Carmel's School of Nursing and has worked at several ICUs in the community. Adam is a friend agreeing to do me a professional favor: lending me context on Mount Carmel and nursing more generally. We both grew up in Grandview, a suburb a mile from the hospital, just north of the brutalist gray loop of concrete on-ramp that strangles Franklinton. When my parents first moved there, the two neighborhoods were not so different. Friends asked them, with thinly veiled concern, why they would want to raise children in a place like Grandview. During the white flight of the 1970s and 1980s, real estate prices fell, houses sat vacant, and gangs invaded the richer suburbs to the north. Stabbings occurred between rival groups of teenagers—or so people claimed in our high school two decades later.

But the neighborhood changed. Both Franklinton and Grandview were built when the city was young, but Grandview rests mostly above the floodplain. Its houses are old and historic, well built at their core, even as they have fallen in and out of disrepair. From the postwar decades, Grandview emerged poised for gentrification and renewal, an old privilege newly realized. Franklinton did not. It is hard now to overstate the differences between these two communities. I remember the school renovations and the local restaurants moving onto the bank block. I remember the bulldozers tearing down the seedy Knights Inn on Route 33 and the pit on 3rd Avenue that sat filled with rainwater and bent spines of rebar for years, until finally someone filled it in and used the lot for luxury condominiums. Now Grandview is full of stationery stores and yoga studios with blown-glass wind chimes clinking out front. It's a neighborhood of new prefab apartments for recent graduates of the Ohio State University and freshly renovated homes originally built in the nineteenth century for wealthy East Coasters who wanted to escape the smog and netted telephone wires of the industrial revolution.

As Adam speaks, a constant rush of suburban traffic hums behind us. I haven't interviewed many people. I keep fiddling with the recorder, afraid it won't pick up his voice. Finally, I give up, and take to scribbling notes furiously, trying not to miss anything essential.

The first thing Adam contextualizes is how fentanyl functions in a medical setting. It's an incredibly useful drug—swift and powerful, but ultimately short-lived. It takes effect in seconds, peaks after five minutes, and fades in a slow taper over thirty or so minutes. Adam uses the word *slug* to refer to the injection of painkillers in bolus, evoking a punch to the stomach or the molten wad of a spent bullet. "Why *slug* a massive, massive amount?" he asks. Why obliterate pain only for it to return shortly after, especially when the drug is so short-acting and when there are high risks associated with using it? Risks that are well known? To medical professionals, sure. But more and more to the public, particularly in a state like Ohio, where the drug's reputation is fearsome and synonymous with untimely death.

No matter what one might think about the case, using a thousand or more micrograms of fentanyl to temporarily control pain is irresponsible and unnecessary. I'm surprised by how unequivocally Adam states this. Later, I will notice this sense of certainty smoldering under most of my conversations with medical professionals. He tells me that no matter the outcome of the trial, trust has been squandered by the perception that Husel acted according to his own ethical principles. This, in a section of town that already struggles with medical mistrust.

Adam is careful to say that he does not agree with what Dr. Husel did or understand his choices, but he is sympathetic with his position. He's had his own difficult conversations with family members hoping against reason for a miracle. He's seen resources spent on patients without brain function, kept alive by machines alone—patients who in some cases may not want to be kept alive after they have experienced brain death. He's called loved ones on a different continent for a patient with a Do Not Resuscitate order, who for some reason was brought into the ICU as "full code," meaning nurses were obliged by the State of Ohio to take every measure to save his life. Adam has worked in the ICU, but he's not bound by it. His degree as a nurse practitioner allows him to practice a range of medicine in various modalities. In contrast, "somebody [like Dr. Husel]," he explains, "who devoted all their life to becoming an ICU physician, they're kind of pot-committed, and that can be confining. It would be awful to practice for a couple years and find that in many ways you're powerless . . . and doomed to continue working in that same arena."

Adam contextualizes more than just the use of fentanyl. He mentions that the bulk of healthcare spending goes into the last forty-eight hours of a person's life, that the majority of GDP spent on healthcare comes in the final two weeks of life, and that medical expenses are the primary source of bankruptcy in the United States—its own form of residual suffering, a suffering that is distributed unevenly. "I've treated one lawyer and one doctor in my time at Mount Carmel," he explains. "Because for the most part they make a *clean escape* from the ICU." I ask about this phrase, specifically what it looks like to make a "clean escape," and he brings up

Kobacker House—an immaculate hospice center just outside of Columbus with large, quiet rooms, soffit ceilings, stained-glass windows, and many well-trained nurses with reasonable schedules and a manageable number of beds. These are the institutions people with money end up in. They are built for transition, spacious, and comfortable not only for the dying but for their families. And they have all the opioids you could ever want.

Adam is deep-voiced and soft-spoken, careful with his words, almost to the point of being struck speechless at times. I suspect his trepidation has something to do with the looming threat of lawsuits in the ICU. Throughout our conversation he speaks in generalities and abstraction to protect patients' identities; only once does he get graphic, when he describes performing CPR for thirty minutes, until "bright red blood was coming out of every orifice." This is what we should be trying to avoid, he explains: protracted pain and suffering, stemming from uncertainty about what a patient wants, and, he suspects, a general discomfort with death. Whether we wind up in Kobacker or the ICU, Adam thinks we need to acknowledge death's inevitability and to prepare for it as much for ourselves as for the people we love. Without that preparation the medical system defaults to doing the least legally risky thing: extending life as much as possible, whether patients want it or not. Even medical ethicists—ostensibly hired to do the hard work of thinking through challenging moral dilemmas in the face of death—often resort to legalistic neutrality, choosing whatever is least risky for the hospital. You can disobey them, Adam notes, but you do so at the risk of your own legal exposure.

I've seen what this can look like, not the disobedience but the preparation. In 2021, I spent several weeks on the cardiac floor of a hospital in Iowa City with a mysterious blood clot. My roommate there was a man named Charlie with a congenital heart disease. He told me his life story one day through the thin cotton curtain that divided the room as we ate from trays of hospital food. How he wasn't supposed to live past ten years old. How his mother told him about his condition when he was sixteen. I tried to imagine the shock of this: living past an expiration date you didn't even know you had. I wondered how his mother must have felt—the joy of seeing her son live, tempered only by the looming questions of how long and how to tell him. She was there with him in the hospital. She held the door open for me once as I wheeled a cart of dripping blood thinners to the bathroom. Some nights, I watched her watch her son sleep, unsure what the future held.

When I met Charlie, he was thirty-four. He had a son with autism and many savvy methods for getting the best food in the hospital cafeteria. It was clear he had spent a lot of time there. He was in the hospital this time because liquid was pooling in his stomach and legs. By then, he had far outlived doctors' expectations, but his heart was extremely weak, his blood pressure extremely low. An impossible decision lay in front of him: he could opt for a heart pump, which would demand maintenance and might not fully solve the defect; or he could choose to have a heart transplant, a much riskier procedure, fraught with years on waiting lists and possible organ rejection by his body, but one that promised him a more normal life in the long run. On the cardiac floor many decisions were like this: a precarious balancing of risk and reward with the highest stakes. There you couldn't walk away from the table. The decision was forced on you, and only you could make it.

My condition was serious but not grave, an essential distinction in a hospital. I could intuit this just from the way nurses spoke to me—blithe happy chatter, even as they asked me about death and living wills. Their general disinterest was a comfort.

Five doctors surrounded Charlie's bed as they explained the

risks and possibilities of a transplant. I could see their feet clustered around the bottom of the curtain dividing our room. The force of their attention was palpable, frightening. It seemed to turn the volume down on everything else. They asked him to consider what he would like the doctors to do in the case his heart stopped on the operating table or if he could no longer eat or breathe without the assistance of a machine. They wanted him to make a plan for his mother, so that she would not have to labor over the questions of when or if to let him go. I remember the stillness as he thought. The raw mortality of the questions felt like staring at the sun, too bright, too intense, too real. It was terrifying to hear someone so young be faced with them. He said he would like to be resuscitated if his heart stopped, but allowed to die if he became "brain dead."

"I don't want to be a vegetable. I'm not good to anyone like that."

I think of these clear directives as their own kind of care, one you pay back to the people who have taken care of you, a strange sort of mercy. You spare them an impossible choice through your willingness to consider death before it arrives. It isn't an easy decision to make. The easiest option is to fall thoughtlessly backward into the default state of medical excess and legal neutrality. But it is the kind of decision Adam hopes more of us consider while we're still healthy.

---

If there is a single concept orienting the case, it is the dichotomy of good and bad deaths. The defense first mentions it in their opening statements. They tell a story about Tracy Young, a former patient of Dr. Husel's. The defense presents Young as tragic figure and an explanation for Husel's liberal use of opioids to treat end-of-life pain. Young spent her final days gasping for air, being delivered more and more painkillers, none of which were enough to alleviate her symptoms, until finally, arduously, she died. Husel's experience with Young, the story implies, taught him that some patients need enormous amounts of opioids to control their pain and that in end-of-life care the management of pain is one of the most essential elements in an elusive good death. But no one had defined precisely what a good or bad death is.

For this, I contact a bioethicist at the Ohio State University, Dr. Ryan Nash. We speak over the phone the summer after the trial. Dr. Nash is patient and lightly Brahminic—a Tolkien character who's stepped unbothered into a life in central Ohio. He takes a walk through a meadow during our interview. A soundtrack of tweeting birds dapples his speech as he defines technical terms like *air hunger* and *agonal breathing* for me. There's something absurd and bucolic about the whole thing, the smash cuts between wildflowers and death. I can practically hear the sunshine through the phone speakers.

Dr. Nash leads with an important caveat: he has no knowledge of the case. He has not reviewed any documents. He hasn't read the reporting on the trial. He does not know what happened, meaning our discussion is in the abstract.

Many people will define a bad death as anything that involves tragedy and suffering, Dr. Nash suggests, and certainly there are deaths of needless pain and excessive suffering that are easily categorized as bad. "I've witnessed patients die with extreme symptoms that should have been managed better. I've seen patients die alone; I've seen patients die scared and without comfort," says Dr. Nash. But good deaths are harder, not only to achieve but to define. If a bad death is characterized by excessive suffering, it is tempting to define a good death as simply its inverse: a death with no suffering at all. Here, though, Dr. Nash is skeptical. We assume a silent body is evidence of a good death, that a dying person who does not moan or cry out, twitch or spasm or respond in any way is not experiencing undue suffering, and so the natural temptation is therefore to tranquilize the body. To exert so much control that the dying come to lack animation. To render them silent. Sitting with suffering, alleviating it when possible, but accepting it as inevitable, Dr. Nash suggests, may be an unhappy but necessary component in a good death.

I want to be careful here not to glorify suffering, or transform it into something divine, but I take the point that a desire to eliminate suffering completely might inflict other unintended consequences. I remember something Adam said weeks before, when he detailed a phenomenon on the ICU floor, in which a sense of pity and dread collects around a patient near death. Nurses do not want to take on a patient who is difficult and unstable. They are emotionally draining, and difficult deaths are notorious among medical professionals for inviting lawsuits. Plunging the dying person into an inert state is easier than contending with suffering. Tranquilization allows nurses and doctors and families to avoid confronting pain at all, but in a single-minded campaign against all suffering, we risk eliminating the sufferer along with it. This is not the clear-cut bad death of Dr. Nash's experience, but it is also not the kind of death I would choose for myself.

On day 5 of the trial, the prosecution calls Dr. Wes Ely, a professor at Vanderbilt University. Several weeks later—after the jury has reached its verdict—one of the members will admit that it was Dr. Ely specifically who put doubt into his head about Husel's innocence. I understand why. Each witness up to this point has been limited by their narrow slice of perspective. They can speak only to their direct experiences: the day a nurse administered a dose of fentanyl, the day a pharmacist first noticed the nervous-system decimating order, the day a sister found her brother passed out in a bathtub from an apparent overdose and rushed him to the hospital. The most common objections I hear from the defense—hearsay, speculation—are on this point: Witnesses are required to describe the world based exclusively on their firsthand experience of events, without assumptions or speculations or logical leaps. Their testimony sketches the broad outlines of a narrative, but each data point is padded with hours of establishing questions and cross-examination. Individually, the testimonies fail to cohere into a clear story, fail to suggest guilt or innocence.

Dr. Ely does something none of the other witnesses have been able to do. He takes a bird's-eye view of the cases. He has examined the medical files of each of the deceased. He knows the facts and contexts of their lives. He has no direct experience to offer, only expertise, and can therefore speak in broad, relatable metaphors. He describes the amount of fentanyl Dr. Husel was using as "driving 250 mph in a school zone," and "enough to take out an elephant." He notes the strange jump in recorded pain levels of patients just before nurses administered large doses of painkillers. "Usually you'd see zero, three, five, six, back down to three . . . but this was extremely consistent zeros then—whammo!—out of nowhere comes a ten." Asked about his conclusions around the death of one of Dr. Husel's patients, he states more plainly than anyone has up until this point: "I think [the medications] stopped him from breathing and caused his death." He is the only one qualified to make such a bold conclusion.

Near the hour mark of Dr. Ely's testimony, the state turns its examination to the question of the deaths happening at night. A palliative extubation "is never an emergency," Dr. Ely says. I had not considered this before. By the time a patient is going to be removed from life support, the assumption is that they are going to die. It is strange to imagine that in this darkest of places there is no rush and no emergency, only waiting and a terrible certainty. But it also makes sense. The patient is being kept alive by machines and kept comfortable with medications. There is no time pressure. In such moments, it is the loved ones who become the center of consideration. "We almost never do that in the middle of night," Dr. Ely explains. "In the middle of the night the family is suffering. They're hurting. They're scared. They are in physical and existential pain. I don't know what sort of conversation they need to say to their loved one to help them heal. I don't want to rush that. I don't want to do it under the cloak of darkness."

———

Another phrase threads through the trial and its surrounding media coverage: the *doctrine of double effect*. In opening arguments, Jose Baez describes it as such: "If a doctor has good intent, and a secondary effect happens—like death—it is fully permissible... If Dr. William Husel intended on giving comfort care and the outcome of the cause of that comfort care was the death, it falls under the doctrine of double effect."

During our interview, Dr. Nash brings up the doctrine of double effect as well. He describes it as the Italian priest and philosopher Thomas Aquinas filtering Aristotle through Christian theology—at which point I ask him to slow down. When Aquinas first formulated the doctrine, he was writing about the ethics of self-defense— is it permissible to do something bad (murder) if it is in service to something good (your own life). But Dr. Nash first learned the doctrine in a more familiar context: opioids. The question in the medical field was whether powerful but addictive painkillers should be used to relieve suffering at the end of life, despite their potential for harm. Dr. Nash admits that the doctrine allows for negative outcomes and considers intention, just as Baez suggests. If, for example, a doctor makes every good faith effort to prevent suffering with a reasonable dose of painkiller, but a patient still suffers or dies accidently because of that reasonable dose, the action is still justified. But the doctrine does not allow a good outcome to be achieved through the bad. For example, the alleviation of suffering, a general good, cannot be achieved by killing a suffering patient or even by administering a dangerous level of painkillers.

All of this, however, may be moot in Dr. Nash's eyes. He isn't sure the doctrine has any domain in this specific case. Opioids are rarely a fatal agent in a medical setting. "In my experience," he explains, "the dose difference between relieving some air hunger [the common end-of-life gasping] and hastening death is quite broad. It's not walking a tightrope between symptom relief and death." Instead, Dr. Nash wonders if this is a case of the last-dose phenomenon, which Dr. Nash explains like this: "In [patients] with a very dismal prognosis," he explains, "there will come a time when they do die, and they will receive a final dose of medication, and there is a question of whether that medication had a role in that eventual death." This, as far as I can tell, has not been mentioned once in the trial.

---

We get so little of Dr. Husel himself. Like many defendants, he never takes the stand. In the video footage of the trial, he is silent, often off-screen. From time to time, as papers are shuffled, or in the dead space between witnesses, the camera pans to the doctor as he whispers to his lawyer, nibbles on a granola bar, or simply sits still, silent, in profile, waiting on his fate.

But there are several events from Dr. Husel's past that might be useful to know. An Ohio native, he was born in Cleveland in 1975. In high school, he was a basketball star and team captain. During the trial, his coach went on record with the *Columbus Dispatch* saying, "He has always portrayed himself in a positive light in our community, and that's why it's such a hard thing to wrap your head around. There are two sides to every story, and hopefully we get to hear from Billy."[7] In college, Billy became William, who would eventually become the Dr. William Husel of first local and then limited national infamy. He attended Wheeling Jesuit College in West Virginia for several semesters before transferring to the Ohio State University in Columbus, Ohio. He completed a four-year residency at the Cleveland Clinic, where he studied anesthesiology. And in July 2013, he began working at Mount Carmel West, a little under two years before the first alleged murder.

His was a largely successful and unexceptional education and career, marked by one extraordinary incident: a pipe bomb he constructed and detonated in a trash can while a student at Wheeling Jesuit. For two years federal investigators worked on the pipe bomb case, and in 1994 they officially charged William with the crime. Their conclusions were that William had been stealing car stereos on campus. After getting caught, he constructed the pipe bomb with the intent of planting it in the car of the man who turned him in. William stored the bomb and bomb-making materials in a dorm room on Wheeling's campus and eventually detonated it in a trash can—likely because he got cold feet. William then attempted to frame another person for the crime by planting bomb-making materials in their car. Unconfirmed details report that this person was forced to change their name for fear of retaliation, and that the bomb was large enough to send pieces of wood flying through the windows of surrounding buildings.

What should one make of these facts? Was he just a juvenile

testing limits? Or did he have a vindictive need for retribution? Of the details, reported and unreported, in this case—the pipe bomb, the stolen car stereos, the chunks of wood flying or not flying through panes of glass—one of the most startling is his willingness not simply to hide the evidence, but to frame another person for the act. I cannot help but think of the young nurses taking the stand at trial, attempting to explain how they were just following orders, straining not to implicate themselves in someone else's possible crime.

None of this history was presented to the jury.

On day 17, as the trial is drawing to a close, the prosecution calls Christine (Chris) Allison as a witness for the prosecution. With her thick black glasses, sharp blazer, and pendant necklace, she gives the immediate impression of someone who is comfortable in a library, but by her own admission she's more comfortable in a bar. That's where she met her late husband, Troy Allison, one of Dr. Husel's younger patients, in 1999.

Over the course of the trial, the prosecution called a number of family members and friends of the deceased to testify: the son of Beverlee Shirtzinger, the friend of Rebecca Walz, and the sister of Ryan Hayes—who found her brother in a bathtub after an overdose. They each have incredible, complicated, heartbreaking stories, but I keep coming back to Chris. She is unlike many of the other witnesses—she is neither the stuttering nurses, fresh out of school, nor the state's expert witnesses, called in to lay out in broad strokes the theory of the prosecution's case. She is earnest and open, unpracticed but confident. She looks like she'd talk your ear off at a pizza parlor only moments after meeting you. Like she has a great capacity to both bother and charm.

The prosecution first asks Chris to walk the court through the events leading up to Troy's death. Chris explains that before he died, Troy had a wound on his leg and was suffering from kidney disease. He had been in the hospital intermittently, given a course of antibiotics and sent home again. On the night of July 15, 2018, he started hyperventilating on the couch. Chris called an ambulance and had him breathe into a paper bag to calm down, its stiff walls collapsing and expanding with each breath. Troy walked himself to the ambulance, as Chris let their dog out. This was not an emergency yet; they'd called simply as a precaution. After Troy was in the ambulance, Chris drove herself to the hospital, still under the impression that this was a relatively routine trip. The next time she saw Troy, nurses were performing chest compressions on him in the hospital. From there everything moved at a blurred pace. Chris was visited by chaplains. She asked questions of the ER doctor. Chest compressions were stopped. Troy was sent for a CT scan in the intensive care unit on the fourth floor. She was visited by more chaplains. And, as the full scope of the emergency was just beginning to dawn on her, the crucial moment came: Dr. Husel asked Chris if her husband wanted to be on life support, to which she said precisely: "Well, no."

"I'm going to take the tube out and make him comfortable," said Dr. Husel. That was the only warning she received.

As I listen to Chris, I'm reminded of something Dr. Nash mentioned: "There is a devaluation of ethics in medicine to a simple matter of permission." Permission becomes both a legal out and a logistical efficiency. Has the patient or their next of kin given the doctor permission to administer the opioids? To extubate the patient? To pull the plug? Then we can proceed. Permission is something of course; it just isn't much. You can secure permission without the hard, searching work of sitting with suffering or dealing with the realities of death.

Of the nurses, working doctors, and medical ethicists I spoke to, nearly all of them agreed on one thing: doctors and patients misunderstand each other frequently. Families have difficulty understanding the difference between heart death and brain death. They struggle to differentiate between allowing and causing a patient's death. They have been taught, incorrectly, a popular-culture narrative of death in which pulling the plug is the ultimate final act, one that triggers a tidy cascade into death. Medical professionals, for their part, do not spend the time or the resources educating patients and their loved ones on palliative extubation, proper painkiller dosages, or the difference between brain and body death—usually because they don't have it.

Chris did not know that taking the tube out meant her husband would die, and she certainly didn't know how quickly it would happen. "He's telling me he's 99.9 percent sure that he's brain-dead and his organs are failing, but you take tests to verify that, right? I mean, we don't go by what he *thinks* you have to go by tests." At one moment in her testimony, when the state's lawyer asks her for a second time what she thought would happen when the tube was taken out, whether she asked anyone what would happen, Chris says, "I don't think you understand. We were not talking about things. We were just doing!"

Chris, however, is not an especially strong witness for the defense. She admits that her husband did not want to be on life support. She admits to watching the trial on TV every day. She admits to filing a civil lawsuit only after she was contacted by an attorney—to having, in other words, a vested interest in the case. She admits that she did not understand what it meant that they were going to take the tube out, but she gave them permission anyway. And Chris does not fit easily into the decorum of the legal proceedings. She has trouble keeping her mouth shut.

Just before the defense attorney steps up for cross-examination, Chris mutters under her breath, "Here we go." She's not exasperated or dismissive, simply acknowledging what's to come: a tough series of questions and combative responses about the exact time she met her husband and the timeline of their marriage, whether he was seeing someone else when she met Troy or was single, and her financial interest in the case. At one point, flustered and desperate after a particularly tense exchange, she turns to the only thing she's certain of. "He killed my husband," she shouts, looking at Dr. Husel. It is a genuine but unseemly declaration, quickly silenced by the judge.

In the end, Troy's brain had probably stopped functioning in those moments of "doing." Without the aid of a ventilator keeping him breathing, he may not have lived for more than a few minutes after the tube was removed. He certainly would not have recovered. But the frustrated outrage of Chris's testimony speaks to an essential element of the case, feelings that exist outside the field of law. She looks victimized by medicine, its jargon and machinations, its cold rationale and efficiencies. "Even with excellent communication," Dr. Nash says, "families experiencing the death of a loved one may not have their expectations met." They will, of course, experience grief, but they may also feel angry and suspicious, fearing they have been taken advantage of. With proper communication families may still feel victimized, but without any communication at all they certainly will.

In the end, Troy was palliatively extubated and given a thousand micrograms of fentanyl. He died three minutes later. The extubation and death happened so quickly and with such failure of communication that Chris missed the event entirely. She didn't see his last breaths. Only afterward, as a nurse prepared her husband's body, did she realize what had happened and screamed, "Is he dead?"

---

On the final day of the trial, this is how things stand. The defense has its star lawyers, they have the trepidation of the attending nurses, the tortured and byzantine nature of drug withdrawals and hospital administration. They have one of the prosecution's witnesses admitting, on the stand, that she gave consent for the hospital to pull the plug on her husband—whether she understood what was happening in those terms or not. They have, perhaps most consequentially, the biases of the American justice system. They have *beyond reasonable doubt*. But still there are those numbers. A thousand micrograms of fentanyl in most cases, two thousand in at least one. The prosecution has the phrase "enough to take out an elephant." And then there are the less tangible considerations, the contested ground on which the case seems to be won or lost: Why had he decided to work at night?

On April 12, 2022, after nearly seven weeks and fifty-four witnesses, the jury leaves for deliberation.

When I explain that I am writing an essay on the trial of Dr. William Husel, many people assume he's a doctor with a god complex or a compulsive, sociopathic need to end life. That, or they believe he is an "angel of death," a maverick with a bleeding heart and a need—perhaps pathological, perhaps unwise, but nonetheless good-hearted—to end suffering. Somehow these tragedies feel easier scaffolded around a coherent plan, a philosophy, no matter how dark: the doctor getting off on murder, the martyr swooping in to deliver relief, the nihilist sick of worrying what another five minutes on earth really means to a person. Which is why I suspect these narratives are so tempting, no matter how extreme; we recognize in them our own feelings and frustrations. By proxy these stories tell us the world is coherent, that we are in control of ourselves, ultimately and fully.

But I find it hard to read Dr. Husel in any of these ways. He didn't administer the medication himself. He wasn't even in the room for most of the deaths. And if he had some deep-seated conviction about the cruel excesses of end-of-life treatment, he kept them well hidden. Instead, Dr. Husel looks to me like an average narcissist, trapped in the realities of his profession. An overworked man practicing in an underfunded hospital where people arrive without a plan or clear directives, a place in which keeping patients alive is expensive and inconvenient. Someone I can have both sympathy and disdain for, but who I fear as an example of what anyone might be driven to do. As the trial closed, the simplest explanation felt correct, if unsatisfying: that he ended these patients' lives because it was the quickest path, an efficient solution to the troublesome problem of excess life. Rather than malice, it is this terrifying absence of motivation that chills me. It feels thoughtless and inhuman. Not the bad death of excess suffering, but the bad death of a failure to consider life at all.

For six days the jury deliberates, informing the judge once that they do not believe they will be able to reach unanimous agreement. The judge, however, assures them there is no group of people more capable of making an informed decision at this time. In the end, they are, in fact, capable. On the final day, the jury returns their verdict: not guilty on all fourteen counts of murder and all lesser charges.

Mount Carmel West is gone now. In 2019, the former hospital was demolished and a new facility built in Grove City, Ohio, to better serve a growing suburban patient population. I missed the demolition, but online I watch a drone circling towers that once housed in-patient rooms. In the video, they're in the process of coming down, a mess of brick, wire, and rebar gasping from their concrete plinths. Occasionally, the camera turns and reveals a stretch of undemolished bedrooms, strangely intact—wallpaper, vinyl chairs, and telephones still hung unsuspectingly on the wall. I would not be surprised to see a nurse step in from the hallway.

Recently, on a trip home to Columbus, I drove to the former Mount Carmel West to see what was left. A nursing school, an emergency room, and some administrative buildings still stand, but the kind of patients Dr. Husel once treated now travel elsewhere, to a suburb farther from Franklinton. Where the hospital once stood is a flat, empty field, edged with the sharp corners of new concrete and freshly rolled sod. It is not desolate so much as simply blank—empty, uniform, too clean and measured.

Franklinton is changing, too. In fact, it is a neighborhood torqued with change. A flood wall was finally built along the freeway, and home prices have since risen. New, cheap apartments have gone up next to the trampled chain-link fence and overgrown sumac of old homes. Some of the old residents are leaving to make way for breweries and artist's lofts, which host monthly open houses next to homes in foreclosure. Many buildings are in the process of renovation, their exteriors naked with fresh lumber, exposed insulation, and Tyvek house wrap, some of it wind-peeled and tattered like bandages concealing a great metamorphosis.

In Franklinton, I stopped by Chris Allison's home and knocked on her door, but there was no answer. In one of several interviews she gave about her husband's death and the trial of Dr. Husel, she said she was willing to talk to anyone about her experiences. A few days later, I sent her a letter—I couldn't find a reliable phone number or email address—and for several weeks I waited for a response. Perhaps she had left Franklinton. Perhaps the rent had gotten too high or the offer to sell too enticing—though I don't know if she owned the home. Perhaps, even with Mount Carmel gone, she did not want to continue living in the house she had shared with her husband. I don't know. The post office returned the letter, unopened.

# Notes

## Inheritance

Sections of this essay, under the name "Annotations," first appeared in *Atlas and Alice*, no. 11 (2018), https://atlasandalice.com/2018/03/29/nonfiction-from-jonathan-gleason (accessed May 28, 2025).

1. Bernard Sachs, *The Normal Child and How to Keep It Normal in Mind and Morals: Suggestions for Parents, Teachers, and Physicians; with a Consideration of the Influence of Psychoanalysis* (New York: P. B. Hoeber, 1926).

2. Bernard Sachs, *On Arrested Cerebral Development with Special Reference to Its Cortical Pathology* (New York: Journal of Nervous and Mental Disease, 1887), 543.

3. Sachs, *On Arrested Cerebral Development*, 543.

4. Sachs, *On Arrested Cerebral Development*, 552.

5. Bernard Sachs, *A Family Form of Idiocy, Generally Fatal, and Associated with Early Blindness (Amaurotic Family Idiocy)* (New York: Medical Journal,1896), 7.

6. Sachs, *A Family Form of Idiocy*, 8.

7. Sachs, *The Normal Child*, 3.

8. Sachs, *A Family Form of Idiocy*, 22.

9. Shelley Z. Reuter, "The Genuine Jewish Type: Racial Ideology and Anti-Immigrationism in Early Medical Writing about Tay-Sachs Disease," *Canadian Journal of Sociology* 31, no. 3 (January 1, 2006); Shelley Z. Reuter, *Testing Fate: Tay-Sachs Disease and the Right to Be Responsible* (Minneapolis: University of Minnesota Press, 2016).

10. Reuter, "The Genuine Jewish Type," 292.

11. Reuter, "The Genuine Jewish Type," 297.

12. Reuter, "The Genuine Jewish Type," 294.

13. Susan Sontag, *Illness as Metaphor and AIDS and Its Metaphors* (New York: Macmillan, 2001), 197.

14. Alan M. Kraut, *Silent Travelers: Germs, Genes, and the "Immigrant Menace"* (Baltimore: Johns Hopkins University Press, 1995), 273.

15. Manly H. Simons, "The Origin and Condition of the Peoples Who Make Up the Bulk of Our Immigrants at the Present Time and the Probable Effect of the Absorption on Our Population," *Military Surgeon* 23 (December 1908): 433.

16. Alfred C. Reed, "Immigration and Public Health," *Popular Science Monthly* 83 (October 1913): 319.

17. W. C. Billings, "The Medical Application of the Immigration Law," quoted in Reuter, "The Genuine Jewish Type," 314.

18. Charles E. Atwood, "Do Our Present Ways of Living Tend to the Increase of Certain Forms of Nervous and Mental Disorder?" *New York Medical Journal* 77 (1903): 1070–73.

19. Reuter, "The Genuine Jewish Type," 300.

20. Sachs, *A Family Form of Idiocy,* 17.

21. Sachs, *The Normal Child,* 5.

22. Sachs, *The Normal Child,* 44.

23. Sachs, *A Family Form of Idiocy,* 17.

24. Harry H Laughlin, *The Eugenics Tree*, block print designed for the Second International Eugenics Congress, September 25–27, 1921.

25. Posters: "Healthy Seed" and "Marry Wisely," Eugenics Society, c. 1930s, at *Wellcome Collection,* https://wellcomecollection.org/works/vzzcqeyx (accessed November 1, 2024).

26. Christine Rosen, "Eugenics—Sacred and Profane: On Orthodox Matchmakers, IVF Clinics, and Genetic Testing," *New Atlantis,* no. 2 (Summer 2003): 79–89, available at www.thenewatlantis.com/publications/eugenics-sacred-and-profane (accessed November 1, 2024).

27. Rivka Weinberg, *The Risk of a Lifetime: How, When, and Why Procreation May Be Permissible* (New York: Oxford University Press, 2017).

28. Robert Pollack, *The Missing Moment: How the Unconscious Shapes Modern Science* (Boston: Houghton Mifflin Harcourt, 1999), 194.

29. Alan Goodman, "Two Questions about Race," posted August 16, 2008, at *learntoquestion.com,* www.learntoquestion.org/resources/database/archives/003348.html (accessed November 1, 2024).

30. Pollack, *The Missing Moment,* 194.

## Blood in the Water

This essay first appeared in a largely different form in the journal *Redivider* (Fall 2018).

1. Richard A. McKay, *Patient Zero and the Making of the AIDS Epidemic* (Chicago: University of Chicago Press, 2017), 289.

2. McKay, *Patient Zero and the Making of the AIDS Epidemic,* 174.

3. "The Allure of a Simple Story," *The Lancet* 3, no. 12 (November 21, 2016): 549, www.thelancet.com/journals/lanhiv/article/PIIS2352-3018(16)30197-7/fulltext (accessed May 24, 2025).

4. Richard A. McKay, "'Patient Zero': The Absence of a Patient's View of the Early North American AIDS Epidemic," *Bulletin of the History of Medicine* 88, no. 1 (2014): 178.

5. Rainbow History Project, "*60 Minutes:* Patient Zero—CBS (11/15/1987)," posted April 1, 2022, www.youtube.com/watch?v=G6YOoamYCfI (accessed November 24, 2024).

6. Randy Shilts, *And the Band Played On: Politics, People, and the AIDS Epidemic* (New York: St. Martin's Press, 1987).

7. SuchIsLifeVideos, "Greg Louganis on *20/20* with Barbara Walters (2/24/1995)," posted July 16, 2014, www.youtube.com/watch?v=VciMA6V7Wp0 (accessed November 24, 2024).

8. McKay, *Patient Zero and the Making of the AIDS Epidemic,* 375.

9. Brian Tashman, "Robertson: Gay People Deliberately Spread HIV/AIDS by Cutting People with Special Rings," *People For,* August 27, 2013, www.peoplefor.org/rightwingwatch/post/robertson-gay-people-deliberately-spread-hivaids-by-cutting-people-with-special-rings (accessed November 24, 2024).

10. Ribbon Community (formerly AIDS Vancouver), "1983: The Forum (the 30 30 Campaign)," posted February 28, 2014, www.youtube.com/watch?v=f5wJXYxNu88 (accessed November 25, 2024).

11. Ribbon Community, "1983: The Forum."

12. John Donne, *Devotions upon Emergent Occasions* (Cambridge: Ann Arbor Press, 1959), 30.

13. McKay, *Patient Zero and the Making of the AIDS Epidemic,* 370.

## Field Guide to Falling Ill

This essay first appeared in *Sun Magazine,* no. 569 (May 2023): 39–46.

1. For the sake of privacy, names and identifying details have been changed in several essays, including "Field Guide to Falling Ill," "Bitter Joy," and "No Harm."

2. Camelia Petrescu, "Teaching Interpreting," *Procedia—Social and Behavioral Sciences* 116 (February 1, 2014): 3266–70.

3. Joy Williams, *The Visiting Privilege* (New York: Vintage, 2015), 3.

4. Roland Barthes, *A Lover's Discourse: Fragments,* trans. Richard Howard (New York: Hill and Wang, 1978), 73.

## Circulations

This essay first appeared in the *Denver Quarterly* 53, no. 2 (2019): 36–45.

1. Rebecca Lindstrom, "Teen Denied, Then Given Transplant Dies in Police Chase," *USA Today,* April 2, 2015, www.usatoday.com/story/news/nation/2015/04/01/teen-denied-then-given-transplant-dies-in-police-chase/70806176 (accessed November 25, 2024).

2. Lindstrom, "Teen Denied, Then Given Transplant Dies in Police Chase."

3. Elizabeth Landau and Jacque Wilson, "Atlanta Teen Anthony Stokes Gets Heart Transplant," CNN, August 21, 2013, www.cnn.com/2013/08/21/health/georgia-heart-transplant/index.html (accessed November 25, 2024).

4. Teju Cole, *Known and Strange Things* (London: Faber & Faber, 2016), 13–14.

5. W. C. Aird, "Discovery of the Cardiovascular System: From Galen to William Harvey," *Journal of Thrombosis and Haemostasis* 9 (July 1, 2011): 118–29.

6. E. Ducasse et al., "Vascular Knowledge in Medieval Times Was the Turning Point for the Humanistic Trend," *European Journal of Vascular and Endovascular Surgery* 31, no. 6 (2006): 603.

7. Susan E. Morgan et al., "In Their Own Words: The Reasons Why People Will (Not) Sign an Organ Donor Card," *Health Communication* 23, no. 1 (January 25, 2008): 23–33.

8. Morgan et al., "In Their Own Words," 24.

9. Charles R. Drew Papers, "Biographical Overview," National Library of Medicine, https://profiles.nlm.nih.gov/spotlight/bg/feature/biographical-overview (accessed December 1, 2024).

10. Yue-Harn Ng et al., "Does Racial Disparity in Kidney Transplant Waitlisting Persist after Accounting for Social Determinants of Health?," *Transplantation* 104, no. 7 (October 14, 2019): 1445–55.

11. R. E. Patzer et al., "The Role of Race and Poverty on Steps to Kidney Transplantation in the Southeastern United States," *American Journal of Transplantation* 12, no. 2 (January 10, 2012): 358–68.

12. Amy S. Chappell, "Toward a Lifestyle Medicine Approach to Illness Anxiety Disorder (Formerly Hypochondriasis)," *American Journal of Lifestyle Medicine* 12, no. 5 (April 27, 2018): 365–69.

13. Tyrese L. Coleman, "Speculum," *Black Warrior Review* 45, no. 1 (Fall/Winter 2018): 62.

14. Lindstrom, "Teen Denied, Then Given Transplant Dies in Police Chase."

15. Morgan et al., "In Their Own Words," 23.

16. Morgan et al., "In Their Own Words," 29.

17. Morgan et al., "In Their Own Words," 29.

NOTES TO PAGES 82–94                                                    223

18. "Charles Drew House," *Black History of Amherst Massachusetts*, n.d., https://amherstblackhistory.jimdofree.com/drew-house (accessed April 26, 2025).

19. Morgan et al., "In Their Own Words," 30.

## A Difficult Man

Sections of this essay, under the name "The Pharmakon," first appeared in *Fugue*, no. 62 (Spring–Summer 2022): 18–29.

1. Robin Hardy and David Groff, *The Crisis of Desire: AIDS and the Fate of Gay Brotherhood* (Boston: Houghton Mifflin Harcourt, 1999).

2. Hardy and Groff, *The Crisis of Desire*, 51.

3. Paul Vitello, "Jerome Horwitz, AZT Creator, Dies at 93," *New York Times*, September 20, 2012, https://nytimes.com/2012/09/21/health/jerome-p-horwitz-creator-of-azt-dies-at-93.html (accessed April 26, 2025).

4. *Burroughs Wellcome Co. v. Barr Labs., Inc.*, 40 F.3d 1223 (Fed. Cir. 1994).

5. Emily Langer, "Researcher Jerome P. Horwitz, 93, Created AZT, the First Approved Treatment for HIV/AIDS," *Washington Post*, September 19, 2012, www.washingtonpost.com/national/health-science/researcher-jerome-p-horwitz-93-created-azt-the-first-approved-treatment-for-hivaids/2012/09/19/0c08c38a-0280-11e2-9b24-ff730c7f6312_story.html (accessed April 26, 2025).

6. "Interview with Dr. Joseph Sonnabend," c. 1983, Joseph A Sonnabend Papers, Series I: biographical files, box 1, folder 1, Manuscripts and Archives Division, New York Public Library, Astor, Lenox, and Tilden Foundations.

7. "Interview with Dr. Joseph Sonnabend."

8. "Interview with Dr. Joseph Sonnabend."

9. "Interview with Dr. Joseph Sonnabend."

10. "Interview with Dr. Joseph Sonnabend."

11. Michael Callen Papers, Audio Tape 149: Joe Sonnabend 8/13/92, record number 10, Lesbian, Gay, Bisexual & Transgender Community Center, New York.

12. Michael Callen Papers, Audio Tape 149: Joe Sonnabend 8/13/92.

13. Sean Strub, "The Good Doctor," *POZ*, July 1, 1989, www.poz.com/article/The-Good-Doctor-1638-8068.

14. "An AIDS Drug, at a Cost," *New York Times*, March 29, 1987, www.nytimes.com/1987/03/25/opinion/an-aids-drug-at-a-cost.html (accessed April 26, 2025).

15. Alice Park, "The Story behind the First AIDS Drug," *Time*, March 19, 2017, https://time.com/4705809/first-aids-drug-azt (accessed April 26, 2025).

16. Joseph Sonnabend, "The Long Road to PCP Prophylaxis in AIDS: An Early History," *POZ*, September 23, 2009, www.poz.com/blog/the-long-road-to-pcp (accessed April 26, 2025).

17. Sonnabend, "The Long Road to PCP Prophylaxis in AIDS."

18. Asha Persson, "Incorporating Pharmakon: HIV, Medicine, and Body Shape Change," *Body and Society* 10, no. 4 (December 1, 2004): 45–67.

19. Gary Braffman, "AZT Is Not a Poison," *New York Times*, February 20, 1989, www.nytimes.com/1989/02/20/opinion/l-azt-is-not-a-poison-953889.html (accessed April 26, 2025).

20. E. Dournon et al., "Effects of Ziduvudine in 365 Consecutive Patients with AIDS of AIDS-Related Complex," *The Lancet* 2, no. 8623 (December 1988): 1297–1302.

21. Concorde Coordinating Committee, "Concorde: MRC/ANRS Randomised Double-Blind Controlled Trial of Immediate and Deferred Zidovudine in Symptom-Free HIV Infection," *The Lancet* 343, no. 8902 (April 9, 1994): 871–81.

22. Elinor Burkett, "The Queen of AZT: To Our Only Weapon against AIDS, Margaret Fischl Owes Everything: Her Fame and Her Infamy," *Miami Herald*, September 23, 1990.

23. Burkett, "The Queen of AZT."

24. Burkett, "The Queen of AZT."

25. Victor F. Zonana, "Bootstrap AIDS Research Giving Patients Active Role—Los Angeles Times," *Los Angeles Times*, December 25, 1988, www.latimes.com/archives/la-xpm-1988-12-25-mn-1447-story.html (accessed April 26, 2025).

26. Sonnabend, "The Long Road to PCP Prophylaxis in AIDS."

27. amfAR, The Foundation for AIDS Research, "Remembering Dr. Joseph Sonnabend, Early Pioneer on AIDS," January 25, 2021, www.amfar.org/news/remembering-dr-joseph-sonnabend-early-pioneer-on-aids (accessed November 1, 2024).

28. Richard Berkowitz, Michael Callen, and Joseph Sonnabend, *How to Have Sex in a Pandemic: One Approach* (New York: Tower Press, May 1983).

29. Letter from Susan Sontag, Joseph A Sonnabend Papers, MssCol 6223, Series 1 Biographical Files, box 1, folder 2, 1963–2004, New York Public Library, New York.

30. Letter from Stuart F. Schlossman, Joseph A Sonnabend Papers, MssCol 6223, Series 1 Biographical Files, box 1, folder 2, 1963–2004, New York Public Library, New York.

31. Berkowitz, Callen, and Sonnabend, *How to Have Sex in a Pandemic;* Michael Callen and Richard Berkowitz, "We Know Who We Are: Two Gay Men Declare War on Promiscuity," *New York Native,* November 8–21, 1982, in Richard Berkowitz Papers, Mss.421, Subseries VIII D, Writings, 1982–2009, box 9, folders 15–18, 1982–1983, Fales Library and Special Collections, New York University, New York.

32. Sonnabend, "The Long Road to PCP Prophylaxis in AIDS."

33. Michael Specter, "AIDS Drug's Price to Be Cut 20%," *Washington Post,*

December 14, 1987, www.washingtonpost.com/archive/politics/1987/12/15/aids-drugs-price-to-be-cut-20/fad89c91-e46b-4159-b4d0-9b01b10cf8cc.

34. Khadija Sharife, "The Great Billion Dollar Drug Scam," *Al Jazeera*, June 29, 2011, www.aljazeera.com/opinions/2011/6/29/the-great-billion-dollar-drug-scam (accessed April 26, 2025).

35. Michael Callen Papers, Audio Tape 147: Joe Sonnabend 8/15/92.

36. Michael Callen Papers, Audio Tape 149: Joe Sonnabend 8/13/92.

37. Michael Callen Papers, Audio Tape 149: Joe Sonnabend 8/13/92.

38. Michael Callen Papers, Audio Tape 101, Michael Callen Papers, record number 10, Lesbian, Gay, Bisexual & Transgender Community Center, New York.

39. Joseph Sonnabend, "An Open Letter to the Residents of 49 West 12th Street," Joseph A Sonnabend Papers, MssCol 6223, Series 4 Legal Case Files, box 4, folder 8, 1963–2004, New York Public Library, New York.

40. Michael Callen Papers, Audio Tape 101.

41. Michael Callen Papers, Audio Tape 149: Joe Sonnabend 8/13/92.

42. Berkowitz, Callen, and Sonnabend, *How to Have Sex in a Pandemic*, 38.

43. Berkowitz, Callen, and Sonnabend, *How to Have Sex in a Pandemic*, 39.

44. Michael Callen Papers, Audio Tape 149: Joe Sonnabend 8/13/92.

45. Michael Callen Papers, Audio Tape 149: Joe Sonnabend 8/13/92.

## Exit Wounds

This essay first appeared in *New England Review*, 42, no. 4 (2021): 120–32. It was later reprinted in *Literary Hub*.

1. "Man Charged in Megabus Hijack Attempt Tells Courtroom He Is Mentally Ill," *Columbus Dispatch*, May 28, 2014, www.dispatch.com/story/news/crime/2014/05/27/man-charged-in-megabus-hijack/24067355007 (accessed November 1, 2024).

2. "Man Charged in Megabus Hijack Attempt Tells Courtroom He Is Mentally Ill."

3. Christopher Payne and Oliver Sacks, *Asylum: Inside the Closed World of State Mental Hospitals* (Cambridge, MA: MIT Press, 2009), 1.

4. Payne and Sacks, *Asylum*, 5.

5. Payne and Sacks, *Asylum*, 5.

6. Payne and Sacks, *Asylum*, 4.

7. Jennifer Jenkins et al., "Fatal Force: 1,122 People Have Been Shot and Killed by Police in the Past 12 Months," dataset for 2015–25, *Washington Post*, www.washingtonpost.com/graphics/investigations/police-shootings-database (accessed December 9, 2024).

8. Wesley Lowery et al., "Distraught People, Deadly Results," *Washington Post*, June 30, 2015, www.washingtonpost.com/sf/investigative/2015/06/30/distraught-people-deadly-results (accessed April 26, 2025).

## Bitter Joy

This essay first appeared in *Michigan Quarterly Review* 61, no. 1 (Winter 2022): 89–101.

1. Marc Kaufman, "U.S.-Built Project Waters Afghan Heroin Trade Poppies," *Baltimore Sun*, March 29, 1997, www.baltimoresun.com/1997/03/29/us-built-project-waters-afghan-heroin-trade-poppies-an-american-water-project-from-the-1950s-is-helping-afghans-grow-poppies-for-the-us-heroin-trade (accessed November 20, 2024).

2. Alice Park, "The Story behind the Viral Photo of an Opioid Overdose," *Time*, January 24, 2017, https://time.com/4634809/photo-opioid-addiction (accessed November 20, 2024).

3. Susan Sontag, *Regarding the Pain of Others* (New York: Farrar, Straus & Giroux, 2013), 6.

4. Reagan Library, "Address to the Nation on Drug Abuse Campaign, September 14, 1986," posted April 27, 2016, www.youtube.com/watch?v=pwpciZ7R8UU (accessed December 10, 2024).

5. Brian Mann, "Opioid Trial in West Virginia Comes amid a National Reckoning for Big Pharma," NPR, May 26, 2021, www.npr.org/2021/05/26/1000435397/opioid-trial-in-west-virginia-comes-amid-national-reckoning-for-big-pharma (accessed December 10, 2024).

## Gilead

This essay first appeared in *Kenyon Review* 43, no. 3 (May–June 2021): 63–74.

1. Patrick William Kelly, "The End of Safe Gay Sex?" *New York Times*, June 26, 2018, www.nytimes.com/2018/06/26/opinion/gay-men-sex-condoms.html (accessed April 26, 2025).

2. Tim Fitzsimons, "U.S. Sues Gilead, Claiming It Owns HIV PrEP Patent," NBC News, November 7, 2019, www.nbcnews.com/feature/nbc-out/u-s-sues-gilead-claiming-it-owns-hiv-prep-patent-n1078346 (accessed December 10, 2024).

3. Jeremiah 8:22; New International Version.

4. Donald G. McNeil, "Who Owns H.I.V.-Prevention Drugs? The Taxpayers, U.S. Says," *New York Times*, November 8, 2019, www.nytimes.com/2019/11/08/health/hiv-prevention-truvada-patents.html (accessed December 10, 2024).

5. Rebecca Robbins, "U.S. Loses Key Case on Rights to H.I.V.-Prevention Drugs," *New York Times*, May 9, 2023, www.nytimes.com/2023/05/09/business/prep-hiv-aids-gilead.html (accessed December 10, 2024).

6. Andy Carstens, "PrEP Failures (Breakthrough Infections)," aidsmap, June 1, 2023, www.aidsmap.com/about-hiv/prep-failures-breakthrough-infections (accessed December 2, 2024).

7. Edward J. Carr et al., "The Cellular Composition of the Human Immune System Is Shaped by Age and Cohabitation," *Nature Immunology* 17, no. 4 (2016): 461–68.

8. Jordan Kisner, *Thin Places: Essays from In Between* (New York: Farrar, Straus and Giroux, 2020), 43.

## Proxemics

This essay first appeared in *Colorado Review* 50, no. 1 (Spring 2023): 35–48. It was later reprinted in *The Best American Essays 2024*, selected by Wesley Morris, series ed. Kim Dana Kupperman (New York: Mariner Books, 2024), 71–82.

1. Lisa Abend, "Inside Barcelona's Unfinished Masterpiece," *Time*, June 27, 2019, https://time.com/sagrada-familia-barcelona (accessed December 4, 2024).

2. Edward T. Hall, *The Hidden Dimension* (New York: Anchor Books, 1990), 4.

3. Sally Elk et al., "Eastern State Penitentiary Historic Site Audio Tour Transcript," Eastern State Penitentiary Historic Site, https://easternstate.org/audio-tour-transcript (accessed December 11, 2024).

4. Elk et al., "Eastern State Penitentiary Historic Site Audio Tour Transcript."

5. Charles Dickens, *American Notes for General Circulation*, 2 vols. (London: Chapman and Hall, 1842), 39.

6. Elk et al., "Eastern State Penitentiary Historic Site Audio Tour Transcript."

7. Hall, *Hidden Dimension*, 119.

8. Hall, *Hidden Dimension*, 121.

9. Gustave de Beaumont and Alexis de Tocqueville, *On the Penitentiary System in the United States and Its Application to France: The Complete Text* (Austin: Springer International Publishing, 2018), 51.

10. Mira Shetty, "Penn and the 1918 Influenza Epidemic," University of Pennsylvania Archives and Records Center, September 15, 2020, https://archives.upenn.edu/exhibits/penn-history/flu (accessed December 11, 2024).

11. Kristin Samuelson, "High Incarceration Rates Fuel COVID-19 Spread and Undermine U.S. Public Safety," *Northwestern Now*, September 2, 2021, https://news.northwestern.edu/stories/2021/september/incarceration-covid-19-spread-public-safety (accessed December 11, 2024).

12. Wendy Sawyer, "The Steep Cost of Medical Co-pays in Prison Puts Health at Risk," Prison Policy Initiative, April 19, 2017, www.prisonpolicy.org/blog/2017/04/19/copays (accessed December 11, 2024).

13. Saneta deVuono-powell et al., *Who Pays? The True Cost of Incarceration on Families*, Ella Baker Center, Forward Together, Research Action Design, 2015, https://ellabakercenter.org/wp-content/uploads/2022/09/Who-Pays-FINAL.pdf (accessed December 18, 2024).

14. Securus Technologies, *Public Lender Presentation* (April 15, 2015).

15. Hall, *Hidden Dimension*, 116.

16. "Interview: James Casebere," *BOMB*, October 1, 2001, https://bombmagazine.org/articles/2001/10/01/james-casebere (accessed December 4, 2024).

17. Rachel Kushner and Caleb Smith, "Discipline and Abolish: Writing, Power, and Mass Incarceration," *Yale Review*, June 28, 2021, https://yalereview.org/article/interviews-discipline-and-abolish (accessed December 4, 2024).

18. Hall, *Hidden Dimension*, 123.

19. Elk et al., "Eastern State Penitentiary Historic Site Audio Tour Transcript."

## No Harm

1. Merrill M. Mitler et al., "When People Die," *American Journal of Medicine* 82, no. 2 (February 1, 1987): 266–74.

2. Jack Healy et al., "One Doctor. 25 Deaths. How Could It Have Happened?" *New York Times*, October 11, 2019, www.nytimes.com/2019/10/11/us/ohio-doctor-overdose.html (accessed April 26, 2025).

3. Ed Lentz, *Columbus: The Story of a City* (Charleston: Arcadia, 2003), 33.

4. Lentz, *Columbus*, 103.

5. Many of the trial scenes from the essay "No Harm" were drawn or corroborated through video coverage of *State v. Husel* provided by the Law & Crime Network under the title "Dr. William Husel Trial."

6. Theodore Decker et al., "Doctor's Past Coming into View," *Columbus Dispatch*, January 31, 2019, www.dispatch.com/story/news/crime/2019/01/31/doctor-s-past-coming-into/4985118007 (accessed December 4, 2024).

7. Decker et al., "Doctor's Past Coming into View."

# Acknowledgments

This book took me over ten years to write. As many debut books do, it changed me both as a writer and as a person. All of the mentors, the friends, the editors, and institutions who supported me, encouraged me, and held me up when I did not think this book was possible had a hand in that change.

Special thanks to Meghan O'Rourke and to the team at Yale University Press—Jennifer Banks, Eva Skewes, Erica Hanson, and Andrew Frisardi—for bringing these essays together. I am grateful to the editorial staff of the magazines where these essays first appeared: details are in the notes section. It was an honor to work with the editors who shaped not only these individual essays but my voice as a writer: Joanna Biggs, Staci Kleinmaier, Will Frazier, Anna Gazmarian, Stephanie G'Schwind, Nicole Dutton, Raina K. Puels, Aaron Stone, Gianna Stoddard, Thirii Myo Kyaw Myint, Carolyn Kuebler, Elizabeth Kadetsky, Kim Dana Kupperman, and Wesley Morris.

All writing, but especially nonfiction writing, demands time. Time to research, time to synthesize, time to live in the world, and of course time to write. To the Elizabeth George Foundation, the

University of Iowa, and the Granum Foundation thank you for the generous gifts of money and time that allowed this book to exist. Many of these essays would not have been possible without access to the lives and recorded experiences of the historical figures that populate them. Thank you, also, to Lou and Luis at the Lesbian, Gay, Bisexual & Transgender Community Center in Greenwich Village; to Tal at the New York Public Library's Brooke Russell Astor Reading Room; and to the Gerber/Hart Library in Chicago for the gift of access.

I am lucky to have had many incredible mentors throughout my writing career. Thank you to Eula Biss and John Bresland, who first made the outlandish dream of being a writer seem possible. Thank you to Hanif Abdurraqib, John D'Agata, Melissa Febos, Brooks Landon, Andre Perry, Bennett Sims, and Inara Verzemnieks for your ongoing guidance and ability to see the potential and possibilities in my work, especially when I could not see it myself.

To Sara Dennis, Colin Hall, and Will Wilhelm—the friends haunting the edges of nearly every essay I write—I am grateful for your insights, your questions, and your endless love. Thank you for experiencing the world with me. Thank you to Tatiana Schlote-Bonne for being my first reader and for living with me through both a pandemic and graduate school. To Andrew Cardenas, Tony John Andrews, Jess Kibler, and Steven Thrasher: thank you for your provocations, your enthusiasm, and all of the copy edits. Thank you to Carrie Meyer and Matthew Oakley for giving me a home to write from. And to the University of Iowa's Nonfiction Writing Program cohort of 2022, thank you for your minds and generosity.

Finally, thank you to my family for your unwavering support of my life and my work.

# Index

Adam (nurse practitioner at Mount Carmel Hospital), 198–201, 205; on the use of fentanyl, 199–200
addiction. *See* pain and painkillers
AIDS: early awareness of, 23, 30–31; early names for, 90; early treatments for, 85, 86; fears associated with, 34–35, 37–38; multifactorial model of, 99–101, 108–9. *See also* AZT
AIDS Medical Foundation, 98
Allison, Christine (Chris), 217; as witness in Husel's murder trial, 210–13
Allison, Troy: as Husel's patient, 210–11, 213–14
amaurotic family idiocy, 7. *See* Tay-Sachs disease
AmerisourceBergen: as distributor of opioids, 148
Anthony, Casey, 192
antiretrovirals: as preventative for HIV, 154
aorta, the, 79

Aquinas, Thomas, 207
Arcade Fire: *The Suburbs,* 143
AZT: costs of, 102–3; disappointing results from use of, 96, 97; early trials for, 87–88, 97; federal grants for, 103; first clinical trials for, 92–93; release of, 102–3; side effects from, 92–93, 95–96; as treatment for AIDS, 85, 86–87

Baez, Jose: as Husel's defense attorney, 192–93, 207, 208
Barthes, Roland, 63
Bell, Mark, 70
Berkowitz, Richard (with Michael Callen): *How to Have Sex in a Pandemic,* 99–102
Black Americans: as less likely to receive an organ transplant, 75–76
Black patients: misunderstandings about, 77
Black people: devaluing of, 69, 74, 75, 77, 80

blood: alarming associations with, 26, 27–28
Boniface VIII, Pope, 72
Brian (pseudonym for interpreter at the free clinic), 41–42, 59–60
Broder, Samuel, 87, 103
Brown, John, 82
Burroughs Wellcome: and the development of AZT, 87; and profitability of AZT, 102–3; and release of AZT, 102–3

Callen, Michael: death of, 112–13; as HIV patient, 103–5; *How to Have Sex in a Pandemic* (written with Richard Berkowitz), 99–102; and recorded interviews with Sonnabend, 90–92, 93, 103–5, 109, 111–12, 113; as supporter of Sonnabend, 109
Capone, Al, 173
Casebere, James: and photographs of paper models of public spaces, 182–83
Castle, Sandra, 197
Charlie (patient with heart disease), 201; and the possibility of a heart transplant, 202–3
Cole, Teju: "Black Body," 70
Coleman, Tyrese L.: *Speculum,* 77
Colin: and the influence of the built world, 181–82
Community Research Initiative: and research relating to AIDS, 98–99
cystic fibrosis, 18

Dalton: Gleason's relationship with, 151–52, 156–157, 158, 162–63, 167–68; parents of, 159; as "undetectable," 152, 160

David (as nurse's aide at Mount Carmel Hospital), 190–91, 196
Denver Principles, the, 90
Dickens, Charles: *American Notes for General Circulation,* 172
Dickinson, Gordon, 97
dilated cardiomyopathy, 69
DNA ancestry tests, 13
doctrine of double effect: as factor in the Husel trial, 207–8
Donne, John: *Devotions upon Emergent Occasions,* 36
Drew, Charles Richard: transfusion refused for, 74, 82–83
Dugas, Gaëtan. *See* Gaëtan

Eastern State Penitentiary: as designed for penance, 171–72; deterioration of, 185; as tourist attraction, 173
Ely, Wes: on Husel's use of fentanyl, 205–7
empathy in medicine: limits of, 62–63
eugenics movement, 11, 13–14

family and kinship: medicalization of, 9
Fauci, Anthony, 94
Franklinton, Ohio, 189, 198–99, 216–17. *See also* Mount Carmel West Hospital

Gaëtan: "exoneration" of, 35–37; Gleason's letters to, 20–39; known as "Patient Zero," 20, 35–36; as speaker at an AIDS forum in Vancouver, 33–34
Galen: *On the Usefulness of the Parts of the Body,* 72
Gallo, Robert, 87
Gaudí, Antoni, 169, 170

INDEX

genealogical societies: popularity of, 12–13
genetic disorders: associated with certain populations, 18. *See also* Tay-Sachs disease
Gilead: multiple meanings of, 164
Gilead Sciences, 154. *See also* Truvada
Gleason, Jonathan: blood clot experienced by, 43–44; and costs associated with medical treatment, 52–53; as creative writing teacher, 56–58; on emotional distance required by medical professionals, 61–63; family tree of, 12–13; and fear of flying, 26; healing as experienced by, 50–52, 53–54, 58–59, 64–65, 66; history of heart disease in the family of, 71; as interpreter at the free clinic, 40–42, 44–45, 48–50, 53–55, 59–60, 61–65; as landscaping worker, 135–36, 137–40, 143, 144; as a lifeguard, 67, 68, 74–75; mysterious illness (Tay-Sachs) suffered by his cousins, 1–2, 5–6, 15–17; and pain associated with his landscaping job, 141–42; as patient, 42–44, 47–48, 50–52, 55–56, 58–59, 60–61, 66; philosophical questions raised by his aunt's choices, 15–17; and summer job with a landscaping company, 135–36, 137–41
Gleason's uncle: letters from (to Gleason's father), 173–74; as prisoner in North Carolina, 169–70, 177–78, 179–80; and relationship with Gleason's father, 176, 179–80, 184–85
Goodman, Alan, 17

Hall, Edward T.: as artist and architect, 170–71; as inventor of proxemics, 171, 175; *The Hidden Dimension,* 171; on public distance, 183
Hardy, Robin, 85–86
Hayes, Ryan, 210
heart, the: early understandings of, 68, 72–73; and Gleason's efforts at resuscitation, 68–69
heart bypass surgery: Gleason's mother's experience with, 71–72
Hernandez, Aaron, 192
heroin, 141
HEXA gene: and mutation causing Tay-Sachs disease, 7–8
HIV: adaptability and durability of, 153–54; as the cause of AIDS, 99, 108; guilt and shame associated with, 29, 32–33. *See also* AIDS; antiretrovirals
Homer: *The Iliad,* 148–49
Horwitz, Jerome P., 86–87
*How to Have Sex in a Pandemic: One Approach* (pamphlet), 99–102, 110–11
Husel, William: concerns about patients dying under his care, 187–88; diverse views of, 214–15; jury verdict in trial of, 215–16; as maker of pipe bombs, 208–10; murder trial of, 186–87, 191–98, 203–16
hypochondria: as family trait, 76–79

illness: and blood, 27–28
immigrants/foreigners: fears relating to, 9–10
incarceration/incarcerated people: statistics relating to, 179

intimate distance, 179
Isaacs, Alick, 88

Jay: as correctional officer in Iowa, 175–76, 184
Jewish blood: fictions about, 9
Jewish immigrants (to the U.S.): fears of disease associated with, 9–11; illness experienced by the children of, 2–5
Jews: genetic diversity among, 17–18
Joel: as Gleason's associate on the landscaping job, 139–41
Johnson-Reed Act (1924), 13
Johnston, Norman, 171

Kaposi's sarcoma, 23, 31
Kisner, Jordan, 167
Kraut, Alan M., 10
Krim, Mathilda, 98
Kushner Rachel, 183

LeChard, Stephanie, 196–98
loneliness: patients' experience of, 56
Louganis, Greg: and diving accident at the Seoul Olympics (1988), 28–30

Marc: death of, 149; Gleason's friendship with, 136–37, 142–43, 145, 150
McKay, Richard A.: *Patient Zero and the Making of the AIDS Epidemic*, 23, 24
medical interpreting: and deverbalization, 46; Gleason's experience with, 40–42, 44–45, 48–50, 54–55, 59–60, 63–65; as a kind of intimacy, 63–64; theory of, 45–46

medical students: emotional challenges faced by, 56–58
mental hospitals: as described by Oliver Sacks, 119–21
Mitchell, Joni, 36–37
morphine, 141
Mount Carmel West Hospital (Ohio), 189, 216; William Husel as physician at, 186–87; neighborhood of, 188–89. *See also* Husel, William

Nash, Ryan: on the doctrine of double effect, 207–8; on a "good death," 204–5, 213; on permission in medical contexts, 211
National Institute of Allergy and Infectious Diseases (NIAID), 93–94
National, The: "Bloodbuzz Ohio," 143

opium: in nineteenth-century England, 139
organ donation: and reasons why people choose (or choose not) to sign an organ donor card, 73, 80–81, 83
organs, human: scarcity of, 69–70
Oxycontin, 142

pain and painkillers: associated with Gleason's landscaping job, 141–42; and poppies, 141–42; prevalence of, 145–49; warnings associated with, 146–48
"Patient Zero": Gaëtan Dugas as, 20, 35–36; *60 Minutes* episode focusing on, 23–24
Payne, Christopher: as photographer for Sacks's *Asylum*, 119–21

penitence and penitentiary, 171–72
pentamidine: as treatment for AIDS patients, 93–94, 97; trials for, 98
People with AIDS Coalition, 93
permission: as factor in medical decisions, 211
personal distance, 174–75
Persson, Asha, 95
pharmaceutical companies: role of in funding and promoting research, 96–97. *See also* Burroughs Wellcome
*pharmakon:* etymology of, 95
*Pneumocystis carinii* pneumonia (PCP), 93
police shootings: mental illness as factor in, 121–22, 131–32; toy guns as factor in, 130–31
Pollack, Robert: *The Missing Moment: How the Unconscious Shapes Modern Science,* 17–19; and theory as to the origin of Tay-Sachs, 18–19
PrEP: availability of, 165–66; costs of, 154–55, 161–62, 163–64; as protection against HIV infections, 152–53, 154, 158. *See also* Truvada
prisons: as experiences, 181; statistics relating to, 177
proxemics: as the amount of space between ourselves and others, 171, 174–75, 176–77
public distance, 183

Radiohead: "Everything in Its Right Place," 143
Reagan, Ronald: drug policies under, 147–48
Reasoner, Harry: and *60 Minutes* episode on "Patient Zero," 23–24

Redford, Ray, 24, 30, 36–37, 39; Gaëtan's letters to, 20
Reed, Alfred C., 10
retroviruses, 32
Reuter, Shelley Z.: writings on Tay-Sachs disease, 8–9
right atrium (of the heart), 67–68
Robertson, Pat: as host of the *700 Club,* 32–33
Rodriguez, Arsenio, 118–19, 121, 133
Rosen, Christine: "Eugenics—Sacred and Profane," 16

Sachs, Bernard: background of, 2; early writings by, 6; *The Normal Child,* 2, 5, 11; and mysterious symptoms observed in babies and children, 2–5. *See also* Tay-Sachs disease
Sacks, Oliver: *Asylum,* 119–21
Schlossman, Stuart F., 100
Schooley, Robert T., 98
Seleskovich, Danica: and theory of interpreting, 46, 64
serodiscordant couple, 157–58
sexually transmitted infection (STI): Gleason's test for, 25–26, 35. *See also* AIDS
Shilts, Randy: *And the Band Played On: Politics, People, and the AIDS Epidemic,* 24
Shirtzinger, Beverlee, 210
shooting incident on a bus (Gleason's experience of), 114–16, 123–25, 129–30; emotional impact of, 116–18, 122–23, 125–26, 132–33, 134; newspaper account of, 118–19, 121; panic attacks associated with, 126–29
Shroyer, Talon, 193

sibling relationships: motto describing, 178–79
sickle cell anemia, 18
Simons, Manly H., 10
*60 Minutes:* episode focusing on "Patient Zero," 23–24
*Skinner v. Oklahoma,* 14
social distance, 176–77
Sonnabend, Joseph: challenges faced by, 105–8; death of, 108, 112–13; and multifactorial model of AIDS, 99–101, 108–9; on pharmaceutical companies, 97; as primary care physician, with focus on treating gay men, 89–90, 94; and recorded interviews with Callen, 90–92, 93, 103–5, 109, 111–12, 113; as research physician, 88–89
Sontag, Susan, 100; *Illness as Metaphor,* 9–10; *Regarding the Pain of Others,* 147
sterilization (compulsory): and the eugenics movement, 14; as extended to ethnic minorities, 14; in the United States, 13–14
Stokes, Anthony: death of, 79–80, 84; as patient in need of a heart transplant, 69, 70, 75–76, 80, 81

Taylor, Jill Bolte, 56
Tay-Sachs disease: as a disease concept, 8–9; genetic screening for, 14–15; as hereditary, 4, 6–7; as "Jewish disease," 10–11; Sachs's article describing, 4, 6–7; as "single-gene linked trait," 18; symptoms experienced by children with, 2–3
tenofovir. *See* PrEP; Truvada
thalassemia, 18
Timmons, James: death of, following a dose of fentanyl, 188
Tocqueville, Alexis de, 177
Truvada: effectiveness of, 166–67; as pre-exposure prophylactic (PrEP), 154, 164–65; profitability of, 164; side effects of, 166

unprotected sex: fears associated with, 160–161

vena cava, 82

Walters, Barbara, 28
Walz, Rebecca, 210
Weinberg, Rivka: *Risk of a Lifetime,* 16
Weinstein, Harvey, 192
White, Ryan, 161
Williams, Joy: "Taking Care," 57
Willoughby, Brian, 33–34

Young, Tracy: as William Husel's patient, 203–4